I'll Drink to That

I'll Drink to That

BEAUJOLAIS AND THE FRENCH PEASANT
WHO MADE IT THE WORLD'S
MOST POPULAR WINE

RUDOLPH CHELMINSKI

GOTHAM BOOKS

GOTHAM BOOKS
Published by Penguin Group (USA) Inc. 375 Hudson Street, New York, New York 10014, U.S.A.
Penguin Group (Canada), 90 Eglinton Avenue East, Suite 700, Toronto, Ontario M4P 2Y3, Canada
(a division of Pearson Penguin Canada Inc.); Penguin Books Ltd, 80 Strand, London WC2R 0RL,
England; Penguin Ireland, 25 St Stephen's Green, Dublin 2, Ireland (a division of Penguin Books
Ltd); Penguin Group (Australia), 250 Camberwell Road, Camberwell, Victoria 3124, Australia
(a division of Pearson Australia Group Pty Ltd); Penguin Books India Pvt Ltd, 11 Commu-
nity Centre, Panchsheel Park, New Delhi–110 017, India; Penguin Group (NZ), 67 Apollo
Drive, Rosedale, North Shore 0632, New Zealand (a division of Pearson New Zealand Ltd.);
Penguin Books (South Africa) (Pty) Ltd, 24 Sturdee Avenue, Rosebank, Johannesburg 2196, South
Africa

Penguin Books Ltd, Registered Offices: 80 Strand, London WC2R 0RL, England

Published by Gotham Books, a member of Penguin Group (USA) Inc.

First printing, October 2007
10 9 8 7 6 5 4 3 2 1

Gotham Books and the skyscraper logo are trademarks of Penguin Group (USA) Inc.

LIBRARY OF CONGRESS CATALOGING-IN-PUBLICATION DATA
Chelminski, Rudolph.
   I'll drink to that: Beaujolais and the French peasant who made it the world's most popular wine /
Rudolph Chelminski.
     p. cm.
   ISBN 978-1-592-40320-2 (hardcover)
   1. Beaujolais (Wine)—French—History. 2. Duboeuf, Georges. 3. Vintners—French—Beaujo-
lais. 4. Wine and winemaking—France—Beaujolais—History. 5. Beaujolais (France)—History.
I. Title.
   TP553.C378 2007
   614.2'2230944—dc22   2007016024

Printed in the United States of America
Set in Electra LH • Designed by Elke Sigal

While the author has made every effort to provide accurate telephone numbers and Internet addresses at the time of publication, neither the publisher nor the author assumes any responsibility
for errors, or for changes that occur after publication. Further, the publisher does not have any
control over and does not assume any responsibility for author or third-party Web sites or their
content.

Contents

When I began researching this book, I was struck by the remarkably consistent—I would even say uniform—reaction by friends and
acquaintances upon hearing that its subject was to be the Beaujolais:
first the smile, then the complicit burst of laughter and one of those you-
lucky-guy remarks to signify that my undertaking was certain to be fun,
but somehow not quite serious. A whole world of predigested assump-
tions underlay this reaction. With the subject of wine enjoying an unprecedented prominence and prestige (attended by its inevitable dance
steps of protocol and snobbery), the general conclusion was that I had
chosen to write a book about a Ford instead of a Ferrari. Everyone knows
Beaujolais, or thinks he does, and everyone has an opinion, one that can
usually be expressed within a few seconds. This opinion-giving is often
wildly erroneous, but it is unfailing. After all, who has not tossed down
a glass of Beaujolais at one time or another in his life, and who has not
read an article about this or that aspect of its singular career? The saga
of Beaujolais Nouveau alone erupts in such a yearly blaze of publicity
that it can scarcely be avoided. For universal name recognition, the only
wine that can rival Beaujolais is Champagne.

The name Champagne doesn't elicit smiles and laughter, though,
and neither do Bordeaux or Bourgogne—that's *serious* stuff. For that

matter, just about any wine you can think of, whether it be from Alsace, Languedoc, Midi-Pyrénées, California, Australia, Chile or anywhere else, will be assessed with similar poker-faced gravity. Only Beaujolais gets the smile and projects this aura of easy familiarity.

But familiarity breeds contempt, as we all know, and Beaujolais has suffered more than its share of obloquy. This, of course, is the ransom of its success, but it is really quite extraordinary that a success and a notoriety of this degree should have come to a wine that represents only slightly more than 2 percent of France's total production and .05 percent worldwide. How it reached this point of celebrity is a story of a few turns of history's wheel, of a certain amount of luck and a certain amount of marketing skill, but mostly of a long background of unremitting drudgery: centuries of hard work poorly rewarded. It is also to a great extent the story of one man, a young peasant winegrower named Georges Duboeuf who at age eighteen revolted against an unfair, illogical distribution system run for the benefit of a dealers' cartel, and did it so well and so thoroughly that he rose to become the biggest dealer of all—but one of an entirely new style.

Beaujolais, then, is a double success story, the wine and the man, but does that make either worthy of being treated in full book length? After all, there are thousands of capitalists wealthier and more influential than Georges Duboeuf, and any number of Ferrari wines of greater prestige than Beaujolais. Naturally I answer an emphatic *yes* to the above question, because beyond the predictable angle of the underdog winning against the odds, the history of the Beaujolais reflects and explains a good deal about the French themselves, "this quick, talented, nervous, occasionally maddening but altogether admirable people" (I'm quoting myself here), among whom I have lived for more than forty years now. As for Georges Duboeuf, capitalism would have an infinitely better reputation today if all the world's Enrons, Tycos and WorldComs had been run by the likes of this model entrepreneur.

More than any other factor, the sudden worldwide prominence that came to the wines of the Beaujolais is owed to Duboeuf. He's a very interesting case, one of those rare persons inhabited by a mysterious kind of driving force that sets certain individuals apart from the rest, causing them to achieve what others don't even think about venturing. We all come across a few of them in the course of a lifetime, and can never quite define what that force is or why it should be there, but it is always clear that it *is* there: he or she is simply different. Georges Duboeuf's rise from modest station to wealth, repute and influence is like the plot of a Thomas Hardy novel, and it is no accident that this rise coincided exactly with the progress of the fortunes of the Beaujolais country and its wines.

For the sake of form, let me establish something right away, lest I be accused of partiality: I count Georges Duboeuf as a friend. I am partial. I am partial to Georges because of his admirable personal qualities — integrity, sincerity, constancy — and for having served as my initiator and guide to the Beaujolais. He generously shared with me his unparalleled knowledge of and love for the country, its people and, of course, its wines, allowing me to partake at least modestly of that knowledge. In his company I explored the back hills, the villages and hamlets and vineyards, and through him I had the luck to become acquainted with the extraordinary, colorful and always engaging human fauna that peoples this beautiful little slice of the French countryside.

Because my expeditions with Duboeuf were not mere tourism. Georges introduced me to an entire gallery of the dramatis personae of the Beaujolais. A short selection would have to begin with the vigneron (winemaker) Louis Bréchard, known everywhere by the sobriquet "Papa," sage and folk historian of the Beaujolais, a man who carried his wisdom all the way to parliament in Paris when he was elected deputy in 1958. Count Louis Durieux de Lacarelle, owner of the biggest single estate in the Beaujolais, presides over his vines, his wine cellar and his lunch table with the melancholy bonhomie of the aristocrat who has seen just about all the world has to offer and, everything considered, prefers his little château in the Beaujolais-Villages country of Saint-Étienne-des-Oullières, where he can follow Voltaire's advice and cultivate his garden in peace. Gérard Canard and Michel Brun were and are passionately devoted professionals of promotion who cheerfully spent their lives spreading the Beaujolais gospel around the globe. (Brun carries his regional loyalty to the point of awarding himself the e-mail address of Michelgamay, appropriating the name of the Beaujolais grape as his personal identity.) Edward Steeves is a poetically inclined Yankee scholar from Boston, a rare and true gent who fell so deeply in love with the wine, the land and the people of the Beaujolais that he settled there, married, produced three Franco-American children and became boss of an important wine distribution house. He will learnedly expatiate at the drop of a hat, in French, English, Latin or Greek, on the relative virtues of Chiroubles, say, as compared to Saint-Amour, Régnié or Chénas, and he does it so well that he is in constant demand as a keynote speaker who politely and convincingly informs the natives about their own wines. Marcel Laplanche and Claude Beroujon, winemakers of the old school, can recite from memory the exact weather conditions of any year from about 1930 onward, how the wine tasted and what price it fetched. My friend Marcel Pariaud is so stricken with the peasant's reluctance to throw anything usable away that at last count he owned seven tractors, none less than forty years old. ("But they all work!" he protests when I josh him about it.) In spite of this rich collection of mechanical antiquity, though, he prefers to do his plowing behind Hermine, his indolent Comtoise workhorse. With her cooperation, Marcel wrings from the soil in and around the village of Lancié a Beaujolais and a Morgon so perfect that you immediately understand why the people of the region stay away from water. And of course there was everybody's favorite, René Besson, "Bobosse" the *charcutier*, sausage maker to kings, the joy and sorrow of the Beaujolais—First-Class Drunkard, as he liked to qualify himself, the laughing, overwhelmingly generous lover of life and good companionship over a shared glass or two or ten, Falstaff to Duboeuf's Prince Hal. Bobosse refused to accept that our short mortal route was but a vale of tears, and he more or less drank himself to death by enjoying the ride too much. Naturally it is impossible to defend irresponsible behavior of this sort in a rational world, but it wasn't rationality that guided Bobosse's life. Where drinking was concerned, he was an *artiste*, and his creativity in expressing his art was Platonic—at a low-flying level, to be sure, but Platonic all the same: divine madness. Everyone knows it must be banned from the city of the sensible, but, lord, how graciously he carried it off.

Denizens of the Beaujolais country like these bear little resemblance to the edgy, ill-tempered Parisians through whom tourists often form lasting opinions of the French national character. One taxi ride from Charles de Gaulle Airport to the center of the capital can be enough to set a negative impression into stone, and that's a shame, because the impressions would be utterly different if these same visitors ever took the time to pass by way of the Beaujolais country. There they would be able to appreciate how inaccurate the tired old stereotypes can be. Contrary to the popular (and largely Anglo-Saxon) legend of Latin hedonism, three-hour lunches and nonstop sexual dalliance, the French are an extremely industrious and hardworking nation with a long tradition of perfectionism in artisan craftsmanship, and few crafts can represent this tradition—vibrant today still—better than that of the individual peasant winegrower.

Beaujolais is the smallholder wine country par excellence. Unlike their wealthy Burgundy and Bordeaux cousins who specialized in wine-making very early in their history, the peasants of the Beaujolais were until quite recent times primarily subsistence farmers who grew grain and tended animals to survive while making wine as an aleatory cash crop. Theirs was a punishing, penurious existence, and most of them remained stuck in anonymous poverty until after the Second World War. That very poverty and relative humbleness of condition, though, made them solid representatives of *la France profonde*, the obscure rural masses at the country's heart, whose life experience and peasant wisdom formed much of the national character as it stands today.

The wine that these and other growers produced has been central to French civilization ever since the Romans backed off and the Gauls took their own history in hand. It is hardly an exaggeration to say that France came to be defined by wine, considering its deep religious symbolism, the stubborn belief in its strength-giving medicinal qualities and, of course, the unique conditions of soil and climate for turning out the enormous palette of wine varieties that made France the world reference in this ancient and still somewhat mysterious art.

Tasting wine, analyzing it and buying it for investment are now fashionable in most of the world's wealthier nations, but as a rule the movement is like a pastime or hobby and limited to the cultured bourgeoisie of the great urban centers. In France, wine is a daily routine that cuts across classes like potato chips and beer in the States. Certainly consumption levels have dropped from the dizzying levels of previous years—the French are becoming reasonable—but wine is no less an everyday part of life, as much a banality as watching the news on television. France would not be France without its wine, and the old traditions are passed on as a matter of course. When a baby is born, Papa still dips his finger into his celebratory glass of Champagne and gives the little newcomer a taste. Does that initiate a lifetime habit? I don't know, but after enough years of living in the midst of this civilization I felt constrained to do it myself, even though both my kids are American, born of American parents in the American Hospital in Paris.

At the embassy, the staff calls this sort of behavior "going native," and I suppose they're right. There's an ever so slight sniff of disdain behind that expression, but for me it was impossible not to fall under the charm of the multitudinous aspects of the wine culture here, beginning with the inevitable epiphany of the first truly Big Bottle (for the record, a well-named Meursault-Charmes of the 1964 vintage). Finding a Meursault seductive is no triumph, of course (approximately equivalent to finding Catherine Deneuve or Juliette Binoche seductive), but it is an excellent way to instill a lifelong respect for the skill of the French vigneron community. Although Beaujolais is a "lesser" wine than the great Burgundies, the devotion that its best artisans bring to their craft is no less impressive. A nation that approaches its wines as knowledgeably as this one can be counted on to respect it and honor it at all levels and in all circumstances, and the mention of my first bottle of Meursault inescapably brings to mind the finest example I have ever heard of this vinous respect and honor. It was delivered by Père Baroillot, who might be termed the unofficial and unbeatified patron saint of French gourmets.

Father Raymond Baroillot is long gone now, but in a single moment of inspired candor a few decades ago, he proved himself worthy of an immortal place in the hearts of wine lovers everywhere. It seems clear that a heavenly power had traced a mission for this wispy, soft-spoken Catholic priest to evangelize the world of wine and food. As a young curé before the war, he had been assigned to take over the parish of Meursault, and he applied himself with such diligence that over the following years he acquired a quasi-professional nose and palate for appreciating the finest Burgundies. Transferred from this dream assignment to the much larger and much less distinguished city of Roanne, he might have assumed his gourmet tour was finished, but as luck had it his sphere of responsibility in Roanne included the area around the railroad station—exactly opposite which sat Troisgros, one of the world's greatest restaurants, directed by Jean-Baptiste Troisgros, an uprooted Burgundian like himself. Father Baroillot watched in admiration as Jean-Baptiste's sons Jean and Pierre Troisgros cooked their way to three Michelin stars. He also ate in admiration because, as confessor, confidant and spiritual advisor to the famous cooking clan, he enjoyed a regular seat at the family dinner table. Before long, his knowledge of gastronomy equaled that of oenology. After Jean-Baptiste died, Jean and Pierre naturally called upon the priest to celebrate a private mass for the departed patriarch. The entire family was present when, at the moment of Consecration, cradling the holy chalice of wine in his hands, he caught himself, turned 180 degrees and ad-libbed a brief bit of professional information for the brothers: "It's a little aligoté from Colin," he said, before giving it a swirl, a sniff and a taste, and then getting on with the rest of the proceedings.

The story would have been just right for my purposes if Father Baroillot had been using Beaujolais instead of aligoté, but you can't always have everything exactly the way you want it. Even so, there's a real connection here to the subject of this book, an almost eerily fitting one, because half a century earlier a French author named Gabriel Chevallier had anticipated Father Baroillot's life story with uncanny accuracy when he penned the satirical novel *Clochemerle*. By inventing the Abbé Augustin Ponosse, saintly of demeanor and scarlet of nose, parish priest of a little village in the Beaujolais-Villages area, he proved conclusively that, in France, anyway, life is often called upon to imitate art. Read on.

I'll Drink to That

I

WHAT A GLASS OF WINE REPRESENTS

*B*eaming, voluble, robust as a workhorse, fairly erupting with energy and good cheer as he performed surgery on his supper with his pocket knife, Marcel sat at the head of a long rectangular plank table supported on sawhorses, presiding over an improbably diverse collection of youth, most of them girls barely out of their teens, med students from Brittany. A second table, same size and parallel to his but over against the other wall, was occupied entirely by men—older, bulkier and considerably noisier than the girls. Nearly forty strong, the harvesting crew filled the little room next to the kitchen with such an ear-shattering din that everyone had to shout to be heard, which of course made the clamor only worse. Never mind: there was some serious chowing down to be attended to, because there was nothing like a twelve-hour day in the vineyards to put an edge on the appetite. After *velouté de légumes*, peasant soup with vegetables from her own garden, Nathalie had delivered four enormous platters of her own *poule au riz*, chicken and rice in cream sauce, cooked up that afternoon on her industrial-sized stove. Cheeses would come after that, and then a selection of Nathalie's tarts and fruit preserves. Pretty soon, once they'd sated their hunger and drunk enough of Marcel's wine, the men would be singing their bawdy songs again, led as usual by Choucroute the Alsatian and Zorro from Toulouse. That was how it always went in the evening.

Glancing down the table, Marcel spotted something amiss: L'Écrivain, the scholarly, ginger-haired young German from Leipzig who also spoke Russian and English and who was always lecturing the girls about Rostand, Proust and Balzac, hadn't finished his chicken leg. Marcel surged to his feet, made a lunge with his fork and spirited the spurned morsel back to his plate at the head of the table. Eyelids squinched down to a crack with epicurean pleasure behind his steel-rimmed glasses, he grasped it in viselike fists and finished it off as neatly as a cat.

Things were going very nicely, even better than he had expected. The harvest was nearly all in, the grapes were healthy and the rain that had been falling all over the country had miraculously spared the regions between Mâcon and Lyon. The new vintage was going to be fine. It was a good time for the Beaujolais.

It was for Marcel Pariaud, at any rate. Sixty-two years of age at the time of this harvest, looking a dozen less than that and charged with the vigor and optimism of a twenty-year-old, he was already in his fortieth consecutive year as an independent wine grower, or vigneron. He had reason for his good spirits, because he had prospered over those four decades — as, indeed, the whole of the Beaujolais had prospered. (And before we go any further, please note the "the" here. It underlines a point that many people do not realize: Beaujolais is a wine, to be sure, but more than that, it is this *place*, an irregular little rectangle of land measuring roughly sixty by fifteen kilometers, framed to the south by Lyon, to the north by Mâcon, and named after the old regional capital of Beaujeu. In terms of geography, "Beaujolais" simply signifies the land lying around Beaujeu, a little ribbon of a town folded into a cleft between hills of chalky clay where grapes can thrive in the sunlight. During several prime daylight hours the abrupt slopes above Beaujeu block the sun from reaching all the way to the bottom of the cleft where the river Ardières flows. The soil down there is no good for grapes anyway, so that's where they stuck the town. Logical: care for the wine always comes first in the Beaujolais.)

I like to think of Marcel as the ideal model of the yeoman citizenry of this stunningly beautiful and still little known corner of France, because wine defines the Beaujolais country the way information technology defines Silicon Valley, and Marcel Pariaud makes it as responsibly and passionately (and deliciously) as any man I know. I admire him because his ebullient good humor never fails him, because no matter how busy he is he will always take the time to educate the ignorant and explain the subtleties of the ever-shifting art of vinification by which the boring old caterpillar called grape juice is transmuted into the gorgeous butterfly called wine, and because in a modern world increasingly dominated by abstractions and virtuality—industries of service rather than creation, economic sleight of hand and "outsourcings," dehumanized manipulations that pluck vast amounts of money apparently from thin air via distant computer keystrokes—it is wonderfully refreshing to discover an embodiment of traditional old ways and virtues. Here is one honest man who built a modest but respectable prosperity for himself and his wife by the sweat of his brow and the calluses of his hands, a man who had truly earned every franc and euro that came to his pockets and who richly deserved the retirement he was beginning to contemplate on that September evening of 2006 as he chomped on his secondhand chicken leg. Reaching his present point of relative financial comfort had been anything but easy, but ease has never been Marcel's strong suit. We'll be seeing more about that, and about Marcel himself, in later pages.

I was about to write that it is difficult to imagine anyone who had worked as hard all his life as Marcel Pariaud, but that wouldn't have been quite right, because there was another one quite nearby, living just down the road hardly more than a mile away, in the neighboring village of Romanèche-Thorins. He was a longtime acquaintance of mine, a man who was quite unlike Marcel but essentially similar, the other side of the same coin. By the time Zorro and Choucroute had begun bellowing their postprandial ditties that evening, this other one had already downed a quick bite and returned to his office to face the mountain of papers on his desk. There were e-mails to answer, phone calls to make, texts to write, reports to read, documents to sign: too much to do. It was past eleven when he finally went home, but next morning he would be up at four-thirty, just like the day before. *Ah là là* he would be muttering, this is no way to live. But he had been living exactly that way for more than fifty years.

His name was Georges Duboeuf, and if on the surface everything about him and Marcel seemed different—antithetical, even—the two men had lot more in common than appearances suggested. Certainly the contrast of physical appearances was striking. Lean, reserved and ascetic where Marcel was hearty, muscular, loquacious and outgoing, Duboeuf chose his words with painstaking care, was given to periods of introspective silence and, poker-faced, spoke in a voice so softly modulated that it could barely nudge a decibel gauge beyond whisper level. Joyous and happy to share his joy, Marcel never stopped smiling and never shut up. The environment at Marcel's place in the little village of Lancié bespoke the true, hands-on, do-it-yourself rural artisan, a little one-man hodgepodge of old equipment and old ways that functioned smoothly only because he had the secret of how to keep it all going. By contrast, the workplace that Georges Duboeuf had built up over the years was enormous: a computerized, high-tech, multifaceted plant of glistening stainless steel and virginal white buildings, one that required 130 or so employees to keep it functioning properly. Marcel was the quintessential small-time winemaker. The vineyards he tended had never measured more than twelve hectares, or about thirty acres, the greater part of it on rented land, and by 2006 he had wound his operation down to his own land, a mere 4.5 hectares. Duboeuf was big-time, a major wine dealer, or *négociant—the négociant* of the Beaujolais, far and away the biggest and most important of them all—a businessman of worldwide scope who year in and year out sold 30 million bottles or more under his label. In fact he was, by the count of bottles sold (more than 7 million a year), the number one exporter of French wines to the United States.

The rich international star of commerce and the obscure peasant did not exactly frequent each other—their life contexts were different—but each knew and respected the other's work. If the yard behind Marcel's vinifying and storage sheds was littered with old equipment rusting in the grass, it only meant that the consumer society had not yet arrived at his doorstep. He was inhabited by the peasant's ancient horror of throwing away anything for which he might conceivably find a future use: he was thrifty. But his rows of vines were as clean and perfectly tended as human sweat could make them, and the wine he made in the old wooden vats inside the big vinifying shed that he had built with his own two hands was the perfect, honest expression of the genius of the gamay grape. If Duboeuf drove a fancy Audi, wore expensive shoes and slung a cashmere sweater over his bony shoulders, Marcel knew that he, too, had been born to the peasantry and had not forgotten it. Each man, within the orbit of his making, was equally estimable. It would be hard to find better incarnations than these two—the winemaker and the wine seller—of the soul and the spirit of the Beaujolais. They represent the forces that brought Beaujolais, against all odds and against the established wisdom of centuries of wine snobbery, to the enviable position it enjoys today as the world's best-known and most popular red wine. There can hardly be a language anywhere in which those three euphonious, easily pronounced syllables "bo-jo-lay" do not trip lightly off the tongue, or a large city (at least in those parts of the world that do not criminalize a touch of the grape) where the wines of that same name do not enjoy the same kind of popularity as back home in France. Worldwide, there is nothing to rival Beaujolais for name recognition save Champagne.

The story of how Beaujolais reached its present prominence is worth a look because it encapsulates so much not only about the wine itself but also about France and the French themselves: this quick, talented, nervous, occasionally maddening but altogether admirable people.

We have to go back a while to get to the start of the story—say, 50 million years, give or take a few million here or there—to when something called the Great Alpine Folding occurred. Under the colossal pressures of this tectonic shifting, the Alps were born, and then the earth's crust gave a secondary shrug as a kind of afterthought, splitting the Massif Central, the high ground in the middle of present-day France, into a series of rocky wrinkles. The easternmost of these wrinkles ended at a plain where the River Saône ambles peaceably along today, leaving a soil heavily granitic in its northern stretches and mostly limestone and clay in the south. Drivers working their way toward Paris from the Mediterranean today can see the result, just a few miles north of Lyon, as clearly as if the process had been laid out on a demonstration board. After the *autoroute* tollgate at Villefranche, the terrain to the right lies flat all the way to the Saône and beyond, interspersed with woods and pastures, and given over to farming and light industry. To the left, though, a dramatically different view appears through the haze: a patchwork of steep, high hills marching off to the horizon in the west—*monts* is the very handy French word for them, for which there's no proper equivalent in English. It means something more serious than a hill, but not just yet a mountain. Until quite recently, this modest portion of upheaved land was just another obscure corner of France's richly varied countryside, little known and little valued beyond its immediate vicinity. *Les monts du Beaujolais* the hills are called.

Geographically remote from the main centers of economic activity, the choppy hillsides of the Beaujolais could, until recent postwar times, have been compared to certain parts of Appalachia. Hunched together in their little villages of yellow stone roofed with rounded Roman tiles, the natives had always gazed down upon the plain of the Saône—today as yesterday France's principal north-south passage—with conflicting emotions. A natural interest in the commerce and novelty that the highway might bring was overlaid with a certain wariness of outsiders, bred no doubt by atavistic memories of the many foreign invasions that their lush, beautiful country had suffered through history. Nor were all of their own fellow citizens to be entirely trusted, either, and least of all the rich or powerful among them, because these hill dwellers were poor themselves—always had been and, it seemed, always would be—and the rich and powerful had a disagreeable historical penchant for exploiting the poor.

I set foot in the region for the very first time in 1965. Strictly speaking, the place where I landed that afternoon was not actually in the Beaujolais, but merely adjacent to it. There is a definite connection, though—I will even say a significant one—between the story of Beaujolais and the town called Thoissey, where I stopped for lunch. This little community of not quite fifteen hundred inhabitants sits on the plain at the base of *les monts du Beaujolais* just east of the Saône and, as nearly as I can tell, has never had anything particular to distinguish it but one: the country inn called Le Chapon Fin. In its time, it was one of the most famous provincial restaurants in France, and its owner, Paul Blanc, enjoyed an esteem among his fellow chefs fully equal to that of media stars like Fernand Point in Vienne, André Pic in Valence and Alexandre Dumaine in Saulieu, the old holy trinity of French provincial gastronomy. Perhaps because of Blanc's bluff, straight-talking manner and his refusal to dandify his décor, Le Chapon Fin never rose above two stars in the Michelin Guide, but by general agreement its food was easily worth three.

Paul Blanc had inherited patriarchal ascendancy over a remarkable cooking clan that continues to dazzle gourmets today. He was the grandson of Elisa Blanc, who had taken over a village inn that her mother-in-law, Antoinette, had founded in 1872 in the nearby town of Vonnas, between Mâcon and Bourg-en-Bresse. Elisa continued Antoinette's style of cooking—perfect execution of simple country dishes prepared with all the best local ingredients—and did it so well that the restaurant, now baptized Auberge de la Mère Blanc, became a famous stopping point for hungry diners from Lyon and travelers en route to Switzerland. Elisa won her first Michelin star in 1929 and then a second in 1931, while somehow finding the time to raise two sons. Her first, Jean, became a wholesale wine and soft drinks dealer, while Paul trekked off to Thoissey, opened Le Chapon Fin and soon made it as famous as his mother's place.

I was totally ignorant of this glorious family tradition when I came to Thoissey in 1965. All I knew was that it was lunchtime, I was hungry, and I was on the N. 6 main road north of Lyon, en route to Paris. The Michelin Guide informed me that a nearby place called Le Chapon Fin had two stars, so I hung a right and headed expeditiously in direction of Thoissey.

My lunch there was a curious experience. Frankly, I wasn't entirely satisfied with the meal. The food was quite good, of course, but I had not expected the mob scene that I encountered when I got there. Every seat in the house was taken, and I managed to find a place only in a distant corner of the terrace. The service was slow, and I was irritated by the long wait. I was younger then, much less experienced in matters French and certainly less patient than I have since learned to be in the presence of serious cuisine. I had not taken into account what should have been obvious: it was August, France's great month for vacationing en masse; it was Sunday, the consecrated day for a proper lunch with the family; and everyone else on the road had also seen those two Michelin stars for Le Chapon Fin.

In the light of the heroic efforts that Paul Blanc and his brigade were expending in their overheated kitchen to get the mob fed, I can now see that my youthful irritation was both misplaced and self-indulgent, but it changed to something like beatitude when my wine order was delivered to the table. Working on the trusty old precept that it is always a good idea to stick with the nearest local wines, I had ordered a simple pitcher of generic Beaujolais, the least expensive choice on the list. I was expecting nothing much as I poured myself the first glass, but when I tasted it my grumpy palate was suddenly greeted with an explosive burst of fruit and flowers.

What was that: raspberries, strawberries, currants? And violets, maybe? I couldn't quite tell, but I knew that I liked it a lot. I stuck my nose into the glass, took a long sniff, tasted again just to be sure. Everything from my first mouthful was still present and maybe even more, too, if only I had the skill to seek it all out. It was one of the finest moments of gastronomic surprise I had ever enjoyed, and a cheap one to boot. Getting up to leave after lunch, I made a point of approaching Juliette

Blanc, the great chef's wife, who was naturally in charge of everything that happened at Le Chapon Fin outside of Paul's kitchen. Wherever, I asked her, did you find such a wonderful Beaujolais to serve in such a plain pitcher for so little money?

"Oh, that's Duboeuf," she replied, in the tone of one stating what ought to have been obvious to anyone but a hick. The name meant nothing to me.

Brute luck, it turned out, had brought me to the very place where, a decade and a half earlier, the eighteen-year-old peasant named Georges Duboeuf had made his first sale. I would be hearing a lot more about this extraordinary character in the following years. So would everyone else.

Five more years passed before I ventured into that area again. Beaujolais had become progressively more popular by the early seventies, and the notoriety of Duboeuf was no longer limited to wine professionals and a limited number of insiders. Things were shaping up nicely as the Beaujolais cantered along with the rest of France into *les trente glorieuses*, the thirty years of economic boom that saw the country heave itself up from the shame and penury of defeat and the wartime German occupation to become a rich and powerful leader of Europe, showing the way to whatever bright future the Common Market might promise. In those happy days, France was still the uncontested center of the wine world, *the* reference for anyone who knew anything about or cared about that miraculous procedure by which the hand of man persuades grape juice to forsake its natural route toward vinegar and detour over into an infinitely more desirable, drinkable alternative. More wine was being produced in France than anywhere else in the world; the natives drank more of it per head (about 120 liters a year, down from 150 in the thirsty fifties, with babies, kids, centenarians, cops, nuns and teetotalers all factored into that impressive figure) than any other population, and the export market, where demand still well exceeded supply, was riding a seemingly permanent upward curve. In the Beaujolais country, some five thousand peasant winemakers were tending individual vineyards, pitching in to the national average by producing a yearly average of a million hectoliters* of the twelve different wines gathered under the Beaujolais label: generic Beaujolais; Beaujolais-Villages; and the ten rarer and more expensive *crus* (growths) of Brouilly, Côte de Brouilly, Chénas, Chiroubles, Fleurie, Juliénas, Morgon, Moulin-à-Vent, Régnié and Saint-Amour. Each one had its own character and its own clientele — the muscle of Morgon, the elegance of Fleurie, the depth of Moulin-à-Vent — but at the same time a very interesting new phenomenon was gaining strength from year to year: the wine called Beaujolais Nouveau was on the verge of becoming an international craze.

Things were looking good for the Beaujolais. It was in this atmosphere of heady optimism that I came back for what was my real introduction to the region. Wine and I were good friends by then, and I was still in those fearless, pack-it-away days of youth when you think you can get away with anything, and occasionally do. In the event, I didn't get away with it, not this time. It was in the village called Juliénas that I made the first of a long succession of overconfident missteps Beaujolais-style, ignorant as I was of the disconcerting fact that the natives enjoy nothing more than testing visitors with as much wine as they can get into them.

I could scarcely have chosen a better place for my initiation, because by itself Juliénas encapsulated the entire sweep of Beaujolais history. The name harks straight back to Julius Caesar himself, conqueror of the Gauls. He wasn't really what you could call an endearing sort of chap: his brand of pacification was little short of genocidal, and he took pleasure in reporting back to Rome on how he had put entire populations to the sword, regardless of age, gender or sexual orientation. Even so, his memory must still be honored in France today, because it was his legionnaires, retiring after hard years of service to imperialism, who taught the surviving natives how to make wine — infinitely preferable

---

*1 hectoliter = 100 liters. Beaujolais represents some 2.2 percent of France's wine production, or .50 percent of total world production.

to *cervoise*, the rough beer with which they had been quenching their thirst until then. Intermarriage with these Roman settlers and centuries of assimilation formed the Beaujolais character such as it is today: tough, stubbornly attached to the soil and the vine, a tad suspicious of outsiders at first view, but jolly and overwhelmingly welcoming once the ice has been broken. This little town's founders named their settlement after their boss Julius, planted their vines and never looked back from winemaking.

Returning northward on a long drive from Spain, my wife and I had veered off the main road into the Beaujolais country in company with our friend Pierre Boulat, one of France's top photographers and a man who knew his way around. There was a pretty good little restaurant in Juliénas, said Pierre, and we rolled into town on a surprisingly balmy October evening. Suddenly the long drudgery of our drive morphed into a wine lover's dream, signaled by an auspicious set of road signs at the picture-postcard main square: Saint-Amour and Saint-Vérand to the north of us, Jullié to the west, Chénas, Fleurie and Chiroubles to the south. Down to the left of the bakery near the marketplace, the spire of a sixteenth-century church soared, as it should in all picture-postcard situations, high over the town. Years later, when I had grown to know Juliénas on more intimate terms, I learned that the regional diocese had deconsecrated the church 1868 and sold it to a local notable, a vigneron, of course, who had promptly put its cool stone embrace to practical use as a *chai*, a wine storage shed. Further progress came in 1954, when a wine dealer, restaurateur and local character named Victor Peyret transformed the church's elegant choir into a *caveau* (wine-tasting cellar), complete with vineyard scenes on the stained glass windows and bacchanalian frescoes on the walls. The church is a drinking place today still, the town's official *caveau*, signaled as such in books, posters and tourism leaflets. It is always just a bit disconcerting to pass under its portal and enter its stony interior only to discover a bar.

Presently we were seated in the dining room of a quirky little bistro called Chez La Rose, with a bottle of Juliénas, cool and fresh from the cellar, standing before us and *andouillettes grillées*, bathed in a reduction of white wine and chopped shallots, ordered and on the way. On the way for me and Pierre, that is. My wife sighed, ordered a civilized roast chicken and muttered insults about savages capable of making a meal out of intestine sausage.

The table next to us was occupied by a curious pair of gents: a short, agitated little man who emitted a steady stream of wisecracking chatter and a massive character, a head taller, with hands like grappling hooks, who bore a vague but still disquieting resemblance to Boris Karloff as Dr. Frankenstein's monster. The first wore coat and tie, the second blue workman's overalls.

Gradually, as the meal drew on, little sparks, little presages of dialogue, grew between the two tables. This was unusual, because the French, when dining, are usually sensible enough to concentrate on the appreciation of what they are eating, and courteous enough to leave space between themselves and those around them. But on that evening a voice perhaps too loud, a comment or two overheard, an accent unmistakably not French—whatever it was—conspired to set off a mutual joshing that was, if not aggressive, at least challenging in some unclear way. A few bottles of wine undoubtedly did their part, too. The upshot was that in the course of the dialogue they learned that Pierre and I were of the journalistic sort. The shorter man introduced himself as Pierre Martray, *régisseur* (manager) of Château de la Chaize; he and his cellar master were dining at Chez La Rose to celebrate the latter's birthday. By the time we were tucking into a cheese platter (some absolutely remarkable goat's milk creations), it somehow became established that we, the interloping outsiders, would be forever marked in history as the merest of churls and *poules mouillées* (wet hens) if we did not accompany them forthwith to the château to toast the birthday and gain an appreciation of different years and different batches of wine from different sections of its vineyard.

Well, now. Château de la Chaize is a big, prestigious name, known around the world. It is one of the brightest stars of the Brouilly growth, and at nearly 250 acres its vineyard is one of the region's largest single holdings. Its enormous vaulted cellar, considerably greater in length than a football field, is the longest in the Beaujolais, and is officially classified as a French historical monument. This was, in short, a serious reference, and Martray's proposition was a serious one that we would have been remiss to neglect.

We accepted. Midnight had come and gone by the time we left the restaurant, and the hostilities commenced without delay. At the wheel of his powerful German car, Pierre found to his dismay that he was hard put to keep up with Martray, who shot away from Juliénas in nothing better than a boxy, battered old Renault van that looked like an automotive caricature of itself. But he knew by heart every curve and bump in the roads winding through the vineyards back to the Brouilly hills, and he negotiated them at breakneck speed. The stock-car race that ensued was pure foolishness, of course, but on we roared after him, up hill and down dale, Pierre manically intent on not losing sight of the shaky tail-lights disappearing around the next bend, and it was probably just as well that in the dark of night we were unable to see just how precipitous were the slopes on either side of us. We arrived at the château with an apocalyptic clamor of brakes, and Martray led us without delay down into his beautiful subterranean domain. Tasting glasses in hand, we were soon treading the cellar's central alleyway of dank clay, preceded at a shambling, languorous pace by our very own Frankenstein, a syringe-like glass pipette in hand. Twin rows of enormous wooden tuns on either side of us stretched away in perfect parallax to a dimly perceived conclusion somewhere at the far end of the ill-lit tunnel. Not even bothering with a ladder, the cellar master clambered skillfully up the supporting framework of one of the first tuns, removed the bung on top, inserted the pipette into the hole and drew forth a column of glistening, ruby red liquid. He nodded at us, and we held out our glasses. He lifted his thumb from the little orifice on top of the pipette, and atmospheric pressure did the rest: before you could say Jacques Robinson, a crimson stream shot out to fill our glasses.

I don't know how many of that endless array of tuns we drank from that night, but I do remember that there was a perfectly plausible oeno-logical reason for every one of them—a different year, a younger or older set of vines, a different *parcelle* of the vineyard and so forth—that our hosts watched intently to be certain that we drank every drop, and that we ended the visit in Martray's office, where Jack and Jacqueline Kennedy smiled down on us from a large photo on the wall. Martray produced a bottle of Champagne, and we drank it in honor of the birthday boy, or of the Kennedys, or of andouillette sausages. (By then it could have been anything at all.) It was close to two-thirty in the morning when Martray finally released us, and Pierre crept away from Château de la Chaize at half speed—which did not prevent him, however, from motoring straight into a cow pasture at the road's first sharp turn to the left.

Although today, nearly four decades after the fact, I can still imagine Martray laughing as he watched us stumble out to the car and inch away from Château de la Chaize, I bear him no retrospective ill will. We didn't have to go back there with him, and we didn't have to drink all that Brouilly and Champagne. We did it of our own free will, and truth be told, we enjoyed it, too, even if we suffered somewhat for our excesses the next day.

This sort of encounter is not, you may have imagined by now, an altogether infrequent occurrence in the Beaujolais. Let me underline, though, that this kind of challenge is not the sole explanation for their behavior. These people are proud of what they labor all year to produce, and sincerely want you to love it as much as they do themselves—but at the same time they also rather like to determine how well you can hold it. Wine is the social grease and catalyst of the Beaujolais, and the natives give it away with a liberality that would scandalize the purse holders of the more hoity-toity growths to the north and west of them, in Burgundy and Bordeaux. Stop at any Beaujolais vigneron's house, knock on the door, announce your presence and intentions; there will be a handshake, a few curt words—and then, inevitably, you will adjourn to his *caveau*. It is only when he is in his element, surrounded by his barrels and his bottles, when he has tapped a vat or pulled a cork to fill his glass and yours, that hospitality will have been served and custom respected. Comfortable now, he will open up and you can start to talk business. The practice is ancient, immutable and immensely agreeable, but carried to the extreme, it can be a test of the simple act of remaining vertical.

Please do not mistake me: by no means do I intend this account to be anything like an apologia for drunkenness. It does happen from time to time, of course, but there are many different degrees of alcoholic euphoria, and they rarely reach downright debauch. Here, as in every vineyard region in the world, wine is a serious business, and the 150 million or so bottles that the Beaujolais produces every year, depending on the vagaries of weather and harvest, represent a serious investment in time, toil and expertise, one that returns a weighty contribution of tax revenues to the French treasury. On the consumer's side of matters, it is obvious that a reasoned investigation of the range and subtleties of wine, rather than just dumb chugalug boozing, is a thoroughly respectable and rewarding undertaking; few activities could be more civilized than the measured—you might almost say sober—consumption that such an investigation requires. Wine tasting, and indeed the whole spectrum of oenology, rife as it is with books, magazines, clubs, computer programs, games, competitions and who knows what other spinoffs, has become a social and business phenomenon of the first order: big money, big pres- tige, big opportunities.

So: wine is fashionable. No need to labor that point any further. But with that fashion, a curtain of tiresome solemnity often descends upon the subject, and we Anglo-Saxons are perhaps more guilty than most when it comes to vinous posturing and affectation. Wine today is ever so gravely classified, parsed and analyzed to death with a vocabulary worthy of the cabala, and the high-end stuff gets bought and sold exactly like stock market shares or sowbelly futures (an excellent investment, I understand). I wish the analysts and speculators every bit of the success they deserve, but for all the times I have rubbed shoulders with the swells of the trade at château tastings in Bordeaux, for all the pomp, pageantry and bizarre costumes I have had occasion to admire at enthronement ceremonies of the Chevaliers du Tastevin, that superbly organized PR stunt of the Burgundy wine establishment, and for all the free Champagne I have swilled at press junkets in the chalky cellars of Épernay and Reims, it is always to the Beaujolais hills that I return when I grow weary of the splendors of our globalized iPod Age and yearn for a less self-important, less technologically correct form of human intercourse. Am I the only one who feels a need to flee the artifice of it all and seek out an earlier, simpler time when my cell phone didn't communicate with my refrigerator, and where I could enjoy a glass of wine without being held to a doctoral discourse? Whatever the case, it is the land of the Beaujolais that constitutes my best cure for the blues. You get your transcendence where you can find it.

Because there is so much more to Beaujolais than just the wine. To begin with, the country itself is soothingly, heart-stoppingly beautiful, far more so than Burgundy, Bordeaux or the Champagne area. All three of these regions make very fine wines, but their landscape and architecture are as boring as flat Perrier water for the most part. The Beaujolais is in glorious, gorgeous contrast to this. It is what a storybook illustration would look like if you sought to depict ideal wine country: a dramatic collection of steep hillsides springing up from the plain and shouldering against one another, forested when the Romans arrived but covered today in an undulant carpet of vines. At the high ground to the west in the direction of Roanne and the Loire is the "Green Beaujolais," a land of cow and sheep pastures, deeply carved escarpments, canyons and pine forests that suddenly give way to a vine-friendly, mineral-rich subsoil of granite, gneiss, clay and limestone, where the vines grow in perfect geometric formation, as neat as cabbages in a curate's garden. Little ribbons of roads—they keep them narrow, lest they eat up too much valuable vine-growing space—wind around the hillsides like seams on a baseball, then dip down into the shaded vales where the villages sit, clustered around the inevitable church steeple.

The villages themselves are masterpieces of rural architecture. In jewels like Bully and Oingt in the southern Pierres Dorées (golden stone) area, the houses are positively aglow with an ochre effulgence, thanks to the iron oxide permeating the locally quarried limestone. Farther north, in the equally beautiful white wine country around Leynes, the building stone reflects the veined, pinkish hue of potter's clay. Between these two extremes, on the hills where the great shiftings of the Tertiary Period littered the ground with crushed granite, the wine is the best and the houses have a bluish tint—in the Beaujolais, you can read the composition of the soil from the facades of the buildings. Nothing is better than this architectural tagging to illustrate the concept of the *terroir*, the localized pockets of rock, soil and minerals distributed throughout the countryside. People built with the materials they took from the ground where they had settled, and it is this ground, this *terroir*, that determines the character of the local wines. A Beaujolais-Villages is different from a simple Beaujolais, and a Morgon from a Saint-Amour for the same reason that a Puligny-Montrachet differs from a Bâtard-Montrachet up in Burgundy: the composition of the soil—the *terroir*—is different, and whatever tricks of vinification are used, it is always the *terroir* that shines through in the bouquet and the taste of the finished product.

"The poorer the soil, the richer the wine," vignerons like to say, and it's not just a casual phrase. Burgundy's most divine white wines, the Montrachet family, come from a *terroir* whose name means "a place where nothing grows." Wine grapes can't deliver the goods in the rich, creamy loam that grains love, but give them a pauper's bed of rocky, pebbly, flinty or even sandy soil, and their clever rootlets will insinuate themselves down through the tiniest cracks and fissures to suck mineral nourishment from the niggardly stone and send it up to headquarters, where the grapes are basking in the sun. Another favorite maxim speaks the same truth: to make the best wine, the vine has to suffer. So does the winemaker: Beaujolais old-timers still remember the days when their fathers and grandfathers had recourse to blasting powder for loosening up the stony ground to plant vines where their picks couldn't penetrate.

It was with this kind of heads-down, single-minded labor that generation upon generation of peasants turned the angular hills of the Beaujolais into the beautifully tended garden that the area is today. Set yourself up on high ground anywhere in the region and you are greeted by the same ocean of green: terrestrial wave upon wave of vine-planted hillsides, many of them so steep that no tractor could possibly work there, and where a man can just barely stand erect to tend the plants by hand.

The best viewpoint, though, is from the crest of Mont Genas, towering above the blessed town of Fleurie. Twice blessed: first by the wonderfully subtle wine produced there, and then again by the Madonna whose statue stands benevolently over the chapel that the locals built at the summit of Mont Genas in 1857 to beg divine protection for their vines against the violent flash storms and hailstones that the physiognomy of the Beaujolais seems to encourage. Due east, yonder far past the Saône, an alert eye can make out Mont Blanc's white flank, but closer to hand, down in the village, some more mundane wonders of the Beaujolais await the interested visitor. There is the municipal water tower that Marguerite Chabert filled with wine in 1960; there is the charcuterie (pork butcher's shop) founded by her father, François, who, upon returning from the trenches of World War I, invented the *andouillette Beaujolaise* as we know it today, the very one that I wolfed down in Juliénas on that memorable night in the early seventies when I got my comeuppance at Château de la Chaize; and there is Le Cep, for my book—that is to say right here, where I'm in control of things—one of the finest restaurants anyone could hope to discover, where Chantal Chagny (bless her, too, while we're at it) stubbornly continues to fly in the face of fashion by serving the marvelous classics of French country cooking with nary a kiwi, a drop of coconut milk or a dash of wasabi.

The Beaujolais has a long tradition of breeding strong women, and both Marguerite and Chantal could be statufied right now as exemplars of that population's character: as strong-willed and uncompromising as they are singular. Marguerite would be somewhat stony up there on her pedestal, because she is long gone now, but her old friend, the (sixtyish)

Chantal, is as present and redoubtable as ever in the Le Cep's dining room, at the cash desk and behind every cook, *commis* and *chef de partie* in her kitchen, making sure that the guys do it her way, and do it right.

Chantal it was who made history by becoming the first chef to voluntarily demote herself in the Michelin, the holy of holies among French restaurant guides. She had opened her little bistro in 1969, single-handedly cooking, serving and washing the dishes for a ridiculously cheap menu (the equivalent of $2) that included appetizer, main course, cheese and dessert. She did it so well that in 1973 Michelin accorded her a star. After she brought in Gérard Cortembert, a talented young chef who became her companion, a second star arrived in due course, and the reputation of Le Cep went worldwide. Unhappily, Cortembert's heart gave out in 1990, and Chantal was faced with the choice of maintaining his sophisticated menu or returning to the simpler home-style regional cooking that she had practiced when she was alone.

Dressed in the black widow's weeds that she has worn ever since Cortembert's death, she went to Paris, strode into Michelin's inner sanctum behind the Invalides and collared Bernard Naegellen, the guide's all-powerful boss. I'm changing my cooking style, she said, in essence—no more complications, no more fancy silverware or china, no more truffles, no more lobster. From now on I'm doing my food—Beaujolais food—so knock me back down to one star in your guide. Bemused and amused, Naegellen shrugged, complied and congratulated her on preserving an endangered national patrimony. Far from losing her customers, Chantal's turnabout made Le Cep even more famous, and it is now one of France's most prosperous one-star restaurants, as acclaimed abroad as it is within the country. About half of Chantal's customers are foreign gourmets who trek to Fleurie in search of the honest rural cooking that is fast disappearing from menus everywhere, in favor of the internationalist fusion style of the currently fashionable Mishmash Cuisine. Chantal pushes her gastronomic audacity to the point of serving coq au vin and even, upon occasion, *boeuf bourguignon*, if you can imagine anything as *démodé* as that, along with consecrated regional specialties like sautéed frogs' legs, genuine Burgundy snails in the shell with butter, parsley and chopped (not crushed) garlic, roast squab, *gratin dauphinois* and Charolais steak with a potent red wine sauce whose punch she sweetens and attenuates by incorporating an unctuous puree of sweet onions. On the plate, it is about as close to perfection as our mortal condition allows.

Marguerite Chabert wasn't one to chop garlic or cook onions. Her thing was just Fleurie—the red wine of Fleurie. In 1946 she became the first and only female ever elected president of a French *cave coopérative*, one of the winemakers' co-ops that are particularly active in the Beaujolais, where eighteen of them produce some 30 percent of the region's wine. A tall, flamboyant, tomboy bachelor lady who lived on the rue des Vendanges (Harvest Street) next to the church, Marguerite dominated the town with her extravagant hats and the overpowering personality of a born persuader. While her brother ran the family charcuterie where papa had invented the famous andouillette, it was she who took over the usually male roles of managing both Fleurie's co-op and the twenty acres of vines that the Chaberts held in *vigneronnage*. Joshing, chivvying and backslapping every politician, administrator, journalist or potential buyer who could possibly do some good for the town and its vignerons, she reigned over a nearly continuous economic boom until her death in 1992.

But it was in 1960 that she had her finest hour. It had been a strange year for the Beaujolais. It rained and rained and rained, swelling the grapes to a size that did no one any good; the excess water made their juice diluted and weak, never a good start for any vinification campaign. Through harvesting, fermenting and pressing, the rains drummed relentlessly on, and as everyone had feared, the young wine proved to be of mediocre quality. But there was a great deal of it, more than any other year in memory—more, in fact, than the tanks and vats of the co-op could hold. Faced with an acute lack of storage space even as more grapes were coming in for vinifying, Marguerite took swift executive action by organizing a convoy of tanker trucks and commandeering

Fleurie's brand-new municipal cistern. Three hundred thousand liters of still-fermenting Beaujolais Nouveau flowed into the big concrete reservoir that September, and the harvest was saved. It would be nice to be able to report that Fleurie's population brushed their teeth and washed their faces in red wine for a couple of weeks that year, but a sense of humor can be carried only so far: Marguerite instructed the co-op's workers to shut down the main valve to the municipal water supply.

"Well, it wasn't a very good year, anyway," a philosophical André Bacot, ninety, told me with a little shrug, recalling the glory days when he was the co-op's cellar master under Marguerite. "But her system worked just fine, you know. When the wine was sold, no one could tell that it had come from the water tower."

Improvisation was the urgent watchword of that bizarre 1960 season. Another veteran of that maddeningly pluvious year, eighty-five-year-old Claude Beroujon, told of the deconsecrated chapel near Jullié that stood in as a warehouse, filled to the roof with barrels of Beaujolais. "We put wine everywhere we could," he said. "It was only the growers' talent for vinification that saved a terrible year and made it acceptable." Unspoken: the vintage was not too watery, after all, by the time it was bottled. In the Beaujolais, the thought of a whole year's wine being tainted with water was (and is) scandalous and abhorrent. Water is certainly acceptable for cattle and for cleaning floors and watering flower beds, but as a drink for human beings it is viewed with deep suspicion.

Even with an equal devotion to the sanctity and comfort of their wine, it is doubtful that anyone could recreate Marguerite Chabert's stroke of genius today. That sort of thing isn't done anymore. With the ever-growing authority of the European Union's bureaucrats in Brussels, a stringent set of health and sanitary rules is slowly squeezing the folklore out of the Beaujolais, France and, indeed, Europe in general. Whole milk and unpasteurized cheeses are in mortal danger from statutory creep, as are a host of kitchen and winemaking practices that used to give a special character to the French table. (French cooking schools no longer teach the old way of making of the veal, chicken and fish

stocks—*fonds de veau, fonds de volaille, fumets de poisson*—the fundamental building blocks of the great classic sauces that were until recent
times the central glory of *la cuisine française*. Young graduates now often arrive in professional kitchens with can openers in their pockets,
for serving up the ready-made pastes and powdered stocks, guaranteed
sanitary, developed by the giants of the food industry.) Prodded by the
nannies of the European Commission in Brussels, while binding themselves progressively tighter with the intricate web of domestic social legislation defining their welfare state, France is fast becoming a serious
nation—serious, glum and humorless.

This is a pity, because the country that gave the world Rabelais,
Molière, Jacques Tati, the Surrealists and the troubadour Georges Bras-
sens has a wonderful native penchant for nonconformity, dissidence and
humor, one that the political-intellectual establishment has been attempting for years to bury under a tsunami of analytical hot air, statistics
and bafflingly complex legislation that hardly anyone understands much
less bothers to obey. In these economically trying times, the Beaujolais is
one of France's last bastions of the ancient, honorable spirit of dissident
laughter. Gabriel Chevallier knew all about that.

Chevallier (1895–1969) was a journalist and author from Lyon
who knew and loved the Beaujolais for its wine and its people, and
habitually spent his vacations in the picturesque hillside village of Vaux-
en-Beaujolais. Taking his inspiration from the traditional French antago-
nisms between right and left, church and state, bourgeoisie and workers,
loyalists and revolutionaries—and, yes, male and female—he composed
his novel *Clochemerle* in 1934 as a kind of extended ode to the Beaujolais. The book was an instant and hugely profitable best seller, translated
into twenty-seven languages, and it remains in publication to this day. In
France, it is one of the great fictional revealers, those fun house mirrors
before which populations can stop for a moment, contemplate their re-
flections and either grin or grimace at what they see. Say "Clochemerle"
to any French man or women, and you will immediately be greeted with
an ironic smile of recognition for the national characteristics, good and

bad, that are revealed through the singular behavior of the citizens of the imaginary little Beaujolais village that Chevallier invented.

The book's convoluted plot is kicked off by the political ambitions of Clochemerle's mayor, Barthélémy Piechut, who conceives of a way to increase his popularity among the town's voters and guarantee his re-election while at the same time infuriating his political opponents. His stroke of genius is to erect what he calls *un édifice* on a town square next to the church, under the windows of a censorious old maid who is, naturally, a religious fanatic. The *édifice* is a public *urinoir*, a convenience known in polite society as a Vespasienne (for the Roman emperor who invented pay toilets), but more commonly known in vulgar parlance as a *pissotière*, or *pissoir*. The series of events kicked off by Piechut's inspiration follows the ripening of the grapes on the slopes around the village as they head toward what promises to be an exceptional year for wine. In the baroque turmoil that ensues, money is made and lost, social climbers rise and fall, husbands are famously cuckolded and political fortunes hang in the balance. Overseeing the village's spiritual well-being is the Abbé Augustin Ponosse, who was sent by his bishop to Clochemerle as a young man, and rapidly adapted himself to the local mores. As village priest, he assuaged his weakness of the flesh with the help of his enthusiastically devoted housekeeper, Honorine, and his temporal thirst with at least two liters of Beaujolais a day, "anything less than which would cause him to suffer."

"This system brought no soul back to God," Chevallier wrote, "but Ponosse acquired a real competence in matters of wine, and by that he gained the esteem of the vignerons of Clochemerle, who said he was not haughty, not a sermonizer and was always disposed to empty his pot like an honest man. Over fifteen years Ponosse's nose flowered magnificently, became a Beaujolais nose, enormous, with a color that hesitated between the violet of the canon and the purple of the cardinal. This nose inspired confidence in the region."

The real village of Vaux-en-Beaujolais (population 850), where Chevallier used to vacation in the curiously named Hôtel des Eaux (a Hotel of the Waters smack in the middle of pure wine country is a flagrant contradiction in terms, but the people of the Beaujolais have never been afraid of jokes, and least of all in Vaux) served as the model for Cloche-merle, and the present-day town council is so proud of the connection that it has based its entire tourism strategy around the book. A splendid Gabriel Chevallier Museum, complete with an interactive multilingual presentation and figurines of the principal characters of Clochemerle, stands next door to the village's *caveau*, where the barmaid is cheery and Beaujolais by the glass is excellent and cheap; one level lower on the hillside, on a terrace shaded by enormous plane trees, old men scheme fiendishly to destroy one another in vicious games of *pétanque* at the *boulodrome*. But Vaux's pride and joy, largely financed by the state, like everything else in this most centralized of European nations, and indicated by arrow-pointing signs lest tourists miss it, is the town's cultural attraction, the municipal *pissotière*. It is entirely male-configured, as these things were in Piechut's day, painted the regulation forest green, and further adorned with Clochemerlesque frescoes by Allain Renoux, Vaux's artist in residence.

"We're not the center of France," the present-day mayor, Raymond Philibert, admitted over a glass of the local Beaujolais-Villages (2005 vintage) in the municipal *caveau*, "but this edifice is important to all French citizens and to those foreigners who have read the book. We owe it to them to give it the prestigious position it warrants."

Tongue in cheek or not, Philibert's heavy emphasis on tourism—the Chevallier Museum alone cost more than $1 million, a serious investment to put into a little burg like Vaux—is a reflection of some hard realities of twenty-first-century customs and economics: times are changing, and not necessarily for the better, for the Beaujolais. Philibert is no fool. He knows that if his gorgeous little village is to prosper enduringly in the coming decades, it behooves him to find some supplementary sources of income to fill out his tax base, just in case. Wine alone may no longer be enough.

"They're worried now," said Bernard Pivot by way of explanation.

One of France's most famous television personalities for his tremendously popular literary programs (he might be called the French Oprah
Winfrey, were it not for the fact that he was reviewing books on the tube
long before her), Pivot was born and raised in Quincié, deep in the
Beaujolais-Villages and Brouilly area, and retains a profound affection
for the place and its people. "The Beaujolais region has been propelled
through three periods, very quickly. The place I knew as a kid was very
much like Clochemerle, very rural and nonchalant. They loved their
wine and they loved to laugh and joke with one another. I don't think
they worried too much about survival, and they didn't ask too much of
life. In general, you could say they were content.

"Then they went through a second phase, the period of triumph —
Beaujolais Nouveau, the easy sales, the sudden euphoria of money that
they had never known before. With that, they made some mistakes and
maybe sold some bad wine. Now they're paying the price. They're learning that there are other wines out there, and that Beaujolais is not universal and obligatory. Their wine isn't just automatically selling the way
it used to. So they're having to adapt to the new realities. The countryside is just as beautiful as it always was, the church bells still ring the
Angelus, the people still play *boules,* and they still sit down to supper to
eat the same soup — but now there's a computer in the room, too. Life is
changing. Fundamentally, I think the people of the Beaujolais are still
as simple and straightforward as they always used to be, but they're worried. As soon as you get them into their *caves,* though, they forget their
worries and become themselves again."

There can be no doubt that the return to one's own wine cellar, to
the faint, sour fragrance of a thousand past tastings, to the familiar heft
of a half-filled wineglass and to the taste of one's own wine, is a wonderful palliative for a wine grower's woes, but that manner of pleasure and
tranquilizing is not reserved for vignerons alone. It is equally present at
the bars, bistros and cafés omnipresent in French urban architecture,
and there is always a writer, a singer, a poet or a scientist to recommend
a little bending of the elbow. The whole world went mad for red wine a

few years ago after Professor Serge Renaud in Lyon announced that its judicious consumption was good for the heart, but long before him the great Louis Pasteur had already labeled wine as "the most hygienic of beverages." Molière composed a wine-drinking song ("Let us drink, dear friends, let us drink, the flight of time urges us on, let us enjoy life to the fullest"), and Jean-Jacques Rousseau nicely philosophized that teetotalers were generally phonies, whereas "the taste for wine is not a crime, and it rarely causes any to be committed. For every passing quarrel it causes, it forms a hundred durable attachments. Drinkers are marked by cordiality and frankness: almost all of them are good, upright, decent and honest people."

But it was two lesser writers, both of them honored devotees of this region, who most convincingly applied the sentiment to the land of Beaujolais. Louis Orizet was chief regional inspector of INAO (Institut National des Appellations d'Origine), France's official registry of product names and quality watchdog, and he loved the Beaujolais and its wines like his own family. His little book À *Travers le Cristal* (Through the Crystal) isn't often seen in shops anymore, but its most famous lines are endlessly reprinted wherever and whenever anyone needs a little persuading about the benefits of a glass of wine. What does a glass of wine represent? Orizet could say it very precisely.

"It is a message of friendship transmitted from year to year by more than a hundred generations of vignerons. It is the prospecting of thousands of rootlets to deliver up the secret of the rocks. It is the sublimation of a summer's heat. It is the fruit of a year's labor. It is the laughter of the harvest hand, the efforts of the vinifier, the love of the cellar master, his vigilance and his skill in perfecting the masterpiece. Everything that is good in mankind is transmitted to the wine: courage, gaiety, strength, perseverance, love, optimism. Everything that is beautiful in nature appears in wine: warmth, strength, light, color, mystery. Wine is matter becoming mind, and all of this can be seen through the crystal."

"You've got to hand it to this place," Gabriel Chevallier wrote after the enormous success of *Clochemerle*. "The people there are never mean drinkers, because Beaujolais is the kind of wine that never does anyone any harm. The more you drink, the more you find your wife pleasant, your friends faithful, the future encouraging and humanity bearable. All the misfortune of the world comes from one single fact: that on this planet there is only one Beaujolais region. This is where you'll always find people with honest, open faces, in good cheer, all of them with their hearts in their hand—the hand that holds the glass, of course."

I'll drink to that.

II

VILE AND NOXIOUS, DOWNTRODDEN AND DESPISED

GAMAY'S LONG STRUGGLE FOR RESPECT

*A*s his name suggests, Philip the Bold was not a man for halfway measures. Youngest son of King John II, he was barred by primogeniture — inheritance to the firstborn — from taking the throne of France, but as duke of Burgundy he wielded quasi-royal authority from his seat of power in Dijon, and his domains extended all the way north, deep into present-day Belgium. A statue for the personal necropolis he built to assure his posthumous glory, carved by the Dutch sculptor Claus Sluter around 1390, displays a strong, boorish face with a fleshy nose, a grim, thin-lipped mouth and a prominent, very determined chin, vaguely reminiscent of Mussolini. Big man, big ambitions, big power. He had a generous helping of problems on his plate — with his brothers he ran the affairs of France during some of the most trying days of the spread of the plague and the Hundred Years War — but in addition to playing the great game of war and international politics, he was also a collector and patron of the arts who did not hesitate to dip into everyday matters of local taste and lifestyle. On July 31, 1395, he issued an edict that, today still, many wine growers of the Beaujolais can cite for you by heart.

The thrust of his edict was as simple as it was uncompromisingly severe: his subjects were summoned to rip out and never again put into the ground "the vile and noxious gamay plant, from which plant comes a very great abundance of wine . . . which wine is of such nature that it is most injurious to the human creature . . . for it is full of a very great and horrible bitterness."

Those who drink it, he warned darkly, have been "infested with grave maladies." Then, soaring on his own rhetoric, he triply underlined the urgency of ridding his duchy of the offending root. It had to be "extirpated, destroyed and reduced to nothing," under penalty of stiff fines. Similarly penalized, he added, would be those who "brought animal droppings (*fiens*) and waste to the vines where good plants were located."

As always with French wines, this edict concerned a matter of *terroir*. Burgundy had the good fortune to possess in its native flora a certain wild grape that had proved, under cultivation, to be exceptionally well adapted to the making of fine wine. It was called by several different names, but the one that predominated is the one still in use today: pinot noir. Over centuries of trial-and-error observation, most notably by the various ecclesiastical orders scattered throughout the duchy, whose peasant monks were often first-rate agronomists, Burgundians had raised the care and husbandry of the pinot vine to a fine art. Wine was an absolute, doctrinal necessity for every Christian mass, however humble, and the brothers in their monasteries reverently partook of it in their daily dietary regimen. And, although the popular imagery of jolly, rotund monks quaffing heroic quantities of wine or beer is certainly exaggerated, there is no doubt that the daily ingestion of the production of the Lord's vineyards would have led many of them to divine inspiration, and hence great expertise in the matter.

The most famous of the monastic vineyards in Burgundy was Clos Vougeot, but green-thumbed monks had, by the twelfth and thirteenth centuries, helped pinpoint a whole array of other superb wine *terroirs* with admirable accuracy: Gevrey, Meursault, Volnay, Pommard, Santenay, Marsannay. There was a downside to this happy story, though: the pinot has always been a finicky, delicate-stalked variety of vine, one that requires constant attention and care, against which it yields a relatively modest harvest of grapes. Hardly surprising, then, that Philip's subjects should have sought to increase yields by spreading the only fertilizer easily available in those times: excrement—and not necessarily just farm animal excrement.

In normal times of peace, the pinot's flighty nature could be dealt with, but the fourteenth century in general was an exceptional, somber and frightening period for France. The conjoined assaults of the black plague and the endless war with England were sapping the very structure of society: the population was thinning out dangerously; villages were emptying of their inhabitants; bandits and groups of apocalyptic religious fanatics roamed the land, rivaling gangs of freebooting soldiers in their depredations; money was tight, taxes extortionate, and manpower dramatically short. Those who could work the vines were often sickly and weak. Some choice vineyards were even being abandoned.

A threat to wine production was a real danger for Philip's duchy. The loss of revenue from the various taxes imposed on the wine trade was bad enough, but in Burgundy as elsewhere, wine represented far more than money. At a time when sanitation and public health were poorly understood at best, wells and streams were frequently polluted, water supplies muddy, brackish and very possibly disease-infested, especially terrifying in periods of epidemic. The wondrous transformation of pure, delicious grape juice into wine, on the other hand, was viewed as a gift of God, one that possessed near-mystical powers. It was considered medicinal and health-giving, a buttress for strength and an uplift for the spirit. It was of capital significance in those deeply religious days that Jesus had drunk it at His last supper and that it ritually accompanied the Eucharist at mass. Commoners who could not afford wine found a second-best alternative in cutting their drinking water with vinegar—turned wine—to disinfect it and disguise the taste of mud and other impurities.

Faced with the need to keep wine production going in these parlous times, Burgundian peasants began turning to a solution that, on the surface at any rate, offered miraculous promise: another variety of vine, one that grew easily in great proliferation on good, strong wood and had a long lifespan, at least equal to that of a human being. It was more robust and easier to work than the pinot noir, tended to ripen earlier, and yielded a much greater bulk of grapes—hence, more wine for less work. And so, logical as ever when faced with the life-or-death choices implied in their treatment of their year's crops, many of Philip's subjects gave up on the capricious pinot noir altogether and massively planted the new vine. This marvel was called the gamay.

But the peasants' logic was not the same as Philip's. Where they saw more wine for less work, he saw this overproductive intruder as a mortal danger to Burgundy's most prestigious product—and, it must be conceded, he was right. Centuries of practice had already shown that the pinot noir vine and the Burgundy *terroir* were perfectly suited to each other. The gamay certainly did fulfill its promise by delivering large quantities of juice, but its wedding with the soil and climate of Burgundy was not a happy one: the quality simply was not there. Bitter, acid and thin when compared to the great depth and character of the best pinots, the wines descended from this interloper were hardly any better than those of the vineyards of Paris and Île-de-France up north. If allowed to continue, the gamay grape could destroy Burgundy's reputation for producing the finest wine in Christendom. Philip acted with the swift dispatch of the true medieval despot, and simply ordered the gamay to disappear. Reluctantly, dragging their feet, the Burgundian wine growers obeyed; in due course, Philip's duchy became virtually gamay-free all the way down to Mâcon.

The land around Mâcon and south, the present Beaujolais, was, then as today, included within the administrative boundaries of Burgundy, but the humiliating truth was this: apparently it was just of no consequence as far as Philip was concerned. Its population was no more than a set of primitive, hill-dwelling peasants, and the wine production there was only occasional, limited to a few fields around a few rural townships. Let them have their gamay. But Philip's eradication program had a strong and lasting effect for the descendants of these hill dwellers.

Like a skillfully orchestrated press campaign, his diatribe launched a persistent and grossly inaccurate canard that continues to have life today still: the assertion that the clear-juiced gamay grape can make only second-rate wines. What the duke could not know was that there was a *terroir* quite nearby that was just awaiting marriage with the gamay to prove him wrong: the clay, crushed granite and limestone in and around *les monts du Beaujolais*.

There was no official certificate, no opening ceremony; the wedding just sort of happened. The Romans had been planting gamay vines as early as the third century A.D. on the hills around Lyon, and the practice moved gradually northward by simple emulation, slowed down by the usual vicissitudes of wars, invasions, backslidings and bungles. As a result, Professor Gilbert Garrier of the University of Lyon, the most knowledgeable and prolific historical expert on matters of Beaujolais wines, dates the true beginning of the region's wine commerce as a separate entity to much more recent times than the Languedoc, Bordeaux or Burgundian wine fields: the early seventeenth century. By then, he writes, the general pattern of Beaujolais peasant life had begun shifting from cattle and subsistence farming to the new hybrid units of self-sufficient family farms with attached vineyards. The gamay grape—the black-skinned, clear-juiced gamay, to be specific—had finally found the *terroir* where it performed best. From that time onward, right up to the present, there has never been any other red wine grape for the Beaujolais.

Beaujolais is gamay, and it can be said with some justice that gamay is Beaujolais, because this is its true home. Certainly there are gamay vineyards elsewhere in France, notably in the Ardèche region south of Lyon and in the Loire Valley, and some plantings abroad (Switzerland, Italy, Australia, South Africa), but of the eighty thousand or so acres of gamay growing worldwide, fifty-five thousand are located within this little vinous rectangle lying between Lyon and Mâcon, and nowhere else does the little black grape express itself so completely and cheerily as in the Beaujolais.

There's always a certain amount of luck and serendipity in matching a *terroir* with exactly the right grape to produce the finest wine possible. Year to year, vintners in the Bordeaux vineyards are constantly fiddling with the blends of the five grapes (cabernet sauvignon, cabernet franc, merlot, malbec and petit verdot) from which their vast palette of red wines is assembled, but if this juggling strikes anyone as complicated, it is as nothing compared to what it was in the old days: toward the end of the eighteenth century, their ancestors were dealing with no less than twenty-seven varieties of red wine grapes. Today's very popular Côtes-du-Rhône red wines are composed from a bouquet of thirteen different varieties, or *cépages*, as they are called in French. There's no lack of choice, because the number of varieties of *Vitis vinifera*, the European winemaking grapevine, is enormous; more than six thousand of them have been named and classified.

Considering the dizzying number of possible permutations between *cépages* and *terroirs*, it is an extraordinary testimony to human ingenuity, perseverance and powers of observation that the Beaujolais and the gamay grape should have come into union, because this particular varietal is extraordinarily sensitive to *terroir* and generally performs poorly in soil other than the granite, limestone and clay in and around the *monts du Beaujolais*. It had to be found in the first place, then brought there, planted, pressed, vinified and given a long trial run before anyone could tell whether it was worth the trouble. It was long thought that the gamay had originated as a vine growing wild in the coastal area of Dalmatia (present-day Croatia), across the Adriatic Sea from Italy of Caesar's day, and that the Romans, as curious and enterprising as they were imperialistic, had brought it with them in their baggage to Gaul and planted it in order to make wine near their garrisons. But recent American DNA research has shown that three of France's (and the world's) most extraordinarily useful *cépages* —gamay, chardonnay and pinot noir—are descended from two parents: a prototype pinot and a grape called gouais blanc. The hamlet of Gamay, adjacent to the very noble Burgundy town of Puligny-Montrachet, may have taken its name from the hybrid that originated there, either by some accident of nature or the experiment of some unknown horticultural genius. One thing is sure, though: it is the Romans who first used the gamay vine to make wine.

"No wine, no soldiers," Napoléon famously remarked, and it was as true around the year zero as it was in Bonaparte's time (or today, for that matter, with the sole adjustment of substituting beer, whiskey or vodka for non-Latin soldiery). The Romans almost got it right, too, when they stuck the gamay into the ground in the hills around Lugdunum (present-day Lyon), capital of the Gauls. If only they had done it a few dozen miles farther north, they would have hit the jackpot, and the story of Beaujolais would be several centuries older.

After the collapse of the Roman empire, the various barbarian invasions, the Dark Ages and all the dimly perceived history attendant to that period, the Beaujolais began evolving as an organized entity with the appearance of its first Christianized lord, Bérard, and his wife Vandalmonde, who in the year 957 set up shop in the rough fortress-castle they called Pierre Aiguë, a Gallic Wuthering Heights anchored on a high escarpment above the poor settlement that was later to become the town of Beaujeu. New to the faith and fired with touching evangelical enthusiasm, this worthy couple made a pilgrimage to Rome and returned with a load of holy objects for the chapel they had ordered built on their vast estate. The collection they proudly brought back with them consisted of the usual religious flimflammery of that period, and included hairs from the Virgin Mary's head, shreds of the gown and shoes she wore while pregnant with Jesus, a hair of Saint Peter's beard and a clipping of Saint Paul's thumbnail.

Religious matters aside, there was already mention of vineyards around Beaujeu at the time of Bérard and Vandalmonde, but it was not until 1473 that the little city came to its great hour of geopolitical glory. It was in that year that Anne, eldest daughter of King Louis XI, was married (at age fourteen) to the youngest son of the House of Bourbon, Pierre de Beaujeu. With that, Anne of France became Anne of Beaujeu. She was a clever, discerning girl, and she rapidly assumed a dominant position in the couple she formed with Pierre, in spite of his twenty years of seniority. Her leadership was not all that surprising, because her father had already predicted great things for her, even if, as it happened in this case, when she married Pierre she had swapped her august patronymic for nothing better than that of an obscure little city in an obscure little wine area. Anne was, King Louis famously allowed, "the least giddy of women, for of levelheaded ones there are none," but in spite of this faint and indubitably sexist praise, she ruled as de facto queen of France for eight years while her baby brother, Charles VIII, waited to accede to the throne. At no time since has the name Beaujeu exercised such influence and prestige. It is a measure of her brains and charisma that while everywhere in Beaujeu today people refer back to Anne, most citizens would have the devil of a time to give you the name of her husband.

Within less than a hundred years of Anne's union with Pierre, Beaujeu had slipped back into the shadows of history, supplanted as the region's administrative center by the larger, more modern and more strategically located city of Villefranche-sur-Saône. As the centuries rolled on, wine replaced politics and war as the great and abiding concern of the area. Even as the acreage given over to vineyards expanded, though, their production seemed doomed to remain a strictly local phenomenon. The twin problems of the frustratingly short life span of wine in general and the primitive state of France's transportation networks were aggravated by the various interdictions, tolls, inspections and special taxes that barred the free movement of medieval commerce. Customs barriers at the entrance to large communities guaranteed that transport was both slow and expensive, and the inspectors and toll collectors of the Burgundian satraps lying between the Beaujolais and Paris could always be relied upon to follow Philip's ancient example and make life hell for any enterprising wine seller from Villefranche, Juliénas or Chiroubles who took it into his head to carry his wares on the main road northward. It was not until the middle of the eighteenth century that dealers in Beaujolais wines were able to establish a regular and fairly reliable liaison with the attractive Paris market, by avoiding their obstructive Burgundian rivals altogether. Improved roads over the hills westward made it possible for heavy oxcarts laden with barrels of wine to reach the river Loire, where horse-drawn barges could take the cargo aboard for the slow plod toward the capital. Even then, though, the vexations and exactions were far from over. Highwaymen frequently attacked wine convoys en route for the river, and the bargees of the Loire were notorious for their great thirst. Adding river water to the casks they broached certainly disguised their theft of Beaujolais, but it did nothing for the reputation of the wine when it finally reached consumers in the big city.

The injustice of the suffocating parochialism into which the gamay's wines had been closeted for so long might have largely accounted for the inward-looking, somewhat suspicious manner of the peasant vintners of the Beaujolais, one that lasted well into our modern times. It was doubtless this sense of injustice that gave birth to the legend of Claude Brosse, a kind of commercial Robin Hood whose exploit is celebrated again and again in the region, today still. Although he is most often described as a vigneron from the Mâcon wine fields, I have occasionally heard claim laid to him as a Beaujolais man, but the exact zip code doesn't really matter, because in any case he is probably mythical. What counts is that Claude Brosse represents the mystique of the Beaujolais in the triumph of an underdog who bursts free of provincial confinement, brings wine to the king—and wins.

He was a giant of a man, the story goes, surely over six feet tall, which was pretty sensational for those days. It was around 1700 or so that the legend has him loading his oxcart up with barrels and trudging northward for thirty-three days, somehow avoiding or bluffing his way through Burgundy's tollhouses and customs sheds until he arrived safe and sound in Versailles. Parking his oxen outside the royal chapel on a Sunday morning, he betook himself to a bench far in the back, the only spot where a commoner like him could expect to attend a mass in the king's presence. At the moment of benediction when everyone knelt reverently, the king's master of ceremonies looked the congregation over and, to his unutterable shock, spied a man in the back who apparently had remained standing.

"On your knees, peasant!" (or something of the sort) he shrieked.

"Well, ain't I on my knees already?" rumbled Brosse imperturbably, still looming over the rest of the faithful. What made the story even more heartwarming for his compatriots down south was that he spoke in the barely understandable patois of his region. And naturally, the story continues, the king sampled his wine, loved it and ordered that it be served thenceforth at the royal table.

If only it were so. In spite of the boosterism of the Brosse legend, the dreary truth was that the wines of the Beaujolais and the neighboring Mâconnais were—as often they still are today—casually dismissed as mere sub-Burgundies: pleasant enough to drink but devoid of big brother's character and nobility.

When Claude Brosse made his legendary trek to Versailles, the French monarchy had less than a century of life left in it. Compared to the debasing serfdom that held most of the kingdom's peasant farmers in bondage, the shared harvest of the fifty-fifty "half-fruit" *vigneronnage* system that prevailed in the Beaujolais was undeniably a real social progress for the personal responsibility and freedom of choice it offered to the skilled winemaking artisan, but considering the essential nature of the ancien régime, it was a humiliating, class-bound structure all the same. Vignerons' contracts tied them to extra chores like cultivating their lords' vegetable gardens, supplying them with a certain amount of eggs, butter and live chickens, maintaining their firewood supply, making their hay, heating their ovens and watching over the cooking of their bread, while their wives were required to clean their houses, help itinerant washerwomen at the river with the twice-yearly laundering of their sheets, bedclothes and household linens and, when needed, to wait on their tables.

After the French Revolution of 1789, the great noble and ecclesiastical estates were broken up, and power and vineyard ownership began shifting downward. With that, the stewardship of the Beaujolais countryside changed to resemble what it is today: thousands of small family holdings, either in a more democratic style of *vigneronnage* or land rental (*fermage*) or, more and more frequently, in outright peasant own-ership of the land. This pattern continued well into the twentieth cen-tury: peasant farmers and raisers of cattle who also made wine. But the forces of history and economics were increasingly nudging them away from the former and toward the latter. Today, just about every square centimeter of ground in the Beaujolais that is favorable to winegrowing is covered with vines, and it is rare to find any livestock at all in a Beau-jolais vigneron's backyard. They used to grow rye in Chénas, Chiroubles was famous for the quality of its turnips, and in any village you could always find a farmer to draw you off a bucket of milk, but all that is from the local supermarket now.

Wine production soared throughout France in the bright new re-publican world of the nineteenth century, spurred on by advances in technique, improved selection of vine plants and the simple fact of greater individual ownership of vineyards. Wine drinking was truly be-coming democratized, and the French took to it with dedication. More wine meant cheaper wine, hence more of it available to even modest incomes. When super-abundant harvests drove prices to rock bottom, deplorable displays of wide public drunkenness were reported, but as a rule wine was treated with the respect it deserved for its undoubted med-ical and spiritual virtues. Infants often had their first little encounters with wine as soon as they were weaned from the breast, and doctors, ever cautious about their patients' health, routinely advised that women and children should drink water only after it had been mixed with wine.

This, then, was the consensus: wine was good, wine was safer and more salubrious than water, and the French soil and climate were ide-al for producing large amounts of wines of a fantastically rich array of types, ranging from the exotic Alsatian gewürztraminer, redolent of rose petals, to the *vin jaune* (yellow wine) of Arbois in the Jura, whose *terroir* imparted a surprising bouquet of spice and walnuts, to the innumerable flavors and textures of the multitudinous Champagnes, to the depth and intensity of the great Bordeaux and Burgundy reds, complex enough to test the vocabulary-making skills of a battery of oenologists. In short, wine was a godsend, and France was blessed as the world's center of winemaking. Hardly surprising, then, in the context of the blithely optimistic nineteenth century, when business leaders, economists, colonialists and men of science had the world nicely figured out and wrapped up in neat theoretical bundles, that some, even among the best, allowed their enthusiasm to run riot.

The most famous of them all, the great Louis Pasteur (1822–1895), was a true giant of scientific research, a pioneer of microbiology who more or less single-handedly invented vaccination against infectious disease and, of course, developed the procedure that carries his name for heat-treating various edibles, notably milk. Pasteur deeply studied the process of fermentation, had vines of his own, and for the first time elucidated the complexities of vinification that for centuries winemakers had been approaching with empirical, hit-or-miss guesswork. That alone would have been enough for him to be venerated in France, but what shot him to the wine community's summit of admiration was a single lapidary phrase he pronounced: "Taken in moderate quantity, wine is the most healthy and hygienic of beverages."

The date and context in which the phrase was born seem to be unclear, but they never let him forget it. The phrase is constantly reiterated and celebrated in France—most often with the first part, the bit about moderate quantity, subtracted—and it is easily the most famous quote attributed to the great man. It has done signal service to the industry, but Pasteur's endorsement was as nothing compared to the passionate convictions of his contemporary and fellow eminence of science, the brilliant medical doctor, agronomist and physicist Jules Guyot. Commissioned by Napoléon III to write a massive study on the state of the French wine industry, Guyot concluded that wine could be substituted for bread at family meals and advised a consumption for an average French family (mom, dad and two children) of at least fifteen hundred liters a year—which averages out to almost 1.5 U.S. quarts per day per individual every day of the year, the two kids included. In Guyot's time, such a recommendation appeared neither unusual nor shocking. It was accepted wisdom that wine—especially red wine—boosted strength and courage, for workers in the field as it did for soldiers in battle, and the concept of alcoholism was little understood among the general population. The good doctor will always be remembered with fondness for a few key paragraphs in *Culture de la Vigne et Vinification*, a study he wrote in 1861.

"A beer-drinking country will never have the mental liveliness and gaiety of the inhabitants of a wine country," he wrote. "The inhabitants of a cider country will never have the candor of the people of a vine country; so it isn't the alcohol that constitutes the value and the goodness of wine, because beer and cider contain just as much and sometimes more. Wine is not good because it contains more or less alcohol. All natural wine, weak or strong, is a good wine if it maintains its organic life and shows it by an honest odor, by a concert of all its elements in a harmonious savor of taste, by an easy digestion, an increased muscular force and a greater activity of body and mind. Whether wine's savor be fresh, sharp and light; whether it be sweet, unctuous and rich, whether it be pungent, warm and austere, wine is good and supports and augments physical and intellectual strength without tiring the digestive organs."

Dr. Guyot's rhetorical flight could scarcely be complete without rendering heartfelt homage to the nation most advanced in the art of winemaking: "I am profoundly convinced that the wines of France are the primary cause of the frankness, the generosity and the value of the French character, incontestably superior to that of all the nations."

Wine = health was a stubbornly ineradicable mantra that for most of the French lasted well into the twentieth century, reinforced by popular maxims like "vegetables make *merde*, meat makes meat, wine makes blood." But the old human tendency to conclude that where a good thing is concerned, more is better, sometimes wreaked havoc on the rationalism for which the French are famous. Professor Garrier points out that around 1870 a new "alcohol therapy" had become quite the rage among the upper bourgeoisie of Paris and that as late as 1930 a couple of professors in the Paris School of Pharmacy were recommending that the grapevine be classified as a medicinal plant. "In 1935," he wrote in his *Histoire Sociale et Culturelle du Vin,* "Doctor Dougnac recommends 'vinotherapy' as an answer to alcoholism; he goes as far as counseling wine for children from the age of five, and maintains that according to a study carried out in the Gironde, students who regularly drink wine have a higher grade average than abstainers."

Whatever their excesses of enthusiasm, the investigations of both Pasteur and Guyot made serious contributions to the art of winemaking, in the Beaujolais as elsewhere in France. Theirs was cutting-edge science for the day, Guyot for the care and growing of the vine and Pasteur for the microbiology of vinification. Nothing bedeviled vignerons more, then as now, than the trade's single, essential fact of life: that Mother Nature intended grape juice to become not wine, but vinegar. Beaujolais peasants were poorly equipped to deal with this problem, and they lived in terror of their precious brew turning. As always, their great battle was with the element that is the most indispensable to us as air-breathing mammals: oxygen. When oxygen gets to iron, the result is immediately visible: rust. When it gets to wine, the result leaps out equally fast in an unmistakable sour pucker: oxidized wine means vinegar.

It is yeasts that are to blame. Naturally present in enormous numbers on grape skins (and today commonly cloned and raised in laboratories), yeasts are teeming, multifarious living organisms that are absolutely fundamental to winemaking. But they are tricky little brutes: if they are allowed to meet oxygen in the winemaking process, they create acetic acid—vinegar. If they are kept quarantined from oxygen, though, they combine with the natural sugar of fruit to produce the joy and wonder of anyone who has ever pressed a grape: alcohol.

Even today, when molecular science and biochemistry seemingly have an explanation for every possible twist and turn of nature's ways, winemakers tread with infinite caution when facing enemy oxygen during the critical period of vinifying their grape juice into young wine and storing it afterward to ensure that it holds still. Two and three hundred years ago, when the natural processes were still largely mysterious, winemakers throughout France were guided by the empiricism of peasant folklore and superstition, keeping a keen eye on the winds and the phases of the moon, and praying to Vincent, the patron saint of vintners. If, in spite of all their precautions, their wine went bad anyway, they resorted to any number of folkloric nostrums and additives to try to bring it back: alum, ammonia salts, plaster, egg whites and wood chips are frequently mentioned.

The only thing worse than wine going bad was no wine at all. Nature being what it is, there were always times when flash frosts, hailstorms or any of a wide selection of diseases and creatures that feast on grapevines destroyed part or even all of a year's crop. Unsurprisingly, in light of the sincere religious fervor that prevailed in the Beaujolais well into the twentieth century, the Church did what it could to allay these menaces. It was customary for priests around Beaujeu to bless candles at Candlemas (February 2), the Day of Purification of the Blessed Virgin. Having brought the holy candles home to village and farm, the faithful lit them at the approach of thunder and hail, while the village curé contributed his efforts by energetically ringing his church bells, on the theory that their pious clangor might ward off Satan's meteorological assaults. When this manner of local prophylaxis went unheeded, mass processions and pilgrimages by vigneron families implored succor from the Almighty or, in the manner of the ancient Hebrews in Canaan, built chapels on high ground, like the ones still standing today above Fleurie or the bigger, more imposing one, Our Lady of the Grape, atop the summit of Mount Brouilly, high point of the Beaujolais wine region. Scholars have found records of ecclesiastical trials in which desperate clergy officially enjoined vine-feeding worms and caterpillars to depart, under threat of anathema and excommunication. Anything was worth a try.

When all avenues of resistance had been exhausted and a dearth of wine was upon the land, Beaujolais peasantry, like their fellow vignerons in other wine areas, turned to homemade substitutes. Various fruits and herbs—a multitude of agents like elderberries, blueberries, sassafras, juniper berries, hollyhocks, barley, nutmeg, dry raisins—could

be infused in water, colored with yet other ingredients and given an alcoholic punch with a few bottles of eau-de-vie or straight grain alcohol.
They were poor substitutes for the real thing, though, and they certainly
did not possess the strength-giving and spiritual powers that folk wisdom
ascribed to true wine.

Lending a helping hand to underpowered wines was an altogether
different matter. Connoisseurs everywhere know that a maddeningly
delicate sensorial balance comes into play where a wine's alcohol content is concerned: too little alcohol, and a wine will probably be thin and
acid; too much, and it is likely to be heavy and out of balance. There is
no absolute rule—some wines may be at their best with only 8 percent
alcohol content, others with 14 percent or higher—but generally speaking, 12 or 13 percent is today considered a happy medium. Since alcohol is produced by the interaction of yeasts with grapes' natural sugar
content, a riper grape will tend to yield more sugar, and therefore more
alcohol. In very sunny southern climates grapes ripen easily and well,
so alcohol content is rarely a problem—in fact, winemakers may even
have to struggle with too much alcohol. But in most winemaking regions
of France the sun cannot always be counted upon to deliver enough
natural grape sugar for an optimum, balanced result in alcohol content.
It was in regard to this fact of life that another famous scientist, this one
a predecessor to Pasteur and Guyot, turned his attention away from investigating saltpeter (vital for gunpowder to use against the English), tar
and various earth salts and had a look at the French wine industry.

Count Jean-Antoine Chaptal was a medical doctor and chemist of
wide-ranging talents whom Napoléon Bonaparte named minister of the
interior in 1801. In that same year, he published a book, *L'Art de Faire le
Vin* (The Art of Winemaking), that proved to be little short of revolutionary. Revised, upgraded and expanded several times, the treatise most tell-
ingly recommended a procedure he had devised, one that is still known
by his name today. *Chaptalisation* consists of adding carefully calibrated
quantities of sugar to the must, the newly pressed grape juice and mash
that is beginning its fermentation toward wine. Faced with this bonus of

sugar, the grapes' yeasts boost the alcohol content of the finished wine a degree or two, filling out its bouquet, mellowing it into a rounder, more interesting and seductive drink—but *not*, contrary to a widely held misconception, making the wine sweeter. The sugar is there only to make alcohol, and it is entirely consumed in the process. In all but the most sun-drenched years, *chaptalisation* is critically important not only for Beaujolais but for the wines of Champagne, Alsace, the Loire Valley, Burgundy, Bordeaux, and elsewhere in France—and indeed, in temperate zones all around the world where the *terroirs* are fine but the sun deficient. In essence, Chaptal only refined and codified peasant empiricism. Off and on, depending on the place, the year and the availability of sugar-heavy products, winemakers had been adding honey or molasses to grape juice in their fermentation vats since antiquity. Today, there is hardly a French wine, even the most prestigious and expensive of Bordeaux or Burgundies, that does not benefit from *chaptalisation*.

As much as Beaujolais winemakers benefited from the painstaking laboratory work of some of the greatest names of French science, the microbiological caprices of winemaking represented only one chapter of the book of travails of the typical nineteenth-century vigneron. Long before the stage of treating grape juice could be reached, a frightening and bewildering combat often had to be delivered on the ground where their vines were growing—or, worse, were *not* growing—if there were to be any grapes at all.

Treasured provider of the pleasures of inebriation for humans, the grape vine does the same service for animals, too, if they happen to feed upon fermenting fruit at the right moment, and it seems to be a particularly attractive target all the way down the line, to the smallest of living creatures. In spite of the tough, gnarled appearance of its wood above ground, *Vitis vinifera* is in fact an extremely delicate plant that requires constant attention by those who make their living from it. Whichever way they turn, they are likely to find some natural predator poised to suck its roots, chomp its leaves, rot its fruit, invade its bark to make their parasitic dwellings or in one way or another threaten its health and make life miserable for the vigneron. My old copy of Alexis Lichine's *Encyclopedia of Wines & Spirits* lists six viral, one bacterial and ten fungal diseases and at least nine ill-intentioned animal parasites that enjoy attacking vines, and there might well have been more added to the list since. In short, there is a discouragingly large waiting list of microscopic critters that want a piece of *Vitis vinifera*. It is a poignant fact of biological life that three of the worst of them originated in America, unintended gifts resulting from the back-and-forth shuttlings of transatlantic cargo ships on which hitchhiking plant predators rode. The malevolent trio was: *oïdium*, mildew and, most devastating of all, phylloxera.

Before their arrival, though, the Beaujolais lived its own endogenous disaster and painfully won triumph with the saga of the little beast popularly known as "the mischievous worm": *pyrale*. Caterpillar and moth rather than a worm, the terrible *pyrale* had been known in France for centuries as a voracious devourer of vine leaves, but never had its depredations been as thorough as toward the end of the first and beginning of the second quarters of the nineteenth century. Proliferating in unheard of quantities, the little caterpillars munched their way through entire vineyards, leaving in their wake a desolation as total as if the vines had been swept by fire. The Beaujolais was not the only wine area under attack—*pyrale* was upon the land everywhere—but it was in the Beaujolais that the saving counterstroke was discovered.

It took a while. Exorcisms, banishments and demonstrations of piety such as pilgrimages to the chapel of Our Lady of the Worm at Avenas, near Beaujeu, which specialized in divine intervention against intestinal worms in children, gave no noticeable improvement. Direct action— sulfur fumigations, sending kids out at night with oil lamps to attract and kill moths piecemeal, squashing eggs attached to vine leaves, rubbing various unpleasant compounds on the stalks, scraping larvae off the bark with rough chain-mail gloves—was an exhausting task that proved equally bootless. In spite of all the effort, the results were heartbreakingly thin: mere mitigation, no cure. In the Beaujolais and Mâconnais, the harvests of 1830, 1831, 1836 and 1838 were three-quarters lost.

It was in this atmosphere of despair that Benoît Raclet settled in Romanèche-Thorins, a little village near Fleurie and Moulin-à-Vent. A minor court functionary from Roanne, Raclet had inherited a Beaujolais vineyard when he married a local girl named Marthe Chaumet. Of course his vines, like everyone else's, suffered from the *pyrale* caterpillar, and it seemed unlikely in the extreme that this newly arrived pencil pusher could have any more success against the intruders than the local peasants, whose agricultural wisdom was almost genetic, dating as it did through generations of ancestors who had worked the same vines before them. But Raclet had a few special circumstances in his favor: his vines grew right up alongside his house; his kitchen plumbing was primitive; and by nature he was orderly, methodical and observant.

One day he put two and two together. Surveying the pathetic remnants of his vines, he could not help noticing that a single one of them continued to flourish, without the least trace of caterpillars or caterpillar damage. As it happened, this vine was planted hard by the drainpipe where hot water from his wife's sink and cooking was unceremoniously dumped outside, for want of a proper septic system. Could water be the answer? And, more specifically, hot water?

Over the following years Raclet began experimenting, first with a simple coffeepot filled with hot water from the house, and then with more complicated systems of his own design for a boiler heated by charcoal fire. Trudging through his vines with his portable fire, his water tank and his coffeepot, he looked like a nineteenth-century Professor Gadget and was naturally dismissed as an eccentric at best and a lunatic at worst. Still Raclet persisted and eventually determined by trial and error that the secret was to douse the vines with scalding hot water in winter, killing the larvae that were hibernating under the bark. The spectacle he and his paraphernalia presented to the ultraconservative peasantry was so bizarre, even vaguely satanic, with its smoke and all, that he became the butt of constant hostile raillery. When he attempted to avoid his neighbors' censorious gaze by continuing his experiments at night, he of course only worsened the situation. In 1828, therefore, when Raclet announced that he had found the way to beat the mischievous worm, he was greeted with only derisive shrugs.

But the derision paled when, the following summer, his vines stood tall and healthy amid the scene of general desolation around Romanèche. Reluctantly, a few of the naysayers swallowed their pride and put their coffeepots on the stove. Over the next years more and more healthy vines appeared in the Beaujolais, and there was no more arguing with success. The Raclet method, as fastidious and time-consuming as it was—a two-man team, one to heat the water at the boiler and the other to treat the vines, could cover only five acres of vine over a ten-day period—proved to be totally valid. In 1842 his boiling water treatment was officially recognized and certified as effective. Equipment manufacturers rushed to design sophisticated portable boiler and hot water delivery systems. The Beaujolais vineyards were saved.

Alas, poor Raclet gained nothing for his decisive discovery, not in his lifetime at any rate. Broke, scorned by his neighbors, his health ruined, he had already moved away by the time his method was universally adopted. Removed to the boring flatlands between Paris and Normandy, where no vines grew, cows populated the fields, and the natives drank cider, he died in 1844. By way of national amends, the French government awarded him a posthumous *Légion d'Honneur*. In 1864, a handsome Benoît Raclet bust was inaugurated in Romanèche's village square, where it still stands today, not far from the little Raclet museum. Now, on the last Sunday of every October, the town gussies up for the annual Fête Raclet in his memory, even if his laborious old pest control method has now been supplanted by modern sulfur-based treatments. On the day of the big celebration, schoolchildren trot out to sing the obligatory Raclet cantata, notables make their speeches, and professionals and buyers get a sneak preview of the year's wines, scheduled for release over the following months.

No sooner had French vines recovered from *pyrale* than they were struck by two fungal diseases. The first, *oïdium*—powdery mildew, as it is known in English—was a spore that came to France after a first appearance in England, probably aboard a popular ornamental vine that had been exported from the United States to Europe in large quantities since the 1830s. Once again, vineyards throughout the country fell under attack: after a fine gray white dusting appeared on leaves, grape bunches turned moldy and then split open, decayed and dried up. By 1854, French wine production had dropped by more than two-thirds, and as usual, any number of ingenious and extravagant ideas were proposed for the fight, but the solution finally proved to be relatively straightforward. English greenhouse keepers, affected by the blight ahead of the French, had discovered that pure sulfur, powdered and applied by bellowslike contraptions, stopped the fungus in its tracks. Picking up the cue, French industry rapidly produced the chemical in large quantities, and soon every vineyard in the country was showered in a dusty yellow fog. Enthusiastic overdoses of the stuff at the beginning of the campaign—the old error of more is better—often resulted in scorched foliage and local epidemics of eye problems like severe conjunctivitis among unprotected workers, but at length vignerons in the Beaujolais and elsewhere learned to control their ardor and their doses of chemicals. Sulfur has remained as a vineyard fixture ever since, not just in France but worldwide. More generally sprayed in a fine mist now rather than delivered in powder form, it is the best and simplest fungicide, and it is used both by industrial-scale producers and organic winemakers.

Late in the 1870s, America's second fungal gift arrived on French shores and proceeded to gain her vineyards. Downy mildew (*le mildiou* in French), it was called, for the mats of whitish "down" it deposited on vine leaves as it began its business of destroying the grape clusters. Strictly speaking a water mold rather than a classical fungus, downy mildew was in fact a cousin of *Phytophthora infestans*, the American-donated organism that brought the terrible potato blight to Ireland. At length this second form of mildew was beaten by a chemical mix patented in 1885 by Pierre Millardet, professor of botany in the University of Bordeaux's faculty of science. Millardet was led to his discovery by the manager of the Château Dauzac estate, who had sprayed his vines with vitriol (copper sulfate), whose bright blue-green color would, he was sure, stop local children from stealing his grapes. What Millardet noticed, though, was something more important than the matter of purloined grapes: Dauzac's vines were mildew-free. Carrying out a series of methodical experiments, he refined the recipe for an effective fungus-killing mixture: 1.5 kilos of copper sulfate mixed with one kilo of slaked lime, to be diluted in water and preventively sprayed over vines.

The *bouillie bordelaise* (literally Bordeaux porridge) that Millardet devised proved to be something of a horticultural panacea. A multipurpose disinfectant and fungicide, it is still widely employed by gardeners today as protection for a wide array of growing things, from apples and tomatoes to roses, potatoes and peaches—and, of course, grapevines. Once again, the vignerons of the Beaujolais set to the task of protecting their livelihood from the parasitic onslaught. At first, they were armed with nothing more sophisticated than buckets of Millardet's porridge and little moplike applicators for brushing it onto the leaves, or little bunches of broom sprigs with which they splashed the stuff in a primitive, hit-or-miss spray, but the process took forever and the results were woefully imperfect. The Villefranche inventor Victor Vermorel improved efficiency by designing a portable delivery system consisting of a metal tank to be strapped on the back, a hand-operated pump for air pressure and a spray hose for the other hand. Laboring through their vines under the torrid suns of July and August with fifty pounds of gear on their backs, the vignerons faced an impossible dilemma: shed their winter work clothes, and they were soon drenched in a corrosive chemical mist that savaged their skin; or cover up, and they would suffocate in the heat. But with their entire year's revenues in the balance, they had no choice but to plug along, bearing it with the dogged stoicism of peasants everywhere. Eventually improved machinery modernized and eased the task, first with horse-drawn equipment and then, decades later, with the tractor, but the basic recipe remained unchanged: a visit to almost any French vineyard today will show the characteristic turquoise hue on the vines' leaves, silent witness to the continuing effectiveness of Millardet's ingenious mix.

Ingenuity has long been a strong point of this country's national character. Inveterate tinkerers and improvers, the French always seem to be able to come up with clever, unexpected and elegant solutions to the most complex of problems that have baffled others. With the providential brainpower of men like Pasteur, Raclet, Chaptal and Millardet having appeared when things went wrong, the vignerons of the Beaujolais might have been forgiven for assuming, along with their winemaking confrères elsewhere in France, that their beautiful, blessed land could go on indefinitely in the production of more and more and better and better wines, for the greater good of their health, their country's prestige and everybody's pocketbooks.

And so, indeed, it appeared to servants of the vine around Beaujeu, Belleville and Villefranche in the two fat decades between 1855 and 1875. Yields were good, prices were high, and production was steadily rising. In the days when Benoît Raclet arrived in Romanèche, the average production of Beaujolais wines had been about 500,000 hectoliters (50 million liters); by 1874, the figure was edging up to near doubling that: 860,000 hectoliters.

Things were looking good. Many peasant landowners of the Beaujolais paid off long-standing debts and got new equipment, while other families that had been stuck in *vigneronnage* for generations were finally able to actually acquire the vines they worked. But under the optimism that the watershed year of 1874 generated everywhere in the Beaujolais, a somber bass note of caution appeared when, that same summer, vine leaves began drying up in the village of Villié-Morgon. The aphid *Phylloxera vastatrix* had arrived in the Beaujolais.

Now it was not just a year's harvest that was under threat, but the very survival of the vines. What happened over the next few years proved to be worse than even the most gloomy pessimists had imagined: the plants that had so generously produced bumper harvests were doomed. In fact, every last vineyard in France was about to be wiped out.

III

RUIN AND SALVATION

*A*t the start, far too many Beaujolais wine professionals succumbed to the old temptation of hubris: this thing won't hit *us*. By
the last quarter of the nineteenth century everyone knew that teeming
swarms of a mysterious, previously unknown insect had been wrecking
vineyards in the south and west for several years, and that the wave of
destruction was marching inexorably northward, but the growers of the
Beaujolais clung stubbornly to an obdurate, head-in-the-sand denial. All
too easily, a hypothesis of folk wisdom developed in the region's cafés
and wine cellars, and once it was out, wishful thinking rapidly turned
to dogma: the invader was a lowland bug that thrived in the year-round
warmth of the Midi, luxuriant land of lotus-eaters. When it came to the
stern frosts and winter winds of the *monts du Beaujolais*, it would meet
its match. When, in spite of some disquieting signs of early leaf damage,
the harvests of 1874 and 1875 proved to be abundant and of good quality, some moralizing voices went as far as to suggest that the southerners
had been justly punished for their notorious sin of overproducing, an
action known everywhere in the rough, colorful idiom of the peasantry:
faire pisser la vigne. Causing the vine to "piss" great amounts of grape
juice had been unworkmanlike. And besides, by flooding the market
with wine it had tended to lower prices.

The folly of the optimistic folk hypothesis was soon demonstrated:

the bug was a survivor, a real champion. What no one realized in those early days was that *Phylloxera vastatrix* was unhurried. In winter it simply lay dormant, and in the spring it picked up where it had left off, taking two or three leisurely years to kill a vine. Those two bumper harvests were the swan's song, sadly sublime, of pre-phylloxera Beaujolais.

Winged and wind-borne, the tiny aphid industriously pursued its business in the Beaujolais exactly as it had done in the south, moving from vine to vine and replicating itself in batches of summer and winter eggs that produced an astonishing quantity of offspring: between March and October, one noted investigator calculated, a single individual could give birth to 25 to 30 million descendants. Dropping its winter eggs on the vine's gnarled bark, it began a furiously repetitive reproductive cycle that moved from the bark to the leaves, drying them and provoking blisters, or galls, in which succeeding generations—born in parthenogenesis, without the need of a fertilizing male—thrived and continued the implacable colonization. Around midsummer, a generation of larvae, or nymphs, moved down the bark and underground to the fine, spidery webs of the vine's rootlets, fixed themselves to the extremities and began sucking out the sap that was the plant's lifeblood. These subterranean feeders in turn laid more eggs, which hatched into nymphs that slowly gained the surface and emerged as winged, adult aphids ready to continue the infernal routine of simultaneously ravaging and reproducing. By the time they departed, the host plants were finished. Desiccated and lifeless, they were good for nothing more than firewood.

The above is only the briefest summary of a three-year life cycle that the British writer Christy Campbell, author of the remarkable phylloxera study *The Botanist and the Vintner*, took several pages to describe in detail. Little wonder that it had baffled quantities of French scientists who had been investigating the insect's behavior for several years before it came to the Beaujolais. By then, though, there was one thing of which the teams of botanists and entomologists that had been tracking *Phylloxera vastatrix* since its first attacks on vineyards near Avignon were certain, and a very unpleasant irony it was: the ravenous little creatures had arrived in France attached to hardy American vines that had been imported in the 1860s because they were resistant to *oïdium*—the powdery mildew that had come from America in the first place. So it was America that had given France—and, indeed, all of Europe, because the aphid's depredations knew no borders—the two most recent and violent aggressors of the vine. But what the scientific community could not know just then was that the irony looped back upon itself: salvation would also appear from the same horizon; a new dawn for the vines would break in the wake of that fatal sunset.

In time, that is. It took a while. By 1874, when there was no more hiding from the fact that the Beaujolais was under attack, the regional authorities had notices posted in every town hall ordering that any vines showing signs of infestation be pulled up and immediately burned and the ground within a radius of five meters dug up and turned over. The measures were useless, of course, and perhaps even worse than useless. Digging the ground could only release tiny buried creatures, and the mere act of pulling up infected vines could attach more of them, or their eggs, to workers' clothing and tools, to be transported wherever they went. In any case, the orders went largely ignored, because human nature was human nature: most vignerons turned a blind eye to the blisters on their vines' leaves in those last two banner harvest years of 1874 and 1875. After all, their grape bunches were still heavy and apparently healthy; and directing a peasant to destroy his present livelihood for some vague future general good was really asking too much. Besides, a fanciful new rationalization had emerged, one that encouraged them to do nothing: Beaujolais vines grew higher than those of the Midi, and someone postulated that the female aphid reproduced with difficulty "in altitude." So the vignerons shut up and carried on as usual, with no one the wiser and everyone hoping for the best. Underground, the little bugs continued feeding.

By 1876, phylloxera was generalized throughout the Beaujolais, and the stock of rationalizations was exhausted. The huge winegrowing region of Bordeaux was already hit, and Burgundy was the next in line, then the vineyards of Italy, Germany, Spain, Switzerland, Hungary and other lands—in short, wherever *Vitis vinifera* was growing, even, in time, California and as far away as Australia. More deadly over its twenty-year infestation than the black plague had been for human beings, phylloxera made a tabula rasa of Europe's traditional wine industry. Not since the terrible winter of 1709 had vignerons known such a catastrophe. In that awful year—which had been bookended by preceding and following winters of nearly equal severity—the entire continent shivered in Siberian temperatures, and crop loss caused widespread starvation. In the wine regions, vines froze solid in the arctic air. Most of France's vines died and had to be pulled up and replanted the following spring; the small numbers that survived were saved only by the drastic surgery of amputation at ground level. Eventually, after a harvestless year or two, the roots gave new shoots and the vines were reborn.

There was no such remedy against phylloxera. Quite simply, no one had any notion of how to kill or control the bug. A long, agonizing period of grasping at straws now took over the Beaujolais, just as it had done earlier in the Midi. Sensibly enough, botanists advised selecting only the healthiest of seedlings to plant in place of dead vines, while thoroughly preparing the ground to receive them and boosting their resistance with potassium-based fertilizers, but heartier young vines only provided the intruders with more nourishing sap. It had already been established that certain southern owners had managed to save half or more of their average crops by physically flooding their vineyards for a couple of months in late autumn, thereby drowning the parasites, but the system was obviously futile for anything but flat, low-lying terrain, and out of the question in the hills and slopes of the Beaujolais. When Raclet's old boiling water method gave no result, peasants were reduced to the heartbreaking task of attempting to physically remove the aphid eggs by hand, in a grotesquely laborious process that involved digging deeply around the vines and cleaning trunks and roots one by one with a chain-mail glove. Although largely useless, the glove at least had the advantage of being cheap, and for a few illusion-filled years it was widely disseminated among winegrowers. Several steps above that were the considerably more expensive high-tech devices of the period like the "injector rod" of the ingenious inventor Victor Vermorel. The apparatus resembled a giant clyster, and featured a cylindrical storage tank, two handles and a foot pedal for squirting carbon disulfide, an industrial solvent, into the ground around the roots. Some minor success had been reported with this compound as an insecticide, and for a few years the government even awarded subsidies for its use, but, like the potassium sulfur carbonate treatments earlier certified by the Ministry of Agriculture, it had the unfortunate side effect of killing the vine along with the insects in anything stronger than light, carefully calculated doses. Vermorel's company also put a "sulfur plow" on the market for delivering an underground stream of carbon disulfide, but the device was expensive and the chemical treatment was highly toxic to the human nervous system, easily flammable and explosive. Beaujolais old-timers used to recount stories heard from their elders of muddle-headed vignerons unthinkingly lighting up for a cigarette break after a few hours with the Vermorel plow or injector rod, and expiring in a horrible, self-inflicted inferno.

The usual prayers, masses and pilgrimages only underlined the degree of disarray that had overcome the winemaking community. For want of anything better, folk and artisanal methods cropped up in patches wherever human imagination sought out the give-it-a-try approach. At the suggestion that the chemical composition of urine might be a palliative, one enterprising army unit in a Lyon suburb diligently collected tanks of horse pee to be ladled out over the vines, and one Beaujolais schoolteacher was reported to have led his schoolboys out of the classroom at recess time to earnestly *faire pipi* in military formation on adjacent vine rows. (For understandable reasons of reigning tenets of modesty, only "masculine urine" was deemed useful for this cure.) The French being a race of inveterate home inventors and undiscovered Thomas Edisons, a vast range of more or less plausible procedures, powders, liquids and chemical compounds — petroleum, viscous tar, sea salt, electrical charges—was proposed and sometimes tried out on the unfortunate vines, all to no avail. Campbell, who went to heroic lengths of research to discover a whole thesaurus of other suggested remedies, enumerated a selection that ranged from snail slime ("rich in calcium") to jellyfish, lard, mustard, turpentine, nicotine, asparagus, parsley, dynamite blasts, marching bands to "drum the aphids out of their underground fastness" to something called a beating wheelbarrow, its mechanical mallets presumably driving the little parasites to distraction by its maddening, endlessly repeated thumping.

As the search went on for a way to stop the deadly bug, French wine production plummeted. In consequence, the decade 1880–1890, and even beyond, was an excellent time to be a seller, if you had wine to sell of course. Those who had laid in good stocks did very well for themselves, and indeed, phylloxera was something of a backhanded benediction for the big wine dealers, who had no trouble at all in unloading even their mediocre reserves. Of course Beaujolais peasants also commanded good prices for their last remaining barrels and sold high, retaining only a strict minimum of bottles for themselves, in case of medical emergency. Wine imports rose dramatically—Italy, Spain and Algeria would still be producing for a while—and, inevitably, ersatz wines soon made their appearance. To the old peasant wine-replacement recipes invented in times of dearth (mostly local fruits and herbs infused in water and boosted with a jolt of pure alcohol) a more up-to-date, scientifico-commercial approach now yielded industrial amounts of fake wine and wine replacements. A common process was to bathe imported Greek and Turkish raisins in warm water for ten days, color the liquid with various essences, some natural, some not, and, to lend a winy bite, with tartaric acid, preserving the result with a dose of sulfur. Far from being back-shed moonshine, the stuff was advertised and sold in the most respectable shops. Three million hectoliters of raisin wine were manufactured in France in 1890 alone.

Professor Garrier of Lyon University told me of an even more crooked product: "sugar wine." This one didn't require any grapes at all, fresh or dried: a mixture of beet sugar, water, tartaric acid and colorings created a drink at eight degrees of alcohol content after yeasts interacted with the sugar. The product could even be dressed up in regional styles by the addition of different synthesized essences like "Bouquet of Pommard, Old Bordeaux, Dried Extract of Bordeaux" or "caramel-malaga" for white wine. Although this was clearly chicanery, it doesn't seem to have been prosecuted with excessive zeal. France was thirsty, and a lot of make-do solutions were more or less tolerated for want of clear laws and instruments for enforcing them. Five million hectoliters of sugar wine were on the market around 1890, Garrier reported in one of his papers, and it was not until 1908, after violent riots and demonstrations by winegrower unions, that this unlovable ersatz was finally put out of business via the simple expedient of a heavy new tax on sugar.

These had been terrible times for France. The country was still recovering from the disastrous war of 1870, which had cost it Alsace-Lorraine (a lot of good wine lost there), the imperium of Napoléon III and a breathtaking quantity of gold in war reparations that had to be handed over to Bismarck's triumphant Prussians. In this unsettled period the political scene of the newborn Third Republic was a roiling theater of passionate debate and controversy, but even with all that the phylloxera scourge continued to be one of the biggest ongoing news stories of the day. French gourmets and politicians did not take lightly to drinking factory-made substitutes, and returning to the genuine product of nature had become a national priority. But how to beat the bug? Once the crackpot proposals had been eliminated, the various investigative and defense committees in the front lines of the struggle soon divided up into three camps: the *sulfuristes*, the *immersionistes* and the *américanistes*. Sulfur compounds had been rewarded with only partial success, and the applications had to be frequently repeated, always attended by the danger of killing the vine by ill-calculated overdose. Immersing vineyards in water staved off total crop failure, but the process was complicated, expensive and practicable only in flat areas near rivers or lakes. The American solution was the last choice, and by far the most controversial.

Since the mid-nineteenth century, American and French wine growers had shown a lively interest in each other's native plants, and it was in all innocence that a certain number of American vines had been imported into France and planted for trials. They thrived, but within a couple of years the native *Vitis vinifera* growing nearby developed ugly leaf blisters and began to slowly perish. By 1869, investigators had made the obvious connection: it was these American vines that had brought a new kind of pest with them from the New World. At the same time, though, a capital characteristic of the imported vines was staring everyone in the face: *they were immune to the aphid themselves.* How this immunity had originated was unknown, but there it was, an inescapable hard fact. Investigators could only assume that over thousands or millions of years of natural selection and adaptation, the vines had developed protective mechanisms that permitted them to remain healthy under the bug's attack, while Europe's *Vitis vinifera*, virgin and defenseless, was easy prey.

Upon the discovery that the culprit was U.S. vines, the first panicky reaction was to embargo any further imports, but the ban was clearly pointless: the damage had already been done; the plague was there, and it was inching unstoppably through the land. It did not take long for a second thought, more logical this one, to replace the first: since the American vines were immune to phylloxera, why not try making wine with them? While the Beaujolais was enjoying its final two years of good harvests, winegrowers in the devastated Midi—or, rather, those who were wealthy enough to afford the expense—had already been replanting their ruined vineyards with strangely named vines from the New World: Jaquez, Cynthiana, Senasqua, Concord, Clinton, Cunningham, Scuppernong. Less fortunate vignerons simply gave up winemaking and turned to raising cattle or growing wheat or rye. The poorest of them suffered a fate similar to that of U.S. Okies. Ruined, their meager savings exhausted, they were reduced to becoming day laborers or moving on, elsewhere in France or in emigration to South America or Australia, where their descendants would be making wines a century or so later that would come into direct competition with those of the land they left behind.

When, in 1874, a specially convened wine congress sampled the first "American" wines produced from the newly planted southern fields, the verdict was unanimous: the stuff was revolting. From that big tasting came a disobliging but conveniently vague quip that went on to become one of oenology's more popular idioms, one that is still in use today. *"Pissat de renard,"* someone said, by way of characterizing the wine: fox piss. But ever since, the sharp, indefinable aroma and taste of wines made from native American vines have been branded with the adjective "foxy" (*goût foxé* in French).

Clearly, then, the U.S. vines would not do as replacements for the cherished European *Vitis vinifera*. With that failed enterprise behind them, winegrowers turned to hybrids, crossing American and French stock in search of the holy grail, the "direct," a single vine that would combine American phylloxera-resistance with the wine quality of *Vitis vinifera*. That ideal never materialized, but there was one hybrid, a crossing of two American stocks, that was received with great enthusiasm by small-time vignerons and farm families who made wine mostly for their own consumption, with perhaps a bit left over for sale to local bars and taverns: the Noah.

The saga of the Noah grape is one of the more interesting sidelights in the vast history of French winemaking. A rustic, hardy and easily raised plant named after history's legendary first winemaker (remember the Genesis story of Noah planting vines after the flood, then getting disgracefully and nakedly drunk in his tent), it yielded abundant quantities of juice and seemed to possess every quality that a vigneron could desire, including a nicely high alcohol content when fermented. And it was versatile, too. It grew lustily in marginal "grain terrain," and the white wine it produced could easily be turned to red by the simple expedient of mixing in a small dose of a powerfully colored red "tinting" wine, like the deep purple of another American grape, the Oberlin. In the stark, desperate years when the vineyards were dying and wine supplies were falling frighteningly short (a shortfall no doubt helped along by Prussia's notoriously thirsty occupying troops), Noah promised a quick way to fill the pressing demand for everyday table and bistro wine. For want of any better solution, many French peasants planted it liberally in spite of its single great flaw: that abiding sin of American grapes, the foxy taste of its wine. But Noah was such a snap to cultivate, and so rich in juice, that it became the *cépage* of choice for many thousands of rural families. In time, they even managed to persuade themselves that the taste of the finished product, *ma foi*, wasn't as bad as all that.

Noah vines thrived in private patches, then, but it was only after a generation of consumption that a second flaw came into evidence, and this one a good deal more serious: the wine did strange things to people. After a first few isolated cases began repeating themselves, it soon became clear that a lot of steady drinkers of Noah were going blind and even, in severe cases, falling into dementia. It was not until many decades had passed that analysis showed just what was going on: fermentation of the American hybrid produced psychotropic ethers, notably methanol, commonly known as wood alcohol, a violent toxin for the human nervous system. In 1930, the Noah vine was formally forbidden in France, a public health measure that paralleled the banning, fifteen years earlier, of the "green fairy," absinthe, a drink credited with scrambling the brains of untold thousands of addicts (even if it seemed to have inspired some of the greatest art of Toulouse-Lautrec). The peasantry gave up their cherished Noah only with great reluctance, dragging their heels through the years and conveniently "forgetting" many a small family patch. Rumor persists that more than a few remain in private cultivation today.

The romance with Noah did nothing, however, for the great sweep of the beautiful Beaujolais vineyards. While the taste of *"pissat de renard"* could be tolerated by home drinkers, low-life bistros or field laborers of rustic palate, it would not do for the sophisticated urban buyers who demanded the high quality and the seductive mouthfuls of fruit that they had come to expect in a glass of Beaujolais. They wanted their gamay back.

It was at this juncture that the Beaujolais produced a second providential savior of the vines, in the person of Victor Pulliat, a man whose energy and determination came to be seen as something like the second coming of Benoît Raclet. Owner of a prosperous domain in Chiroubles, the most westerly and the highest of the Beaujolais *crus*, Pulliat was an original thinker and dedicated student of the vine who was not afraid to fly in the face of accepted wisdom. As the phylloxera calamity wiped out one vineyard after another, an intense anti-American sentiment became generalized within the French wine community. How could anyone trust a nation that had delivered mildew, *oïdium*, the phylloxera aphid and then, as a bonus, had apparently thrown in the new plague called black rot? All this was undeniably true, but Pulliat had an inspired thought: rather than carping on what was wrong with the American vines, it would be more constructive to put to use what was right with them. His plan was simple but breathtakingly (and literally) radical: to make the American vines the entire basis of the wine industry, not as hybrids or foxy *directes*, but as something altogether new that he had been experimenting with at his domain: a binary plant. *Vitis vinifera*, he proposed, should be physically grafted onto phylloxera-resistant American rootstock. The U.S. plant would be the foundation, gamay the structure above.

Like Raclet half a century earlier, Pulliat was greeted with hoots and catcalls, or even worse. Where Raclet had been dismissed mostly with amused tolerance as a lunatic, Pulliat was often denounced as a public danger bent on propagating the damned Yankee infestations. It was only common sense, after all, that the American roots were bound to deliver an altogether different, foxy character to the valiant French grapes struggling to assert their native personality up above. Pulliat rejected the argument. Deliberately ignoring the embargo on U.S. plants, he went on with his trials at Chiroubles. By 1879, even the most hidebound traditionalists had caved in when the entirety of the Beaujolais was officially declared *phylloxéré*. Finally recognized as pointless, the embargo was lifted, freeing the way for any and all experiments. Pulliat began offering vigneron families free grafting classes after Sunday mass in Chiroubles's twelfth-century Church of Saint Germain.

Surprise: the wine from his binary vines didn't taste foxy at all. It looked, smelled and tasted just like what it was—gamay. Pulliat's intuition proved to be entirely correct. It was the grafted vine after all, and not the rootstock, that produced the character of the finished product. Beaujolais was saved—and a good deal more than Beaujolais, too, because there was no arguing with the success of *la méthode Pulliat.* Grafting was quickly and universally adopted. The denunciations of America ceased in measure with the vines that once again began flourishing throughout the land. Today, apart from a few small and isolated exceptions that may be called lucky freaks of nature, there are no more pure, native *Vitis vinifera* vines in France—or, indeed, anywhere else on the continent. The most modest and the most extravagantly expensive wines alike, from a simple *vin de table* to La Romanée-Conti and Château Pétrus, are pressed from grapes now growing on American roots, and they fear phylloxera no more. The grafting procedure has become so commonplace and so widely and skillfully organized that nurseries, cooperative agencies and individual growers distribute binary seedlings as efficiently and easily as pure stock ever was in the past. A handsome bust of Pulliat now stands opposite the church in Chiroubles, and, like Raclet's *fête* in Romanèche-Thorins, the great man's memory is honored with a solemn annual tasting on the last weekend of April to determine the year's best batches of the ten prestigious Beaujolais *crus.*

The traumatic phylloxera episode had a wide-ranging and permanent effect on the wine industry. Since the nationwide annihilation of the vines had wiped the slate clean, the replanting with grafted vines finally brought a certain degree of modernization to an extraordinarily antiquated and toilsome enterprise. In our machine age, it is easy to forget just how punishing the work of the vine had been in the old days, right through to the end of the nineteenth century, when industrialization was in full swing in Great Britain, Germany and the United States. It is no exaggeration to say that the Beaujolais peasant had lived under a sentence of hard labor to produce that light, friendly drink so prized by city folk. Up before the crack of dawn to tend to the animals, he worked all day long in his vineyard at the endlessly repeated seasonal drudgery, sustained at lunchtime by a chunk of salted fatback, a loaf of dark, homemade bread and a little barrel-shaped container of *piquette* or *vin de repasse*, the thin, acid drink confected from a re-pressing of his grapes' dregs infused in water, offering a slight alcoholic nudge of four or five degrees. (His true wine was far too valuable a commodity to be wasted on personal consumption.) Tramping back to the house at sundown, he took the same familiar peasant supper that his neighbors in the village would be eating: soup, bread and perhaps a chunk of homemade cheese, washed down with more *piquette*. Almost invariably, the soup was composed of whatever vegetables had been stored in the cellar or were in season. A frequent, economical version was made of boiled nettles, and when vegetables were scarce an alternative was a mush of oats or other grains, not unlike the *puls* that had been the common sustenance of the invading Roman armies of ancient times. It was only on Sundays that most farm families expected to have any meat on the table. Bread was the everyday staff of life, endowed with a near-mystical status that was fully equal to that of wine, and never a crumb was thrown away or intentionally wasted. To do so would have been shocking behavior, akin to blasphemy.

Until the great social and economic upheavals caused by World War I, the Beaujolais peasant housewife customarily ate her own supper standing in the kitchen after serving husband and family. Why did she not sit and join them? The answer isn't clear. It was simply the custom, and customs changed slowly in the fiercely conservative atmosphere of the countryside. Perhaps the explanation lies in the reigning imperative of hard physical labor that governed their lives. She had no time for dawdling. There were more important things to do. Balancing this apparent gender indignity were the strict social observances that peasant children learned at a very young age. Women were honored with a simple, courtly grace that has largely disappeared from modern societies.

Outside the immediate family cell no male, young or old, would ever think of remaining seated when a woman, or even a teenage girl, entered the room. If the encounter took place outside, he would be viewed as a shameful boor if he did not doff his cap in her presence.

Women were, as they remain today, absolutely indispensable for the smallholding Beaujolais vigneron, and their workdays were as long and exhausting as his. Although generally spared the hardest labor of pick, sledgehammer, mattock and maul, the housewife joined her husband in the fields for the fine work of removing buds and tying up vines, and cared for the farm's animals with hardly any less devotion than she gave to her own children. When not out among the vines, she baked her bread, drew water from the well, cleaned house, cooked supper, sewed and mended, made and laid down preserves, and then joined her husband and any others present—the older children, often her parents-in-law, perhaps a *valet de ferme*, one of the hired workers who lived in the house as a virtual family member—to work until late at night by the fireplace repairing tools, preparing stakes, stripping and splitting willow branches for baskets, or any other of dozens of seasonal chores. It was at this evening gathering in the darting shadows of the waning fire—*la veillée*—that the web of intercourse that defines a region's culture was woven and its society welded into a like-thinking unit. The intercourse was strictly local, and the language was Beaujolais patois rather than the French that they had learned in their few years of basic schooling. Gossip was exchanged, local history recounted by the elders, aphorisms, tips, and words of wisdom passed on, old tales repeated and embroidered, folk songs softly sung. Today, the *veillée* has been predictably shouldered aside by the television set on the kitchen table.

Up next morning with the chickens, the vigneron family carried on with the sempiternal routine. Ever since the earliest days of winemaking, all the multiple operations of tending the vine had been carried out by the force of human muscle power alone: preparing the ground with a heavy pick or mattock, planting, pruning, loosening up the soil in the months of growth, packing it around the plants to help them survive the winter, digging them free in the spring, carrying eroded soil back up to the top of the slopes from which it had washed down, delivering fertilizer, hoeing against adventitious weeds and grasses come to compete with the vines for water and nourishment, carrying out preventive sprayings and, of course, picking, pressing and vinifying the grapes. The family cow occasionally could be harnessed to pull the cart that moved manure or delivered barrels, but that was the limit of the vigneron's surcease from hard handwork. It wasn't that much of a surcease, though. Even for limited calls on their strength, cows are not really satisfactory beasts for work. Shambling, difficult to harness and virtually untrainable, they are not naturally suited for anything beyond grazing and giving milk, or their own selves for meat. Further, most Beaujolais cows were weak and stunted: with natural grazing land taken over by vines, they ate poorly, being reduced to foraging for the limited grass growing on roadsides. Hay being an expensive commodity, they rarely ate anything better than straw in the wintertime. The ox, if the peasant was prosperous enough to own one, was a fine worker, the bulldozer of the day, but limited to specialized chores. A slow but immensely strong puller, he was used exclusively for pure power jobs like ripping out vines, dragging logs or drawing heavily laden carts.

Phylloxera's total destruction introduced a radical rethinking of the ancient ways. Now, for the first time, beasts of burden—or, rather, traction—entered the vineyards: mules, horses and, occasionally, for those who could afford nothing better, the cow, the poor man's tractor. On the surface, it appears surprising that it was not until the very end of the nineteenth century that animal power was brought to the wine fields. It seems like such an obvious solution for making chores easier and faster—but it wasn't, for the simple reason that since the Middle Ages Beaujolais vineyards had always been something of a chaotic hugger-mugger, planted en foule, "in throng." The peasant reproduced and extended his vines by the ancient practice of marcottage, burying a living vine branch, still attached to the trunk, until it produced the roots that would become the foot of a new vine. Since vines were tended one by one, it made no difference how unevenly the plants were distributed. The vigneron moved from plant to plant, working each one by hand exactly as his father and his grandfather had done, and all their ancestors before them. No horse or mule, or even less a cow, could ever enter the vineyard without trampling vines and making a big mess of it.

When the peasantry was forced to start the wine fields all over again from scratch, they were able to benefit from the advances of the Industrial Revolution. The revolution had come late to France, but by the last quarter of the nineteenth century clever inventors and entrepreneurs like Vermorel were mass producing gear that for the first time could mechanize many of the ancestral gestures of the vine. Technology could replace—or at least supplement—technique. Animal power was the obvious solution for pulling the heavy equipment to plow the earth and spray the vines, but for animal power to be practicable, the vines had to be planted in dead-straight, geometrically perfect rows between which the horse or the mule could navigate under the vigneron's gee and haw. (The ox was too slow, the cow too clumsy, to make a proper job of it.)

But the modernization didn't happen without controversy and dissent. Conservative as ever, most peasants were initially suspicious of the idea of allowing great, heavy quadrupeds to come lumbering through their precious vines—sure as rain, they would trample more plants than they would help. Their opposition was only another sign of the relative poverty in which the vignerons had always lived. They were unfamiliar with horses because few of them had ever possessed any. And why should they have? Horses were expensive and skittish, and they ate twice as much forage as cows without giving any milk in return: a very poor investment. Peasant logic is always correct when it is based on experience, because it is the old ways that have allowed them to survive year to year, as their ancestors did. Where novelty and speculation for the future are concerned, though, their stubborn resistance to change can often settle them deep in error.

So it was at first with their opposition to the horse. Marcel Laplanche, seventy-five years old when I met him, was a retired vigneron who vividly remembered his parents speaking of their amazement and shock at their first sight of a horse in a neighbor's vines in 1912. "He's mad!" they had cried, certain that they were about to witness a disaster. But when they saw with what delicate intelligence a well-trained animal could pick its way through the vines, they could only accept that it was progress, after all. For most peasants, though, that acceptance came very slowly, as it had for Pulliat's wild idea of grafting onto American roots. It was not until the end of World War I that the rectilinear vines tended by a man behind a horse became the rule in the Beaujolais. In a macabre kind of way, this modernization was spurred along by the fact that France had been bled white by the scarcely believable mass butchery of the Great War: manpower had become rare. It is a sobering experience to visit the *monument aux morts* of any little French village and contemplate the neatly chiseled row upon row of names of the local boys who at Verdun, the Vosges and the Somme had served as fodder for cannon and machine gun — the kill-power of war, too, had benefited from the Industrial Revolution. The Beaujolais needed all the help it could get.

Although its introduction was slow in coming, the horse was the first great labor-saving revolution to come to the Beaujolais, Papa Bréchard once explained to me. Eighty-nine years young when I met him in his village of Chamelet, Louis Bréchard had earned the sobriquet "Papa" by his evergreen longevity (he finally died at age ninety-three in 1997), his exemplary winemaking career and his political importance for the region. Progressing from simple vigneron in the beautiful yellow-stone country near Bois d'Oingt to mayor of his village, to leader of a wine-growers' union and finally to deputy in the National Assembly in Paris, he had rubbed shoulders with the movers and shakers of the government of Charles de Gaulle, including *le Grand Charles* himself. Although at ease among the mighty of the land, he remained the constant, imperturbable icon of and spokesman for his rural constituency, a stocky, broad-shouldered, mustachioed peasant who rolled his R's and delivered crushing handshakes with calloused palm. The great man was the memory of the Beaujolais.

"Most of the villagers were surprised to see that horses didn't damage the vines," he said. "The animals were light on their feet, and they actually seemed to understand the work they were doing. They were a lot smarter than people had given them credit for."

The young Louis Bréchard was himself a perfect example of the need for modernization. He had become *chef de famille* and taken over the family's nine-acre vineyard at age fourteen, when his father was killed in the trenches near the end of the war. In conversation with me and in the book of memoirs he composed with the Lyon journalist Jean-Pierre Richardot (*Papa Bréchard, Vigneron du Beaujolais*, Éditions Stock, 1977) he evoked the amazingly different world of his youth. Before the end of the First World War electricity was nonexistent in most Beaujolais villages, water entered the house in a bucket from the communal well, and it was economized as a precious rarity and utilized in a careful cascade — first wash your vegetables with it, then your hands, then throw it over plants. It was a time when peasants' feet were still shod in sabots, the universal wooden shoes of rural France, hand-carved from walnut or birch blocks, and straw was used instead of socks; when the courtyard harbored pigs, chickens and rabbits (raw material for future feasts) in addition to the cow and the horse; and when the kitchen, the single great farmhouse room where the family lived around the fireplace, frequently had a floor of beaten earth and was lit by the fragrant flames of walnut oil lamps.

The casual visitor to an archetypal country scene like this one might well have concluded that the Beaujolais vigneron lived in the same timeless, unchanging routines as his forefathers and would go on that way through the generations, but the reality was quite different. Winegrowing families were often subject to sudden, dramatic change, and had to be quick on their feet to adapt. Papa Bréchard's great-grandparents had grown hemp on the family property, stripping the plant's fibers and weaving them into rough cloth that they whitened with successive washings in the acidic waters of the River Azergues and eventually sold for making sheets. But the next generation felt the heat of the Industrial Revolution, and factories using machines and chlorine bleach were already turning out sheets whiter and faster. His grandparents, then, slowly gave up hemp and moved into mixed agriculture and grapes. By the time his father took over, hemp was entirely gone and the family exploitation was half-farm, half-vines. Under the young Bréchard's stewardship, it turned almost entirely to the making of wine. Then as today, the vigneron could never insulate himself from the forces of change or the need to readjust his life to them.

The switch to animal power and rectilinear planting meant that Beaujolais peasants were obliged to rapidly learn how to handle that useful but very difficult and demanding creature, the horse, and how to improve the quality of their wine to cover the extra expense that this implied. Then, barely more than twenty-five or thirty years later, the horse was out in favor of the tractor—different methods, more expense. Shifts of this sort underline the unusual, and unusually demanding, nature of the vigneron's trade. It is a complicated business, one that requires him to master several different disciplines. For most of the year he is a simple peasant, husbanding his crop of grapes as close as he can to perfection, itself an undertaking that requires a great variety of instruments and seasonal skills. In the autumn and early winter he becomes a biotechnician, transforming the crop into the delicate, capricious artifact that is a well-made wine. Next, he goes into the storage and warehousing business, before entering the world of commerce and salesmanship when he puts his year's production on the market. Not everyone is capable of handling all these steps with equal felicity or can afford to buy and maintain the modern equipment they require, and the typical vigneron often might have envied his cousin in the grain business who simply plowed, planted and harvested. It was this multifaceted complexity of the wine trade that early in the twentieth century was to give birth to a system of *caves coopératives,* the co-op wine cellars that today bring together thousands of small growers who are not willing or not equipped to perform this multitude of tasks by themselves. Today, co-op cellars vinify and store more than half of France's wine.

The old Beaujolais of Papa Bréchard's childhood was far from such up-to-date facilities. The vines planted *en foule* before the days of the horse were extraordinarily dense, with anywhere from twelve thousand to fifteen thousand and sometimes even twenty thousand separate plants per hectare.* That's a huge number, and the vineyards often must have looked very much like jungles. When the horse and the tractor brought rectilinear order, the number of plants per hectare in the Beaujolais dropped and stabilized at around ten thousand, but even this was (and is) high for France, where most winegrowing areas average between four thousand and seventy-five hundred plants per hectare. This greater number of plants means more work, of course, especially the demanding handwork of pruning, removing buds and tying branches to stakes and wires. But work was always the essential identifying characteristic of the Beaujolais vigneron's existence, and he had no choice but to stoically accept it as part of the inevitabilities of life.

"When I took over the farm," Papa Bréchard told me, "my mother and I had to work nonstop, just plugging along from one day to the next, making ends meet. It wasn't easy to get by in those days." In his memoirs he gave descriptions longer in detail on just how hard that work could be. Probably the most trying and frustrating job was dealing with the erosion that constantly threatens the steeply sloped vineyards that are so commonplace in the Beaujolais.

"Erosion frequently caused gullying," he wrote, "and that made the work really tough, because whenever a storm carried the soil away it had to be brought back up on your back. I did it myself. We had *hottes*, [wickerwork baskets] and we shoveled the earth that had been carried away into them and brought it back up to the top in order to have a layer of arable soil in place. It was like coolie work; the method wasn't very much different. On each trip we brought 50 kilos [110 pounds] of earth up the hill—now, that's a good load! We brought up as much as we had to, day after day. It was easier to walk when the ground was frozen, be-

---

*One hectare = 2.471 acres.

cause then it didn't give way under our feet. So we carried up earth to the point of exhaustion."

The *hottes*, as he explained them, resembled hod carriers' troughs, entirely made of wood in those days before the arrival of the plastic containers that have now become the common tool of vineyards all around the world. Supple willow branches that had been stripped and split during some earlier night's *veillée* were woven together to form the basket itself, which was held in a solid wood framework and supported by a couple of stiltlike legs, which the field worker could grasp as he clambered uphill. He filled the basket, humped it up and shuffled forward, bent almost double on the slope in order to keep his center of gravity stable, planting the two legs on the ground for support when he stopped for a breather. In the steepest sections of the slope, he would sometimes be on all fours. The jolly winemaker of popular imagery was a beast of burden himself.

Then there was the work of pickax and mattock. The earth always had to be loosened up for the vine, and before the introduction of horsepower that meant human elbow grease. "A good pick man, a really strong one, if he could do 600 square meters a day, he was a master," Papa wrote. "That's really something, 600 meters. He needed almost two weeks to handle one hectare. And he had to have decent weather, too, because when it rained hard the soil firmed up like cement. A certain number of days would be lost, but still we had to keep at it, chopping, chopping, chopping. It was very hard work."

A less exhausting but potentially dangerous chore occurred each year when the grapes were brought in for vinifyng. True to the stereotypical imagery, the old Beaujolais vigneron trampled his grapes after they had been dumped into the big tuns and were on their way to transformation into wine. The standard practice was to do the job "in the costume of Adam," as Papa put it—emphasizing, however, that they washed up first, using a basin of water and sometimes even soap. But those same tuns, vast and deeper than a grown man, could become death traps if the trampler was ever unwise enough to work unaccompanied, because the undetectable carbon dioxide gas rising up from the purplish, fermenting fruit could coldcock a man as surely as a blackjack. The lone, naked vigneron who keeled over into the seething mass of grape skins and juice might be discovered only hours later, asphyxiated by his own crop. There were victims every year, said Papa.

The center of village life was always the café. Some vignerons went to mass on the Sabbath and some didn't, but none ever missed the Sunday morning gatherings in the village café. These informal get-togethers were vital, much more important than mere social or recreational outings. For want of any other plausible venue, the café played the role of the local business and convention center. In a cloud of acrid black tobacco smoke from their pipes and the cigarettes they rolled themselves, seated around a few half-liter *pots** of Beaujolais, the men exchanged information about the incessant struggle for the health of their plants, the progress of ripening in different sectors, the prices their wines were fetching, any new regulations that might affect their livelihood, projected harvest dates, or any of the numerous other topics of daily concern to the wine trade. After lunch they might return to the café for a spirited game of *boules*, the Beaujolais equivalent of *pétanque*, but the Sunday morning meetings were all business.

Life was local and slow, lived at the pace of the seasons and the natural cycle of their plants. National news was distant and spotty, apprehended by newspaper and word of mouth, because radio was nonexistent and television not even imagined. When, once every few years, a vigneron was called for family reasons, pressing legal business or some truly extraordinary errand to make the twenty-five-mile trip to Lyon, the regional metropolis, few expected to get there by any other means than shank's mare. There was the train at Mâcon, Belleville and Villefranche, to be sure, but it was expensive. Instead, the Beaujolais winegrower preferred to walk, and he did it with the same plodding peasant determination that ruled the rest of his life. "We would leave for Lyon at three in the morning," Papa

---

*A thick glass carafe measuring forty-six centiliters.

Bréchard remembered. "Quite often in wooden shoes. Leaving at three or four, a good walker expected to be back by that same night. He needed six or seven hours to get to Lyon, walking at a normal clip. He did his business and came back that evening, almost always carrying a load."

The reason for departure in the middle of the night was, of course, to avoid missing a full day's work upon his return. As it was with thrift, the work imperative was absolutely constant, graven into the vigneron's psyche and never allowing him to breathe completely easy. Certainly peasant life in the late nineteenth and early twentieth centuries was beginning to edge into many of the conveniences of the industrialized world, but the typical Beaujolais attitude toward work, as described by Papa Bréchard, had hardly changed since a striking portrait in words sketched by an anonymous eighteenth-century observer that the Lyon historian Raymond Billiard cited in one of his books (*Trois Siècles de la Vie de Nos Ancêtres Beaujolais*, Éditions du Cuvier, Villefrenche, 1945):

> *Men of this sort have to be hard-working, and in fact they are; never an instant of respite, always harnessed to the hardest and exhausting labors. To give you an idea, it's enough to know that the women, apart from their housework and their care for their family and animals, share with their men all the toils of the vine, scythe the meadows, plow the earth, harvest and thresh the wheat.*
>
> *The Beaujolais peasant does not much fear death; he suffers and speaks with indifference of the end of his days, regarding it as the end of his misery. He takes care of his earthly business and then goes to his tomb. Four days later his widow is remarried, for she must have help to carry on with the inheritance with which she is charged.*

More than his winemaking brethren almost anywhere else in France, the Beaujolais vigneron had always been hostage to unpredictable vagaries of weather. However well things were going, however healthy his vines or how good the prospects for the next harvest, there was always a distant dread lurking in a corner of his subconscious: what would the sky deliver next? Years of too much rain could wash away his soil, bring fungal attacks and make the juice of his grapes thin and watery; drought would certainly shrivel the grapes and lower his yields, perhaps dramatically. He could deal with those kinds of conditions, though; they were a normal part of his bargain with natural forces that were, on the whole, benevolent in the Beaujolais by comparison with other, less hospitable, parts of the world. But it was the unjust and unpredictable that spooked him—the aberrant moments when nature went mad, bringing destruction to him with capricious, irrational cruelty. Nothing, it appeared, could ever be entirely free for the Beaujolais vigneron. Where nature gave with one hand, it took away with the other.

"On the plus side, the *monts du Beaujolais* are beautiful and the *terroir* is perfect for gamay," Professor Garrier explained, "but there's a negative side to that: the lay of the land creates a local microclimate that is propitious for storms. It's a simple physical mechanism: if winds from the west and northwest are carrying water when they hit the hills, that means trouble. When the wind sweeps up over the top of the mountains, the water drops can freeze, and that means hail. It's just nature, and it's particular to the Beaujolais. The hail problem is much worse here than up in the Côte d'Or. And in Bordeaux they've got no such problem at all."

More than mildew, rot or even insects, hail is the most terrifying calamity a winegrower can imagine, because it strikes suddenly and without warning and can devastate an entire area in a matter of minutes. Reminded of the subject, Papa Bréchard unhesitatingly harked back to 1929 and 1966, displaying yet again that extraordinary faculty that seems to inhabit all vignerons: the unerring memory of annual events all the way back to their earliest youth. These people think not in days or weeks but in segments of *millésimes* (vintage years), and the longer you speak with them the more total their recall seems to be. In the awful August of 1929, Papa remembered, a cataclysmic hailstorm hit southern Beaujolais just before harvest time. So intense was the storm, and so enormous the hailstones, that the vines were not merely stripped of their leaves and grapes, but in certain vineyards the trunks themselves were snapped off by the barrage. In 1966, again just before harvest, he personally witnessed in Morgon a pile of hailstones nearly a yard high.

How can you fight against visitations like that? You can't, really, but they tried. Less fatalistic than their ancestors, most vignerons by the turn of the century were unwilling to place their faith in holy candles, prayers and church bells anymore. Instead, they turned to the new religion of modern technology. What Our Lady of the Vine had not consented to protect, perhaps science and industry could. Rationalism, invention and the fantasy of triumph over nature were very much in the air of the time; Jules Verne was already a classic, and H. G. Wells was just hitting his stride. Surely hail could be defeated by machinery and mankind's clever manipulations.

First up in the battle with the sky was the military approach: cannon aimed upward. Obscure and totally undocumented reports had claimed battlefield experiences wherein the rumble and smoke of artillery fire had chased clouds away. No one knew whether it was the noise or the rising gunpowder smoke that did the trick, but it was worth a try. Around 1890 the first anti-hail cannon appeared in the Beaujolais. Facing upward, the weapons' muzzles were surmounted by sheet metal cones in the shape of three-storey-high megaphones, the better to aim and concentrate the noise and the smoke—whose particles, it was ardently expected, would cause ice to turn to rain. Papa Bréchard remembered his childhood's bucolic peace being shattered by thunderous midsummer explosions, but nary a hailstorm was prevented. The failure, in fact, was Europe-wide, because the cannon experiment had been tried in several different vineyard zones.

Where artillery had failed, the more sophisticated approach of rockets was next in line: now cloud seeding became all the rage. Potassium iodide crystals that would precipitate rain, it was posited, could be sent by rockets high into the center of clouds, where cannon fire had not been able to reach. Alas, this early space age idea also flopped, even if the idea of cloud seeding has had a longer life. It is still occasionally attempted today in various parts of the world, in hopes of delivering rain to drought-stricken areas. The seeding element of choice is now silver iodide rather than potassium iodide, but the result is approximately the same.

The last gasp of scientific approach was the contraption called the Niagara (presumably named in anticipation of the floods of rainfall it would produce). In 1912 the Beaujolais Agricultural Union laid out a considerable sum to have seventeen of them erected at strategic points around the most hail-susceptible areas, and very impressive they were, too—all the more so since they were designed to use that mysterious new magic, electricity. Giant pylons like mini Eiffel Towers stood fifty yards high, topped with electrodes not unlike certain TV antennas of the future. These upper electrodes were connected by a copper cable to a second set buried underground, in contact with the water table. State-of-the-art for the time, the Niagara was based on an advanced and appropriately fuzzy logic. Somehow, its backers promised, differences of polarity would prevent the formation of hail by lowering the electrical tension of approaching clouds (whatever that meant). One more flop.

"Crooks!" snorted Papa Bréchard in appropriate praise of the Niagara's inventors. The last pylons were finally dismantled in 1922 and sold for scrap. Beaujolais vignerons today have returned with a shrug to the old fatalism. Like death and taxes, hail will come when it comes. There's always hail insurance to be bought, certainly, but it is expensive. Most growers just take their chances.

By the time the fourteen-year-old Louis Bréchard took over the family vineyard and farm in 1918, there weren't many holdouts for the old ways left. The Beaujolais was modernizing, and not by machinery alone. Agronomic science was improving plant selection, and the big phylloxera scare had brought a greatly increased attention to cloning and grafting on a semi-industrial scale. Effective pest-control chemicals and potassium-rich fertilizers derived from the slag of the steel industry in eastern France were becoming available, while progressive industrialists like Vermorel were regularly disseminating information sheets on rationalizing traditional agricultural methods. As a result, wine production soared throughout the country even as the total acreage under cultivation dropped. Progress marched forward in the Beaujolais as everywhere else, and yields per acre jumped. To those who had known the old days, this came as a divine surprise. As matters turned out, though, the alchemy of greater yields proved to be very much of a mixed blessing. And how could it be otherwise? For the fatalistic vigneron, every plus always dragged a minus along with it.

"When I was a boy we used to dream of getting thirty hectoliters of wine from one hectare of vine," Papa Bréchard told me in 1993—a time when any grower in the Beaujolais could easily produce two or three times that amount, if he hadn't been restrained by the quality-control limits imposed by INAO (the National Institute of Certified Names). By the time I met him, the problem throughout French vineyards had become not how to produce enough wine to satisfy the national and international demand, but rather how to keep yields down within reasonable limits, thereby maintaining good prices and constant quality. The ancient worry of not enough wine to go around had flip-flopped into the new economic bête noire of oversupply.

This dilemma of too much wine and not enough buyers was to be a recurrent and painful theme in the ongoing history of French winemaking. Ironically, it was phylloxera that brought that dilemma to center stage for the first time. In those years of dearth, the commercial wise guys had learned how to make wine ex nihilo, or almost, and the parasitic sugar-wine industry continued to run full steam for several years even after the country's vineyards had been reconstituted with phylloxera-resistant grafted plants, to produce real wine the old way. It was a curious and surprising anomaly—who, least of all among the French, could possibly prefer fake, factory-made "wine" to the real thing? A lot of people, as it turned out. Sugar wine was bulk stuff, aimed exclusively at the low-end of the spectrum—a cheap drunk—but there was a market for it, and a combination of dirt-cheap pricing and weak, unclear consumer-protection legislation made it possible. After all, why bother with all that specialized field labor and fastidious vinifying when mixing up a bit of cheap wine from Algeria or the Languedoc region with a jolt of tartaric acid, sugar and yeasts, all of it thinned out with plenty of water, delivered a nicely profitable drink that could be labeled with any fanciful name?

Sugar wine finally disappeared in 1908 when the government applied a new sugar tax specifically designed to deal with it, but it was not before peasants in the south, whose wine prices had been dramatically undercut by the factory-made stuff, had set off a series of violent demonstrations that turned to bloody rioting. In June 1907, six people were killed in clashes with police in Narbonne, and in nearby Perpignan the regional administration building was burned to the ground. With a quasi-insurrectional climate upon the land, the army had to be called in to restore order. It was high time to get rid of the vinous counterfeiters once and for all.

Through it all, the Beaujolais remained dead calm. Theirs were "lesser" wines than those of their rich and noble Burgundian cousins up in the Côte d'Or, but they were honest, traditionally made and sincere, miles above the sugar-based industrial plonk that was causing all the trouble down south. Since Beaujolais was in a higher category of prestige and price, there was no head-to-head competition, and hence no cause for strife. So the vignerons plugged along with their specialty, the peculiar little gamay grape that they knew better than anyone else and which apparently was happier on their granitic slopes than anywhere else, turning out the pleasant wine that over the years had conquered a modest but respectable corner of the national market. None of them could have illusions of accumulating anything like wealth from their labors; in fact, all the way through to the end of the Second World War, the Beaujolais could only have been classified as one of the poorer regions of France.

"It wasn't so easy to be settled into neediness the way we were," Papa recalled in a moment of retrospection, "but I suppose we weren't all that ambitious. As long as we had about enough to eat and people liked our wine, and the neighbor liked it, too, we had a certain kind of contentment with our life. Everything considered, our misery was joyous enough. We might have been living close to the edge, but we were living, after all."

Right up into the 1950s, the old ways and customs continued very much as they had been in Papa Bréchard's youth, and the atmosphere of the Beaujolais country remained generally slow-paced and thrifty, closer to penury than to prosperity—getting by. But things were about to be shaken up. In March of 1957, France, Germany, Italy, the Netherlands, Belgium and Luxembourg signed the Treaty of Rome, the founding document of the European Economic Community. The Common Market was just around the corner, and the enlarged European Union was being sketched out on the horizon. It was to grow into the greatest market in the world, the economic powerhouse that over the next half century was to become one of the principal motors of the astonishing wealth-creating machine that now goes by the name of globalization.

The Beaujolais was to profit mightily from this wealth machine when the rest of France, and then Europe and finally the entire world, woke up to the fact that the much-belittled gamay had been given a seriously bum rap by Philip the Bold. That was a secret that the population of Lyon had known all along, of course. Because it was there, in France's second city, that Beaujolais's extraordinary run to worldwide popularity had begun.

IV

THE THREE RIVERS OF LYON

*S*cratch a grumpy French intellectual, and the chances are pretty good that beneath the bark and the bombast you'll find an insecure little gourmet yearning to climb out. Léon Daudet (1867–1942) was an unabashed reactionary, a fire-breathing author, critic, politician and polemicist who hated just about everything in Republican France and democracy in general, and who was always ready to put up his dukes or his pistol (he is said to have fought at least fourteen duels) to lay low anyone who disagreed with his radically royalist and retrograde opinions. But set him into hot intimacy with the winsome breast and well-turned thigh of a Bressane hen, or the *volupté* of an elegant wine, and the Savonarola turned into a milksop.

"There are three reasons why Lyon is the capital of French gastronomy," he wrote in 1927, doubtless with a tear in his eye and a glass of Brouilly or Moulin-à-Vent standing within easy reach. "The first is that this incomparably gastronomic city is neighbor to the Bresse region, with its unctuous quenelles and the best chickens in the world, raised the wise old way, and ringed with layers of golden fat.

"The second is that in her markets she has the crayfish that can't be found anywhere else in the world and, when they are in season, black morel mushrooms.

"The third is that in addition to the Saône and the Rhône, she is served by a third river, the Beaujolais, which never dries up and is never muddy."

If it was Pasteur who gave drinkers everywhere the ideal rationalization for having another glass (wine being the most hygienic of drinks), it was the ill-tempered Daudet whose riverine image became the single most famous and frequently repeated phrase used to characterize both France's second largest city and the wine it loved to drink more than any other. As long as anyone could remember, the house wine in the wonderful restaurants for which Lyon was justly famous—often, in the simplest of them, the only wine available—was Beaujolais. For a gent sincerely zealous about his thirst like Daudet, it could, indeed, appear that Lyon was awash in a river of the wines of gamay. So fitting was Daudet's image that the inveterate Beaujolais drinker became a national stereotype as the star attraction of the Lyonnais marionette theater invented by an out-of-work Lyonnais *canut* (silk worker) that continues to thrill French children today in spite of continuing aggression from the cathode ray tube. These hand-puppet shows feature a whole vocabulary of colorful characters, but the two principal ones are unfailingly Guignol in the left hand and Gnafron in the right. Guignol is the Lyonnais Everyman, the typical *gone* (guy in the street): quick, skeptical, bright and subversive. But it is Gnafron who gets most of the laughs, because he is both recognizable and irresistible—the barfly with a W. C. Fields nose as red as Abbé Ponosse's, an amiable shoemaker who neglects his work in favor of homespun philosophizing and wicked political commentary over a *canon* of Beaujolais, the standard bar wineglass measuring an eighth of a pint.

Like Gnafron, Lyon's food-loving, joke-loving population took to Beaujolais and adopted it as their very own wine, because it was good, plentiful and inexpensive. Beaujolais became as much a part of the city's identity as the rich local argot and the peculiar drawl of the Lyon accent, as different from Paris chatter as Boston's is from New York's. The real-life Gnafrons who hung around bars and cafés with a finely tuned sense of what counted in life and what did not knew that November 11,

Saint Martin's day, was a pivotal moment in the year's cycle of Beaujolais winemaking. Peasant empiricism, perhaps reinforced by a lingering belief in succor by divine intervention, had determined that each year's new vintage, or at least a part of it, could be ready for drinking only two months or so after harvest. By common accord, the date they chose for this early release was heavily symbolic, the day of France's patron saint. The good, charitable Martin, he who had given his cloak to a freezing pauper, could always be counted upon to bring success and comfort. In Lyon of the eighteenth century, when preserving wine was still a hit-or-miss matter of luck, the barrels in the drinking places were often oxidizing and turning sour by the end of summer, so the arrival of the new year's fresh wine was an eagerly awaited event. Ritually, then, Lyonnais bar and bistro owners trekked north to Villefranche, Belleville and Beaujeu as of November 11 and fanned out through the countryside to taste, select, haggle and finally buy their barrels of new wine, or *primeur*, as they named it. Still fermenting its residual sugar, needles of CO_2 burping, Champagne-style, through a straw stuck in the bung, the barrels were loaded aboard horse-drawn barges for the easy walk down to Lyon, coasting on a Saône so tranquil, as Julius Caesar himself had remarked in his *De Bellum Gallicum* nearly two millennia earlier, that you could hardly tell in which direction it was moving.

The closer to November 11 the *primeur* arrived in town, the better it was for the dedicated drinkers of Lyon, because there was this special quality about Beaujolais: it was good when it was young, even very young. Fully finished Beaujolais wines—especially the more complex *crus*—required six months or more of ageing, and by tradition were not released until they had "done their Easter," but Lyonnais throats grew dry in November, and the rite of having a taste of the year's wine in its juvenile state, still tingling on the tongue with CO_2, gradually became institutionalized as one of the city's characteristic annual events.

For the best part of three centuries, while communication was slow and people tended to live out their lives in or near the areas of their birth, most outsiders were unaware of the Lyonnais's November wine-drinking eccentricity. Those who happened to come into contact with it probably gave the ritual no more thought than the indulgent smile reserved for local folklore. In modern times, though—that is, after World War II—everything accelerated, and the custom of drinking *primeur* in mid-November began spreading outward from Lyon to the rest of France and thence to the world at large. That proved to be both a blessing and a damnation for the peasant vignerons of the Beaujolais, because after enjoying the giddy pleasures of worldwide stardom they would soon be confronted with its hangover, in the form of a fundamental rule of the business: wine drinkers can be very fickle.

Niagaras of ink would be spilled, pro and con, on the subject of *primeur* in future years, but the essence of all the brouhaha was disconcertingly simple and innocent. It just so happened that the gamay variety of *Vitis vinifera* was happy on the Beaujolais hills, and its marriage with that particular *terroir* was such that its juice could be vinified extremely young into a pleasant, unpretentious little wine that was enjoyable to drink. This happy state of affairs, it appeared, was unique to the Beaujolais gamay. It didn't work with the pinot of the great Burgundies, and even less with the multiple *cépages* of the noble Bordeaux. (The tannic attack of a new Bordeaux was "like having a porcupine in your mouth," remarked Professor Garrier with a shudder, recalling a tasting experience he had lived in a moment of departure from his academic duties.) When, all the way back in the fifteenth century, the Burgundian Philip the Good (1396–1467, grandson of Philip the Bold) presciently warned that the wine of the gamay grape was dangerous because "it flatters foreigners" in its young state, he apparently had assumed that no genuine Frenchman could be taken in by a wine made by and fit for serfs. But the Lyonnais people, the most gastronomically inclined of all French citizens, knew better: the serfs were no dummies. So they stuck to their little ad hoc November *primeur* pleasure, grateful for the cheer it lent to the cold, dreary days leading up to Christmas. That little eccentricity was destined to have an astonishing surge in later years.

The French Revolution gave a serious boost to the special relationship between Lyon and the wines of the Beaujolais. The newly installed republican government desperately needed money, and one of first steps it took to harvest ready cash was to sell off communal grounds, Church holdings, and the estates of landed gentry who had fled abroad to save their necks from the guillotine's hungry bite. There was plenty to sell: depending on the region, 20 to 30 percent of France's land had been owned by clergy and nobility. In principal, this big sell-off ought to have immediately endowed the French countryside with hundreds of thousands of new, individually owned farms of peasants released from serfdom. In reality, though, what happened was what always happens in such situations: most of the land fell into the hands of wealthy speculators. Rather more rare were the prosperous peasants who had laid aside enough money to pay for newly released acreage. Consequently, the greatest part of the confiscated lands fell into the hands of Lyonnais bourgeois—but they had neither the time, the strength nor the inclination to work it themselves, and any casual hands whom they might think of hiring were unlikely to possess winemaking expertise. They were, then, obliged to deal with the peasant winemakers who had been there all along. The result was a large expansion of the fifty-fifty "half-fruit" *vigneronnage* system, as Beaujolais peasants began making wine for absentee landowners sitting in Lyon townhouses rather than for locally resident nobility—but now half of the production became theirs. Squirreling away their petty savings year by year, often in the form of gold coins hidden in the proverbial straw mattresses, more and more of them managed to fulfill the peasants' eternal dream of actually getting full title to their very own land. Patiently, hectare by hectare, year by year, they bought up vine space as the bourgeois shaved off sections of their big holdings, creating the patchwork of small family exploitations, most of them no more than five or six hectares, that still characterizes the Beaujolais today. Often this patchwork was split into odd shards—perhaps a bit of land in Villié-Morgon, a bit in Lancié or a bit in Chiroubles, as the *parcelles* became available. Beaujolais vineyards are not always handily and contiguously disposed around vignerons' houses, and it is common for winegrowers to work several different fields in different *terroirs*, some owned, some rented.

By the twentieth century, the Lyonnais absentee landowners had disposed of most of their properties in the Beaujolais, keeping only the *résidences secondaires* they had built for summertime rustication with their families. The symbiosis between the city and the wine country had taken a new turn. From landowner to sharecropper, the social model changed to independent artisan interacting with the occasional visitor from the big city.

It was a curious relationship. The Lyonnais and the typical Beaujolais vigneron were fundamentally quite similar in character, and in fact many of the Lyonnais were descended from the pure Beaujolais stock of ancestors who had trekked down to the big city to make their fortunes. Both sides of the divide were marked by a wicked sense of humor and a penchant for pranks and shenanigans—a penchant unerringly encouraged by a procession of *canons* of Beaujolais—but the traditional rural-urban standoff was inevitably present nonetheless. The city guy wondered whether the crafty peasant was trying to pull the wool over his eyes one way or another, and the country guy was always a bit defensive lest the city guy display any sense of superiority, with his money and his urbane ways. The Lyonnais loved to visit the Beaujolais on weekends, all the more so if he owned a house there; the denizen of the Beaujolais enjoyed nothing more than inviting him into his *caveau* and getting him good and drunk.

But there was one aspect of life about which the two were in total agreement, even harmony: the planning, preparation and consumption of food. If Lyon had become the gastronomic center of France (and thereby the world, of course; no one ever had any doubt about that), it was at least partly due to its proximity to the wine country that it cherished. Because there was this that had to be said for the Beaujolais peasantry: they were poor, most of them, but when the time came to celebrate special occasions, they knew how to pull out all the stops and do it with style.

Madame Rolland, a leading *passionaria* of the French Revolution (who in 1793 paid with her head for being in the wrong political wing at the wrong time), remarked in one of her letters that in the Beaujolais "the least bourgeois house a bit above the common offers meals more delicious than the richest houses of Amiens and a great number of very wealthy ones in Paris. Ugly little house, delicate table."

Pity she hadn't gone all the way down the social order with her slumming and mingled with the peasantry, because there she would have learned about *really* serious eating, of the kind that Papa Bréchard remembered from his youth. It wasn't exactly delicate. "The meals lasted twelve hours," he recalled, "if not twenty-four hours. Twenty-four hours was a little long, but twelve was the minimum."

The marathon chowdown he was describing was not the most frequent, but it was the most important one — the village wedding. Naturally this had to be celebrated with the utmost vigor, but weddings were occasional events that happened at unpredictable times. More reliably fixed on the calendar were children's First Communions, Christmas, Easter and the *fête des vendanges*, the blowout meal cooked up by vignerons' wives for the grape pickers after the final baskets of the harvest had been brought in. During the long days of grape picking, the harvesters were fed well enough with good, traditional country fare — cabbage soup with fatback, potato and bean salads, omelets, noodles, pumpkin flan and the like — but when all the grapes were in, the poor peasants of the Beaujolais threw aside the frugality of their everyday lives and briefly entered the Lucullan world of Roman emperors. Professor Garrier posits that the magnificence of the harvest celebration had a triple significance: first, in an unwitting hangover from the magical invocations of their pagan ancestors of pre-Christian days, as a kind of propitiatory gesture to ensure that future harvests would be as plenteous as the meal being offered; and then two others which could not possibly be more practical and down to earth — to outshine the neighbors, and to make such an impression on the harvesters that they would be certain to return for more of the same the following year.

The typical post-harvest feast always centered around that rarest and most luxurious of comestibles: meat. Unlike the usual peasant paucity, here an orgy of meat was glutted to overdose proportions, prepared in the three classical manners. In the first course it was boiled: either chicken or beef in the form of a pot-au-feu, ritually preceded by a bowl of its own broth. Next was a meat dish slow-cooked in sauce (*boeuf bourguignon* was a perennial favorite), and finally a big roast, usually veal. With each dish, the housewife presented her personal vegetable and starch creations, and a selection of tarts and pastries wound the meal up in proper splendor. Fired to enthusiasm by the profusion of wine, the guests sang and danced well into the night, for as long as their energy lasted. Anything less than a celebration of these proportions would have been considered vaguely shameful, a loss of face in the village.

If the *fête des vendanges* was a series of individual events celebrated separately at each vineyard, the weddings concerned the entire village. "There were hundreds of guests," Papa Bréchard recalled. "It was a mobilization! We borrowed crockery and dishes in every house in the village. Everyone helped out. It was the local festival."

As it still frequently is in all of France today, the typical Beaujolais wedding was a double affair, and by custom it took place in the morning, in order to leave the afternoon free for feasting. The first stop was the town hall for the official republican ceremony, pronounced by *Monsieur le Maire* who, resplendent in his tricolor sash, married the young couple before the state. The marriage before God came next, in the church, with *Monsieur le Curé* saying an impressively lengthy mass, blessing the union and enjoining the couple to raise their children as good Catholics. Then the feast began at the house of the bride's parents.

"We sat down at 2:30 or 3:00," Papa Bréchard wrote. "The wedding feast started rather late, in general, but it lasted at least until noon the next day. That was a minimum. These meals were truly Pantagruelian: abundant, varied, solid, with all the meats and all the fowl. To tell the truth, it was completely exaggerated. . . . We ate enormous amounts. Chickens, ducks, venison, huge chunks of meat of every origin, roasts that would be enough to scare people today. No one made a menu with less than six main courses without counting the desserts, also extremely abundant—six main courses, to which they added the indispensable vegetables. But the essential basis of it was fowl, rabbits and venison. Hares were abundant in the country then, and partridges, too. We ate a lot of them. Then there were also legs of lamb, and roast beef in industrial quantities. It was enough to knock you out."

Naturally the father of the bride served his best wine to the hundreds of guests, setting up a barrel with a wooden spigot at the bottom, free to anyone who cared to draw off a glass or a pitcher. When the barrel was emptied, out came another one from the cellar, and the dancing, singing and eating continued through the night, to the more or less expert notes of one or more of the village's accordionists. When energy flagged, there was always at hand a bottle of the winemaker's rough white lightning, *marc*, made from the re-pressed and distilled grape mash, to crank it back up again.

As with these stupefying wedding feasts, the workers sitting down to the once-yearly *fête des vendanges* were allowed to drink the vigneron's wine—his real wine this time, not the thin *piquette* with which they had quenched their thirst while out working in the vines. Such generosity represented a real expense, but to do otherwise would have been bad for business, because guaranteeing the return of happy harvesters was of first importance: no grape pickers, no wine. An army of harvesters some thirty thousand to forty thousand strong invades the Beaujolais every year in late August or early September, and the winegrowers would be lost without them. Unlike most other wine regions of France, winegrowers of Beaujolais-Villages and the ten *crus* share with their rich professional cousins up in Champagne the distinction of being *required* to pick their grapes by hand. In both cases, this requirement is related to vinification: the grapes must enter the vinifying vats undamaged. Harvesting machines are much cheaper to use than hand labor, but even the best of them cause some damage to the grapes. It was only in 2004 that mechanization was permitted in vineyards of the lesser, "generic" Beaujolais.

Whatever the overindulgence at the wedding or harvesting blow-outs, though, and however aching the heads, the Beaujolais vigneron and his *vigneronne* would be back to the flinty realities of work at dawn the next day, he in the fields or the vinifying shed, and she with the children, the animals and the house. The feasting had briefly allowed them to thumb their noses at the relative penury of their existence, but the single, unyielding imperative that gripped them was to ensure the self-sufficiency of the family and the farm, the basic unit for survival. In those days, the vines were still a mere adjunct. In a good year, they might provide enough extra money to buy new equipment, pay off back debts or perhaps fulfill the ancient peasant's longing for more land. In a bad year—or worse, in a succession of bad years, when the wine was poor and the prices low—the vigneron and his wife had to rely on the farm alone to get through to the next harvest. The family survived mostly on home-grown vegetables, milk from their cow, and whatever cheeses the lady of the house was clever enough to make.

"We could never be certain of getting through tomorrow," remarked Papa Bréchard matter-of-factly. Every Beaujolais peasant could recall miserable seasons when hail, drought or attacks of insects and fungus came close to wiping out an entire year's crop of grapes. "Very often, the baker was the banker," Bréchard explained, "because we weren't always able to pay him for his bread."

The credit list at the baker's is a thematic memory that always returns in conversation with elderly retired vignerons who had known the period between the two great wars when subsidies were nonexistent, social protection mostly a matter of charity, and when an informal cartel of wholesale wine merchants, the most powerful of them based in Beaune and Dijon, ruled the roost. Those were the hard times, the days when the little window in the dealers' offices in Villefranche symbolized the quasi-feudal commercial subjection that bound the winemaker to the big dealers. Mondays—it was always a Monday—the vigneron brought his sample bottles to that little window, where a clerk took down his name, address and noted how much of the stuff he had for sale. Come back in a week, he said, and that was that.

"A week later we'd go back to see whether or not they had accepted the wine, and if they did, at what price," one of these veterans of innumerable Beaujolais campaigns told me. "Then it was take it or leave it—period."

"We were all alone against the dealers in those days," Papa Bréchard explained. "We weren't organized, and we didn't have any unions or anything like that. We had a lot to learn."

In those days a real corporatist antipathy separated vignerons and wine wholesalers, because the latter were the only significant commercial outlet for the former, who were consequently in a permanent position of weakness. On-site direct sales at the vineyard or farm were virtually unknown, because few peasants owned anything other than the most rudimentary of bottling equipment, and the automobile civilization that would eventually see thousands of tourists and weekend drivers from Lyon and elsewhere cruising deep into Beaujolais territory did not even begin developing until the mid- to late fifties. The little window in Villefranche—or the Café des Promeneurs, or Chez Coco, the two bars where wholesalers' reps commonly received petitioners in preference to their stuffy offices—were, then, the frowzy little mini-Meccas to which the typical vigneron was obliged to entrust his hopes for a year's revenues.

"It was impersonal and it was humiliating," said Gérard Canard, the passionate son of the Beaujolais who for thirty-five years directed the Beaujolais Wine Promotion Committee. "There was no harmony, and certainly no fellowship between the two trades, none whatsoever. It was two completely separate worlds. The dealers didn't even have to invest in the personnel to go around and seek out the best wines—with their system, the vignerons came to them. The dealers' reps just sat around in the cafés and drank *canons* all day long. They exploited the peasants, of course. Very often, the guys didn't have enough money to pay their harvesters, so they would borrow from the dealers, with their wine as collateral. Naturally, this put them at a big disadvantage when it came to negotiating the price of that wine."

The dirtiest trick of all—again, a canker that repeatedly arises in conversation with old-timers—was the village credit rating scenario: the most ruthless dealers would occasionally send investigators around to interview bakers and butchers in order to discover which vignerons owed the biggest tabs. The deeper the debt, the worse would be their bargaining position for the price of the year's wine. It was pretty unscrupulous stuff, and word of the practice quickly flew around the village, of course. The animosity between grower and buyer grew even more solidly entrenched.

Down in Lyon, the *canut* silk weavers had been similarly exploited by both the big silk dealers known as *les soyeux* and by the owners of the hundreds of small, family-owned workshops that dotted the city. Like the rural artisans of the Beaujolais, these urban proletarians—for the most part peasants who had removed to the city in search of a better life—worked twelve- to sixteen-hour days at their looms in stuffy, overcrowded firetrap ateliers and earned a pittance that barely lifted them above the minimum for their families' survival. Theirs was a Dickensian existence of economic wretchedness, as pinched as the hard times that Papa Bréchard remembered from his childhood up in the wine country. But history avenged the workers of the loom, because today, when the old silk-weaving industry has disappeared, it is the skeptical, rebellious, wise-guy *canut* who is acknowledged and proudly held up as the true representative of the soul of the place, the one who exemplifies Lyon's character the way the cool, unflappable *titi parisien* does for the capital city up north.

Like the Beaujolais vigneron, his cousin in austerity, the *canut* fed himself and his family on day-to-day rations of extreme modesty, with the traditional Sunday chicken in a casserole or boiled beef pot-au-feu being the only truly respectable meat dish of the week (heavy on the leeks, carrots, turnips and potatoes, more miserly on the beef). Daily fare centered mostly around bread, cheese and the evening soup, as it did with the rural peasantry. To this was added a whole vocabulary of poor man's nourishment of a style as surprising, rib-sticking and delicious as the American soul food that owed its invention to the same kind of poverty. Named with the wry, self-deprecating humor that is native to the city, all of these specialties are inextricably bound up with the culinary identity of Lyon today. Mention any item on this list to a food-conscious citizen anywhere in France, and the spark of recognition will be immediate—it can only mean Lyon. A short compendium, far from inclusive, would have to include:

- *Gratons*, fatty pieces of pork, discards from the noble cuts, that have been melted down in a large pan, then grilled into browned, irresistible, bite-sized cholesterol bombs. (The run-off fat from the pan is sold as lard.)
- *Matefaim* (literally, hunger-tamer), a swaggering, rib-sticking omelet reinforced with flour and sometimes rum, with further additions *ad libitum.*
- *Paquets de couenne*, ham rinds tied into little bundles, poached and then sautéed with lard and parsley. Also known (derisively) as *pigeons ficelés* (bound pigeons).
- *Crasse de beurre* (butter crud), the whitish residue that comes to the surface or sticks to the side of the pan when butter is melted—highly recommended for spreading on slices of bread.
- *Tablier de sapeur* (sapper's apron). While the bourgeois were treating themselves to gorgeously sauced *quenelles de brochet* (fluffy "omelets" of chopped and mashed pike flesh), delicate, buttery frogs' legs, or truffled chicken, Lyon's working class was eating sheep's feet and testicles, donkey snout *en gelée*, and this most typical of proletarian delicacies: *tablier de sapeur*, a slab of ruminant's stomach or honeycomb tripe large enough to imagine a resemblance to the leather apron traditionally worn by sappers or military engineers. Breaded and grilled, it was (and still is) served with a *sauce gribiche*, a kind of herbal vinaigrette thickened with chopped egg yolk.
- *Andouillettes*. This somewhat intimidating tripe sausage can often be a rough experience elsewhere, but Lyon's version, more delicate, is made with calves' mesentery, the fatty lining of the abdominal cavity, rather than the intestine itself. (This nuance of the awesome Yuck Factor is not immediately apparent to all visitors to the city.)

- *Cervelle de canut* (silk-weaver's brain). This well-named specialty is whipped *fromage blanc* (uncurdled cottage cheese) that has been lent an unexpected Sunday punch by the addition of oil, vinegar, chopped shallots, garlic and a cocktail of herbs.
- *Fromage fort*, a redoubtable, supercharged paste made by mixing odd scraps of dry cheese with white wine. Poor *canut* families updated it almost daily with whatever other bits of cheese scraps were left over, vigorously mixed into the crock where it was stored.
- *Gratinée de pain* consists of nothing more elegant than bread slices and cheese, layered and wetted with bouillon, then oven-cooked until a nicely appealing golden crust appears.
- *Soupe de farine jaune*, probably the most arresting example of this food of the urban poor. "Yellow flour soup" is the city dweller's equivalent of the Beaujolais housewife's pinchpenny nettle soup: cornmeal mush that has been elevated to a modest gastronomic level by the addition of milk and strips of pork rind.

By common assent, nothing went better with Lyon's traditional cooking than the friendly, fruity, refreshingly tangy wine of the gamay from up north. Like the food itself, it was plentiful, free of artifice and easy on the pocketbook. Through the nineteenth and twentieth centuries, Beaujolais automatically accompanied Lyon's rise to its enviable situation as the gastronomic capital of France, the city uniquely situated to take advantage of the ideal natural larder that lies at all points around it: poultry of unparalleled quality from the Bresse, beef from the Charolais, freshwater fish from the Rhône and the Saône, magnificent crayfish and cheeses from the Jura, fruits and vegetables from the Rhône Valley and, a bit further to the south, the profusion of seafood, oils, herbs and spices of the Mediterranean regions.

By geography alone—it lies at the confluence of two great rivers, next door to Switzerland, Italy and the Mediterranean but at a safe distance from the intrusions of plunderers and rapparees from England, until recently the most aggressively, never-endingly expansionist of nations—Lyon was a much more logical choice than Paris to be chosen as France's capital city, as it had been for the Gauls in Caesar's days. For a while it seemed that history might just turn out that way, because the great monarch François I had taken a liking to the place, so much so that he was considering settling there for good. Alas, in 1536 in Lyon his son the dauphin François shocked his system by draining a glass of chilled water after a particularly heated game of *jeu de paume* (court tennis) and died shortly thereafter. That water may not have been entirely innocent—suggestions of poisoning have floated around the story ever since—but King François removed his crown and his court to Paris, and Lyon never had a second chance.

No matter. The Lyonnais have liberally consoled themselves ever since with food and drink and humor, and no one feels worse off for the bargain. The city's aura as the world's capital of great eating was already growing in François' reign, when the Dutch humanist scholar Erasmus remarked that he didn't understand "how the innkeepers of Lyon manage to serve such sumptuous food at such modest prices." Even those who for one reason or another did not hold the place in affection were forced to admit that it harbored special talents where food was concerned. "I know of only one thing that they do very well in Lyon" wrote Stendhal, author of *Le Rouge et le Noir*. "You eat admirably well there and, in my opinion, better than in Paris."

The Lyonnais naturally agree, and most of the French along with them, even if judgments of this sort tend to make Parisians cross. But once the inexhaustible quarrels about the relative merits of the greatest temples of *haute gastronomie* have been put aside, even the most chauvinistic of Parisians will concede that nothing in the capital can rival Lyon's proudest institution, the one that virtually defines the city: the low-down, low-price *bouchon*, the Lyonnais version of the bistro. Working-class gathering and drinking places par excellence, these little family affairs evolved over the centuries from rough-hewn bars to a special category of humble, one-room "restaurant." I use the slightly demeaning quotation marks because most of these places were so simple that there was rarely space for more than two or three tables, and the cooking equipment usually consisted of nothing better than a sink and a little coal stove, which in more modern days became gas or electric. It was in these improvised cubbyhole kitchens that proprietors' wives turned out ragouts, stews, soups and runny omelets of sorrel, cheese and tripe, while their husbands sliced bread and sausages at the bar and poured *pots* of Beaujolais. Served up to order, often consumed standing at the bar, inexpensive and delicious, these meals were little masterpieces of simple, honest gastronomy — fast food à la Française — and precursors to the culture of *les mères Lyonnaises*, the celebrated "Lyon mothers."

That was another category, a notch or two up from the *bouchon* and every bit as admirable. A succession of these rather more imposing restaurants, run by intractably perfectionist, frequently ill-tempered but endearing female chefs, became gloriously famous both in France and abroad, and they are remembered in Lyon today with a kind of sepia, Proustian nostalgia for a more comforting time before globalization spoiled all the fun by making life efficient.

The *mères Lyonnaises* were truly grandes dames, and memories of La Mère Guy, La Mère Fillioux or eccentrics like La Mélie or Léa are enough to bring a tear to a Lyonnais eye. Léa, whom I had the honor and advantage of meeting toward the end of her career, and whose kitchen floor I happily trod, engulfed in a savory microclimate of slow-cooking aromas, was one of the memorable local characters of downtown Lyon, a wild eccentric who doubtless struck some casual strollers as half-mad. Bright and early every morning, she left her restaurant, La Voûte, on a dark little side street behind Place Bellecour, and made her way, shouting and gesticulating at drivers who presumed to get in her way, through the traffic to the farmers' market on the Quai St. Antoine along the eastern bank of the Saône. Further accentuating the spectacle was the outlandish wheeled contraption that she pushed, not unlike a Sabrett's hot dog cart or a Good Humor ice cream bin, to which she had attached an oversized rubber-bulbed bicycle horn which ever and anon she honked as she thrust her way forward. There was plenty of room inside her pushcart for her day's provisions, and a bright sign on the front warned: FAIBLE FEMME, FORTE EN GUEULE (Frail Woman, Loud Mouth). Léa picked through the day's fresh offerings with fiendish determination, and she got exactly what she wanted. Whether it was tripe, foie gras or just a perfect lettuce, the results showed spectacularly in her little one-room restaurant. Léa was mad like a fox.

La Mère Fillioux, who ran her little restaurant in the Brotteaux section of town from 1890 until her death in 1925, was as renowned for her cooking as for her steely determination to do nothing but her own recipes, turning aside all culinary fads and fashions with the scorn they deserved. "I have spent my life making four or five dishes," she famously declared, "so I know how to do them. And I won't do anything else."

What were these marvels? The list was so short that to most long-menu restaurateurs it would have appeared laughable: a rich, smooth truffle soup; pike quenelles in crayfish butter, browned in the oven; artichoke hearts with foie gras; chicken *demi-deuil* ("half in mourning" in reference to the black truffle slices under the skin, slow-cooked for an hour in bouillon); and, on special order, lobster *à l'américaine*. But her specialties were turned out with such generosity and devotion to perfection that in her time they made her famous to gourmets the world over. (It is an interesting game to speculate whether Michelin, the great arbiter of restaurant quality, would have had the courage to award three stars to a place with such a limited card, but we'll never know the answer—the famous system of one, two and three stars did not enter the red book until 1933.) Her signature dish was the chicken, of course, and someone once figured out that she must have sliced up half a million of them during her thirty-five-year career, always using the same little knife. Worn to a fraction of its original size by successive sharpenings, the faithful instrument is now on display in the Escoffier Museum of Culinary Arts in Villeneuve-Loubet, near Nice.

There's a nice little anecdote about that knife. One evening in the early twenties, it seems, a world-famous surgeon—some say American, but the stories vary on this detail—perhaps fired to excess of confidence by the flow of Beaujolais that had passed his gullet, asked for the unusual privilege of being allowed to carve his own chicken after it had been lifted dripping from the pot and freed of its cheesecloth wrapping. La Mère Fillioux reluctantly handed over her precious tool, and the surgeon squared his shoulders and set to work. No more than a few seconds had passed before a cry of anguish passed her lips: "Stop, unhappy man, you are murdering it!"

The highest achiever of this wonderful sisterhood was Eugénie, La Mère Brazier, who was among the twenty-one to be awarded three stars when Michelin's first rating system appeared in 1933. She was a peasant girl who had begun life tending pigs, but she rose to become Lyon's most renowned chef until Paul Bocuse came along with his own brand of perfectionism and promotional genius. But Bocuse would not be what he is today if he had not served as a foot soldier under Eugénie Brazier's command—she was one of the several chefs under whom *le grand Paul* apprenticed in the early days of his ascendancy toward the imperial status he now enjoys. La Mère Brazier taught her apprentices the old-fashioned way, setting them a work schedule that broke the will of many of those who made the climb up to her place on a hill (col de la Luère) above Lyon. Rising at 5 A.M. and rarely to bed before 11 P.M., young Bocuse chopped wood, hoed the vegetable garden, milked Eugénie's cow, did her laundry and starched and ironed her tablecloths before he even got a chance to do any cooking. With that experience under his belt, followed by stints with the great Fernand Point at La Pyramide in Vienne, and Lucas-Carton in Paris, he was ready for any challenge the world of cuisine could possibly put in his path. It is no accident, then, that Bocuse holds the world's record for the longest incumbency (forty-two years and counting) in Michelin's top three-star rating.

In the early seventies, Bocuse introduced me to another archetypal Lyonnais institution: the *mâchon.* I suppose I should have known it would involve an encounter with Beaujolais, and rather more matutinally than I normally would have preferred. The *mâchon* (from *mâcher,* to chew) is an extra meal that the Lyonnais invented, a solid little bit of feeding too serious to be qualified as a mere snack and yet not quite a meal: an emergency measure to fill that perilously empty gap between the *café-croissant* and lunch. I had been honored to join Paul on a revictualing trip to Les Halles, Lyon's central market in the Part Dieu section of town, riding on the floor in the back of his famous blue Renault delivery van, the one with the Gallic rooster and the "PB 1926" logo painted on the side to indicate the owner's identity and birth date. (As if there could be anyone in Lyon who didn't already know all about both — the man is far more famous than whoever happens to be the current mayor.)

I was riding on the floor because my wife was up front in the passenger seat next to Paul, enjoying the view of the city and appraising his skill at the traditional French sport of slaloming through traffic. After less than an hour's shopping, Paul had filled the van with such a profusion of vegetables, fruits, meat, seafood and dairy products of all description that I felt like a participant in some surrealistic reconstitution of an Arcimboldo painting — foodman! — complete with potato nose, beef filet cheeks, bunches of grapes for hair and cherry eyes, careening through town in a turbo-charged vehicle with a stuntman chef at the wheel. There was a bump when Paul pulled over and parked the van halfway across the tiny sidewalk of the rue du Garet near the Rhône embankment and led us into a little room behind a streetside façade of dark wood.

Chez Georges, the place was called, and before I quite knew what was happening I found myself faced with a plate of sliced *rosette* sausage, a *cervelas* salad, a bowl of *rillettes d'oie* (goose pâté thick with luscious fat) and a *pot* of Beaujolais-Villages. It was about nine in the morning, more like my usual orange juice and toast time, but who was I to dispute ethnic culture and custom? I plunged in dutifully, and it wasn't really all that much of a sacrifice, because the food was delicious and the Beaujolais superb — but I couldn't help noticing that Paul only symbolically raised his glass to his lips before placing it back down on the bar. He watched me closely, though, and so did Georges. Over the following years I was to become a good deal more familiar, both in Lyon and in the Beaujolais country, with this routine of being tested with an avalanche of food, mirth and drink that stopped only when you cried uncle. (The point being to see how far you will go before you *do* cry uncle. The game can be hazardous.)

There was a spring in my step, or was it an incipient totter, when I marched back to Bocuse's food wagon that morning, but I was grateful for his unscheduled stop there, because it was my introduction to the culture of the *bouchon*, my first serious glimpse of a shard of urban folk history that was already centuries old. It was in 1913, in just such a *bouchon* as Chez Georges, that the *Société des Amis de Guignol* was founded, which in a moment of luminous inspiration nineteen years later organized a quirky little competition that proved to be of serious importance for the future of the wines of the Beaujolais—the *Concours du Meilleur Pot.*

The Society of the Friends of Guignol was an informal grouping of writers, journalists and men-about-Lyon who were devoted to honoring and preserving the *canut* traditions that had made Lyon different from all other great French cities: the puppet shows, art, folklore, literature and craftsmanship—and, of course, the food and drink. On this last subject their devotion was total, and their 1913 inaugural dinner, wetted down with a small river of Beaujolais, was the city-dweller's equivalent of the wedding feasts dear to Papa Bréchard's memory: beginning with poor man's food, it moved on to the more elaborate creations worthy of special occasions. Naturally *paquets de couenne* and *gratons* had to come first, and this time they were accompanied by the rather less commonplace *os de China*, or grilled pig's tail. Appetites sharpened, the table companions moved on to destroy a stuffed breast of veal, scalloped potatoes *à la Lyonnaise* (with onions), turkey with chestnuts, a salad of mule's muzzle, herring and dandelions, and finally the cheese platter, inevitably starring *cervelle de canut*. Dessert could only be sugared *bugnes*, feather-light, deep-fried wisps of sugared pastry that make the American donut seem like an anvil in comparison.

The journalist Henri Béraud, who died in 1958, was a faithful friend of both Guignol and the wines of the gamay grape, and he left behind a poignant little vignette evoking that curious mixture of merriment and melancholy—lachrymose joy—that is the mark of the true philosophical drunk. "We were Lyonnais *gones*, drinking Beaujolais according to the venerable custom in a little café, where the emptied *pots* lined up on the table formed a handsome grillwork, through whose greenish bars we drinkers exchanged handshakes, vows of friendship and words of deep wisdom."

Barhopping was not the only activity of the Friends of Guignol, but this time-honored, largely masculine act of purposeful circumambulation unquestionably formed a serious part (personally, I suspect it was the backbone) of the society's raison d'être. By the mere act of paying solemn visit to *bouchon* after *bouchon* to sample *pot* after *pot*, these gents would have noticed, compared and commented upon the differences in style and quality of the Beaujolais they had drunk in each. It was this wide range of differences, the fruit of each proprietor's scouting trips into Beaujolais country to buy his yearly supply of barrels, that gave birth to the first *Concours du Meilleur Pot*, in 1932.

The point of the competition was to discover the best over-the-counter Beaujolais in town, and if at the outset it gave the self-appointed jurors a magnificent excuse to indulge in some exceptionally assiduous barhopping, it grew, sui generis, without need for any promotion or money injection whatsoever, into an event of far greater importance than any of them had expected, because it was a natural winner for the press. Gimmicky feature stories like these leap directly into print, because journalists love them: they are fast, easy to write and probably entail free drinks. Enthusiastically covered by all the local papers, the competition soon assumed formal rules and procedures, and Lyonnais bars and *bouchons* fell all over themselves to offer free samples, electrified at the prospect of the stampede of new customers that a winning entry would ensure. With that, the easygoing barhop that lay behind the idea in the first place succumbed to the chore of a formal *dégustation*, a comparative tasting session of dozens of sample bottles, complete with grading sheets and spitting buckets.

The joyous troupe of gamayphiliacs succeeded so well in their enterprise that they defeated their original purpose of innocently irresponsible merriment and became something very much like a movement.
The competition for the best *pot* of Beaujolais was destined to outgrow
Lyon and move on, first to Paris and other major French cities and then,
eventually, to the world at large.

By the late thirties, the luck of the Beaujolais really seemed to be
turning. The unassuming drink was gradually gaining recognition beyond its regional boundaries as a respectable growth that could take its
place alongside the *grands seigneurs* of France's unparalleled palette of
wine varieties. Beaujolais was not merely legitimate, in spite of the
oïdium that had been heaped upon the gamay grape since Duke Philip
took his famous umbrage in the fourteenth century: it was *good*.

But history runs in cycles. Now, just as matters were beginning to
look very good, calamity struck again, this time in the form of human
folly: World War II was upon the land. Catastrophically overconfident
in their strategic thinking, the French military brass entirely misjudged
the capacities and ingenuity of the German forces, and their modern,
well-equipped army was ridiculed by Hitler's *blitzkrieg* tactics. Five cruel
years of occupation began on the day that German troops marched down
the Champs Elysées.

As matters turned out, the Beaujolais country had relatively good
luck, to the extent that luck could be considered good in hungry, distressing times such as those. The Germans' agreement with the col-
laborationist Vichy government split the country roughly in two, and
the east-west demarcation line left Mâcon, Villefranche and Lyon in
the southern "free zone" under Vichy, while the Germans occupied the
northern half, which of course included Paris (and Champagne).

In the wine country, life slowly returned to something resembling
normalcy. Mourning the hundreds of their brethren who had died in the
fighting, the Beaujolais peasantry returned to the vine and the familiar
seasonal gestures of its timeless life cycle. There was more handwork
now, and more horse and mule work, because the severely limited sup-

plies of gasoline and oil were monopolized by the German forces, with only a tiny fraction allowed for the official vehicles of the Vichy government. Gas-powered machinery gathered dust and rust in their hangars, and chemical fertilizers and products for protecting grapes from mildew and insects became things of the past. There was no more sugar, so chaptalization, too, was finished. In spite of themselves, and for want of any alternative, vignerons throughout France went over 100 percent into the camp of what today would be called organic winegrowing.

Lacking the usual artifices for helping the vines along and giving their wines' alcoholic content a nudge, the Beaujolais peasantry may have felt disarmed, but Mother Nature generously intervened, delivering a series of wonderful, even fantastic years. In 1941, 1943 and 1945 the output per hectare dropped severely, averaging scarcely better than thirty-five hectoliters per hectare, but the quality of the wine was astonishingly good. In 1947, wartime shortages and restrictions still remained, but the rains came at just the right moments and the sun was unfailing. To these ideal maturing conditions was added a month of September so infernally hot that Beaujolais vignerons found themselves obliged to harvest at night, lest their grapes begin fermenting in the transport bins before they could be dumped into the fermentation vats—but it made a truly memorable wine.

"We got 15.7 and even 15.8 degrees of alcohol that year without the help of any sugar at all," remembered Marcel Laplanche, a veteran vigneron in the Beaujolais-Villages town of Blacé. In that same memorable year, the famous vigneron and wine dealer Jules Chauvet, father of modern wine-tasting methodology, reported hitting a high of 17 degrees with some of his *parcelles* of vine in La Chapelle de Guinchay. "The wine was so strong that people who were accustomed to swallowing a certain amount when they tasted in the *caveaux* were staggering all over the place when they emerged into the sunlight. Restaurant owners complained that we were deliberately getting their clients drunk. But it wasn't our fault."

Harsh years, great wine—the antithetical ironies continued to pile up, and in the end it had to be said that, as appalling as it was for the country as a whole, the German occupation proved in the long run to be beneficial, in a delayed, unexpected, backhand kind of way, for the wines of the Beaujolais.

Once again, as so often where wine is concerned, the reason was directly related to the press. With the debacle in 1939, thousands of northern dwellers fled southward to take up residence as best they could in the Vichy-administered zone. Parisians were heavily represented in this impromptu refugee flow, of course, and among them were large numbers of newspapermen, many of whom had signed anti-German tirades that were now frozen in print, marking them out for retribution by the occupiers and the various quislings who flocked to help them. For the duration of war, then, Lyon became something like the journalistic capital of France, but the journalists were effectively muzzled: although the southern zone was free of Germans, the Vichy authorities were just as zealous as their Wehrmacht tutors to the north in imposing a draconian censorship over the press. And so, bored and *désoeuvré*, the typical Parisian hack did what he always had done best when not holding a pen: he held a glass.

Haunting the *bouchons* in companionship with his Lyonnais confrères, dozens of these Parisian exiles discovered the Lyonnais habit of merry melancholy and passed the war years philosophizing over innumerable *pots* of Beaujolais in little back corners of little cafés on little back streets, where they could remake the world in peace and quiet.

It didn't take them long to acquire a lasting taste for the wines of the gamay grape, and at war's end they returned to the capital with a deep affection for the city that had harbored them in their time of distress and for the Beaujolais that had made their exile bearable. That affection was to serve the Beaujolais well as French life slowly returned to normal in the fifties and then during *les trente glorieuses*, the thirty glorious years of uninterrupted economic growth that began in the early sixties and rocketed the country to a pinnacle of prosperity the likes of which it had never known before.

Part of the fun of enjoying this prosperity was the *Concours du Meil-leur Pot*, which the formerly exiled newspapermen imported lock, stock and barrel from Lyon. It was only natural for this same band of journal-istic elbow-benders to lend their editorial support to that other curious Lyonnais institution that would soon be arriving in the big city: the mid-November tasting of the new Beaujolais wine.

Cynical, jaded old Paris took to both of these adventures with sur-prising, almost juvenile enthusiasm. In a trice, Beaujolais became the capital's darling—and what Paris loved, the rest of the world would soon be adoring. Down around Villefranche, Belleville and Beaujeu, peas-ant vignerons just one generation removed from the hardscrabble days of the credit list at the baker's and the cow as social security rubbed their eyes at the sales figures and wondered how it all had happened. It seemed almost too good to be true.

As usual, peasant good sense had seen clearly. In a way it *was* too good to be true. The Lyonnais were already beginning to grumble about this theft of their traditions and the commercialization of their confi-dential little pleasure. Nothing succeeds like success, they say, but then nothing goes out of fashion as fast as fashion, either. The newly suc-cessful peasants of the Beaujolais had never concerned themselves with fashion, not a whit. But in time they would be suffering from it.

V

INTERLUDE

*J*t is a proven scientific fact that prominent among the identifying characteristics of *Homo journalisticus* is a partiality to liquid solutions of the alcoholic variety, most especially cherished if they are free. It was, then, a stroke of purest promotional genius when, in September of 1934, a Lyonnais newspaperman turned vigneron named Toto Dubois teamed up with grower-dealer-hustler-restaurant owner Victor Peyret (the very one who had transformed a sixteenth-century church into a wine cellar and bar) to invite the editorial team of *Le Canard Enchainé* down from Paris to dine at Peyret's restaurant, Le Coq au Vin, located smack at the crossroads in the center of Juliénas. As the story has it today, the guys simply strolled out onto the street, hailed a passing cab or two and (doubtless having figured a way to charge the boondoggle to their expense accounts) made the five-hour trip in familiar Parisian comfort on the old pre-*autoroute* roads. On Peyret's menu that evening were hot Lyonnais sausages *en brioche*, crackling andouillettes, coq au vin, steak grilled over grapevine twigs and trimmings, *gratin dauphinois* (scalloped potatoes wallowing in butter and crème fraiche), salads, a selection of cheeses and tarts—and, of course, limitless bottles of wine from the fields surrounding the village in every direction.

In essence, Dubois and Peyret were only carrying on with the grand old Beaujolais tradition of getting visitors good and drunk, but since in this case the visitors were journalists, they naturally bent their backs and elbows to the task with professional application. The result was, according to local legend, one of the most glorious acts of mass intemperance that the town had ever witnessed. Grateful for the food, the drink and the break from the dreary Depression-era routine of reporting on yet another strike and yet another government crisis, the *Canard* remained steadfastly loyal to Juliénas and the Beaujolais ever afterward, not hesitating to testify, in print, to its pivotal role in some of the newspaper's most important editorial decisions.

The *Canard Enchaîné*, the exotically named "Chained Duck," is a French institution, a hybrid weekly that artfully combines political analysis, satire, gossip and enough whistle-blowing to topple governments or ruin the careers of politicians caught with their pants down or their hands in the public till. Free of ads and fiercely independent, the little paper punches far above the nominal weight of its slender eight pages: everyone who is in power or simply interested in power reads the *Canard*. It is respected, feared and very influential. The *Canard*'s account of the evening at the Coq au Vin, augmented afterward by regular references in its columns to the healthy, restorative powers of its preferred wine, proved to be a godsend for sales of Juliénas, thenceforward known as "the most Parisian" of the Beaujolais *crus*.

Where the *Canard*'s team led, other brothers of the corporation were not far behind in helping the cause along. Returning to Paris after their wartime sojourns in Lyon, a coterie of refugee journalists who had advanced the principles of the Friends of Guignol by emptying uncounted *pots* in back-street *bouchons* decided to found their own similarly dedicated fellowship. The Académie Rabelais, they named it, and its mission was to bring to the bistros of the capital the noble Lyonnais tradition of briefly playing hooky from the responsibilities of adulthood with the help of several delicious *ballons* of cool Beaujolais. In 1954 the academy awarded its first Parisian

Coupe du Meilleur Pot to a now-forgotten bistro, and if the impact of the story in the Paris press was not quite as striking and immediate as it had been in Lyon, where wine always has been a matter of serious and scholarly concern, the good word began spreading around town nonetheless. And "good" was the operative word, because times were at last beginning to look a little less grim. If memories of wartime deprivation, humiliation and destruction were still acute, the detested food rationing of the occupation was a thing of the past, France was rebuilding fast, and her shattered economy was approaching a mighty springboard of economic growth. For the investment of a few francs, a glass of the amiable thirst-quencher from the gamay grape was like a foretaste of the better life that lay just around the corner.

The symbiosis between Beaujolais and the press was well and truly launched, and the French were drinking wine again with gusto, averaging 150 liters a year per person by the early fifties. Beaujolais enjoyed its part in this renewal of the country's traditional thirst, of course, and presently a new word was finding its way into the national vocabulary, an adjective of undocumented origin but pointedly specific application: *gouleyant*. A *gouleyant* wine was one that was light, supple and benevolent, free of complexes and pretension, one that slipped with pleasurable ease down the gullet. The adjective could be properly applied only to Beaujolais. With no other wine did it make any sense at all. Beaujolais owns *gouleyant* the way the Loire Valley's white wines of the sauvignon grape own their curious nose of *pipi de chat* (cat pee) or gewürztramin-ers their characteristic signature of rose petals and litchis.

It was in this crucial period of reorganization and reconstruction that the French authorities finally managed to make some real headway in the huge task of putting their wine house in order. The vector for this redoubtably complex undertaking was INAO, and its primary weapon was AOC. We need to spend a little bit of time on these two cabalistic acronyms because, as baffling as they are for most foreigners (and for a lot of the French, too, for that matter), they are crucially important. INAO is *Institut National des Appellations d'Origine* and AOC is *ap-*

pellation d'origine contrôlée: the National Institute of Certified* Names and name of certified origin. Anyone with any interest at all in French wines should be familiar with some of the basic history lying behind the initials INAO and AOC, because they constitute the bedrock on which the entire industry is based.

Although not reaching its full effectiveness until postwar days, INAO had been founded in 1935, when the wine situation throughout the country was in chaotic disorder, and had been that way for half a century or more. It all went back to the phylloxera plague, a viticultural earthquake the aftershocks of which had continued for decades. The desperate wine shortage of the worst years had birthed the worrisome new habit of import—wine from Italy, Algeria, Greece or any other place that could help stanch the national thirst—and spawned the monstrous industry of fake wines that not only contained no grape juice at all, but were occasionally grave dangers to health as well. Then, from undersupply to oversupply, the pendulum swung in the opposite direction after desperate vignerons around the country planted and overplanted, sometimes with native grafts on U.S. rootstock, sometimes with foreign "direct producers" and sometimes with various hybrid novelties like the notorious, high-yield Noah. When too much wine flooded onto the market, prices collapsed and growers found themselves once more on the brink of ruin. Clearly a fix of some sort had to be found, because allowing unregulated market forces to run wild had led only to mayhem and violence.

With riots, destruction and even death marking peasant revolts that had required the army to be out restoring order, the Ministry of Agriculture had tried to take remedial action as early as 1905. There were several obvious priorities: get rid of fakes; stop or at least limit imports; rationalize production by codifying the country's huge palette of wines; and put a halt to overplanting in order to keep yields down to manageable levels that would not burden the market with unsellable wines. The

---

*Literally, "controlled" (or "checked" or "monitored" or "verified") origins, but I feel that "certified" renders the French meaning better. Others would use the term "designated." Difficult translation here.

overarching goal was to establish a national map of designated areas where the various different wines should be made, to limit them to those areas and to award specific place names to wines originating in them, according to "local, loyal and consistent custom."

It was a dauntingly complex project. France was the powerhouse, the world's number one wine producer, but the makeup of her soils and microclimates, and the grapes that performed best in each, were so tremendously varied that it was imperative to identify the best of each growth and each *terroir*. After all, a Volnay first-growth Clos de la Rougeotte was not the same thing as a Volnay first-growth Fermiets-Clos de la Rougeotte, was it? And certainly a Brouilly ought not to be confused with a Côte de Brouilly. It was only judicious to indicate these shades of difference, these nuances, so that connoisseurs could make their choices intelligently. The intention was laudable. Translating it into practical, user-friendly reality was another story.

The ministry's earliest efforts at reform had failed miserably, mostly because local politicians and winegrowers always got involved, yanking the covers over to their side of the bed and demanding special favors for "their" wines. After the 1905 reform flopped, so did following ones in 1911, 1913 and 1919. After the First World War, with lawsuits crowding the courts, recrimination flying and a detestable atmosphere of nascent rebellion overlying the industry, the government finally learned from its failures and got serious in 1935, with a new, comprehensive set of regulations that drew clear and realistic limits around France's best winegrowing areas, stipulating that only vineyards within these limits could enjoy the privilege of using their names: a Côtes de Beaune had to really be from the Côtes de Beaune, and a Haut Médoc really from the Haut Médoc. But that wasn't enough. In order to be certified, each wine would have to present "particular characteristics due to natural and human factors." In other words, they would have to be good, proper, honest wines—and someone would be watching to make sure that they were. The goal was to give a clear message and guarantee to consumers: these wines are what the labels say they are. The French state vouches for them.

The vehicle doing that vouching for the state would be INAO, a mixed government-private organization based in Paris and carrying the official stamp of the Ministry of Agriculture. Significantly, its all-powerful oversight committee was made up not of bureaucratic officials but of wine professionals who knew the business intimately: two-thirds growers and one-third dealers. They were the ones who delivered AOC, the stamp of approval.

Fundamentally, INAO sprang from the same sense of urgency and the same philosophy of response that gave birth to the European Common Market two decades later: there was a big mess, and a strong organization was required to fix it. Institution-building, rule-making and certifying were very much in the air during the cataclysmic period between and after the two great wars that had torn Europe to shreds. Now a new set of wine assessors was organized and given some surprisingly tough regulatory powers. INAO controlled the number of individual vine plants that could be grown per hectare of ground, the quantity of wine that could be produced from them, its alcoholic content, what fertilizers and chemical agents would be allowed, in what manner the vines should be pruned, staked and tied up, the dates when harvesting could begin and even such details as the order of words on labels. The requirement of respect for "local, loyal and consistent custom" was clearly a statutory shot at sugar wines and other fakes, and the flat, across-the-board prohibition of irrigation* underlined the concern for producing wines naturally, in reflection of the true nature of different *terroirs* through years both good and bad—in other words, the "particular characteristics due to natural and human factors."

The heaviness of INAO's regulatory hand (as in the rules of behavior in the old Soviet Union, everything that is not forbidden seems to be obligatory) often strikes modern newcomers to the winemaking business—North and South Americans, Australians, New Zealanders—as an overweening

---

*In December of 2006 a change in the rules allowed limited irrigation, upon declaration, but to be applied no later than August 15 of each year.

form of nannyism that would make life hell for imaginative entrepreneurs, but that's precisely the point: France had *had* plenty of imaginative entrepreneurs after the phylloxera crisis, and they had come close to discrediting the entire trade. The time had come to impose some order. Everything considered, then, it's hard to fault the reasoning that inspired INAO's powers. The fake wines, the shady commercial practices of mixing, flavoring, tinting and mislabeling, the occasionally grotesque overproduction (*faire pisser la vigne*) that sent supply soaring over demand and ruined prices—all of this had to be brought to heel if the wine industry were to be prevented from lurching from crisis to crisis.

Papa Bréchard put it succinctly: "INAO put an end to a century of fraud in French wines."

Unfortunately, if the reform was healthy and necessary, it was also subject to the same political pressures and human frailties as the Ministry of Agriculture's earlier efforts. Once the process of INAO certification began in earnest, everyone naturally clamored to be awarded the AOC stamp, and too many got it: eventually 45 percent of France's total production received the precious label. Result: nearly five hundred AOC wines, grouped into regional, subregional and local growing areas of twelve principal "basins of production." Not all of the wines were really good enough for the coveted AOC; the rules that governed them were not universal, but varied from one area to another; and in any case the rules were often opaque or even contradictory. Making a complicated situation even more complicated, another category intruded into the clutter: VDQS, *vins délimités de qualité supérieure*, for "superior quality" wines—a consolation prize for production that was good, but not quite up to AOC standard.

With all that, INAO tripped itself up. By earnestly trying to do too much too well, it created a model of labyrinthian complexity that was maddeningly difficult to understand, even for the French themselves, who rather enjoy complexity. Overzealous, the institute had composed a parochial canon by and for specialists—winegrowers, dealers, brokers, sommeliers and the like—but which entirely neglected another segment of the wine chain, perhaps the most vital one of all: the last one down the line, the ordinary consumer. Having set themselves the task of classifying and bringing order to the wines under their supervision, INAO carried it through in a typically rational, Cartesian manner, but without lending thought to eventually selling the wines. It was all for theory and nothing for practice: the French disease.

For the moment, it didn't matter. As the world's leading producer of fine wines—nearly a monopoly—France ruled the roost, and demand nicely exceeded supply. Good or bad, French wines sold easily, because the market had no other choice. Half a century later, after the rest of the world discovered the pleasures of drinking wine and the profits to be made from producing it, the French would be biting their fingernails for having locked themselves into such a highly specialized system. No one had anticipated the depressing truth of retail: the average wine buyer in Los Angeles or Hamburg—let alone in Peoria or Gelsenkirchen—didn't really care about the nuance between Volnay Clos de la Roche and Volnay Ferniets-Clos de la Roche.

Today, when the vastly simpler modes of naming and classifying wines from the United States, South America and the antipodes—often little more than the name of the grape and a flashy trademark—are running commercial circles around the complexities of the French wine trade, it is fashionable to laugh off the AOC system as archaic and somehow symptomatic of French intellectual arrogance, but INAO's founders deserve credit all the same. In their high-minded manner, they were only trying to inform intelligent buyers, to protect them from fraud, and to underline a reality that every serious wine lover at the time took for an obvious truth: different *terroirs* create different wines, each one of which changes from year to year, depending on what sort of weather the vines have experienced. This kind of detailed information and this kind of protection are not offered by the great masses of semi-industrial varietals that fill supermarket and liquor store shelves in today's globalized world. The idea of wines that remain constantly the same, year in and year out, like tonic water or Diet Coke, is repugnant to the French

mentality and contradictory to the logic of nature. And, as for the difficulty of fathoming INAO's labeling system, the French can legitimately
ask whether consumers are better off with too little information than
with too much.

In 1935, when the reform creating INAO was promulgated, the
growers around Villefranche, Belleville and Beaujeu may have turned
their eyes toward Paris with a certain anxiety, but they were quickly reas-
sured: the wines of the gamay had definitely earned the respectability
that Philip the Bold and his descendants in the Côte d'Or had always
refused them. The six *crus* of Brouilly, Fleurie, Chiroubles, Chénas,
Morgon and Moulin-à-Vent earned their AOC label in 1936, and generic Beaujolais and Beaujolais-Villages followed in 1937. One year
later Côte de Brouilly and Juliénas were similarly honored. The prettily
named Saint-Amour, the northernmost of the *crus*, had to wait until
after the war, in 1946. And the nine *crus* became ten when the intensive
lobbying of vignerons in the little village of Régnié finally paid off in
1988 with the AOC label which, they were certain, they had deserved
all along.

At the end of the war, when the Germans had been chased away and
the vines were slowly incubating the fabled *millésimes* of 1945 and 1947
over long, hot summers, a casual observer who dropped into the Beaujolais would have encountered mostly idyllic, timeless scenes that might
have tempted a Millet or Corot. The five or six thousand vigneron families working the land still lived in something like autarky, growing their
own vegetables, drinking their own milk, making their own cheeses, and
keeping rabbits, goats, chickens and a few pigs for the traditional feasting
days. The man of the house, perhaps still in wooden shoes, manhandled
a plow behind his horse in the vines, his wife either worked at his side
or in the house, and the kids walked to the village school. It was still
very much a time of handwork and horsework. Where horse and plow
couldn't go—high up at the top of the steepest slopes where the ground
was the best, the sun stayed the longest, and where the old vines gave the
finest wine—the vigneron labored with nothing more sophisticated than

clippers, pickax and hoe, unless he was one of those who had invested in a winch, a strange-looking machine that first began appearing in the vineyards in the mid-thirties.

The winch formed all by itself a curious little side chapter of the Beaujolais story. Heavy, ungainly and powered by a putt-putting gasoline engine, winches gained special popularity in the steeply escarped vineyards of the Côte de Brouilly and Vauxrenard, near Fleurie, but they demanded a lot of work. First they had to be humped up to the top of the slope and firmly anchored with heavy crowbars. Then, with the gearbox set in neutral, the winch's long cable could be pulled down to the bottom of the hill and attached to a plow. Grasping the wide handles behind this mechanical horse, the plowman slowly let himself be pulled uphill, fighting to keep the plow steady and the furrow straight as he advanced up to the summit while the winch's drum ate the cable back in. This mechanism offered the advantage of power against gravity, but it also obliged the vigneron to make his vine rows not only rectilinear, but also in a straight up-and-down direction—which of course made it easier for winter rains and summer flash storms to cause erosion and gullying. This could be parried, or attenuated, by scraping up earth on the hillside with long, sideways scarrings, but it was all that much more work. Labor-saving devices often have a way of creating more labor.

Even so, the winch was a significant harbinger of the modernization and mechanization that would soon be sweeping over not just the Beaujolais but the entire French winegrowing and winemaking trade. Immediately after the war, a limited number of standard agricultural tractors—primitive, underpowered little ponies, but tractors nonetheless—began arriving in the region, but most vignerons had little use for them beyond the usual farm chores. Too low and too wide, they were unsuited for working in the vineyard rows, where they would flatten the vines as they passed through. But then, first in 1949 and in a steady stream in the succeeding years, came the *enjambeuse*: the "straddler." This narrow, high-legged rig on wheels, pulled behind the vigneron's horse, had enough ground clearance to pass right over the vines, straddling the rows without damaging them. Furnished with a central tank, a pump and spraying arms that reached out on both sides, the rig could spray four rows of vine at a single pass. That was a real revolution for the vigneron who had been accustomed to slogging through his vines with a copper tank on his back and a single spray hose in his hand.

"Four rows!" recalled Claude Beroujon, an eighty-five-year-old retired vigneron from the village of Blacé, his eyes glowing with pleasure at the memory. "We were absolutely captivated. But they were expensive— 230,000 old francs. I bought one in 1951, and it lasted me ten years, until the motorized *enjambeuses* arrived."

That was the logical progression. In the normal course of things, inventive manufacturers like Vermorel went on to develop autonomous, fully motorized *tracteurs enjambeurs,* and these skinny, lanky little specialized machines, standing high on their stiltlike legs, are now standard equipment in French vineyards. Apart from a few nostalgic holdouts and a limited number of stubborn devotees of uncompromisingly organic viticulture, the days of horses in the Beaujolais vines ended in the early sixties. This was also the period when classical standbys for treating vines—sulfur, *bouillie bordelaise*—began encountering competition from various synthesized compounds generated by modern chemical manufacturers for keeping mildew, *oïdium* and crawling and flying pests at bay. Over those years, the Beaujolais peasants, like their confrères throughout the French wine industry, slowly swung over from the hand and horse to new high-speed, high-tech ways.

That proved to be a mixed blessing. By the mid-sixties the most archaic tools of the trade—the pick, the hoe and the plow—appeared to be in danger of disappearing when the winemaking community discovered the chemical marvel of *désherbants*: weed killers. Generalized by the seventies, these compounds offered appreciable and immediately visible advantages. By killing adventitious grass and weeds, they cleaned up the vineyards, made it easier to work on the vines and eliminated competition for nutrients in the soil, to the advantage of the vines. Eliminating these low, ground-level growths also eliminated the humidity they captured, and by consequence the various forms of fungus that would spontaneously generate within it. The immaculate rows of lush, green vines marching in military order straight up and down the hills of the French wine country, the earth between them a perfect, tawny carpet, made a quite strikingly beautiful sight, but to many who viewed these picture-postcard landscapes, nature tamed to that extent just didn't look quite right.

It didn't sound right, either, as bees, ladybugs and birds massively deserted the vineyards and took their business elsewhere. At length it was clear that overuse of chemical agents was sterilizing the soil and killing off its microbial life. As a result, the next step, again perfectly logical, was to bring on yet more chemicals—fertilizers, this time. Compacted by heavy machinery and rarely aerated by plowing, the soil became more resistant to vine roots searching for nourishment in the depths, so they did what any self-respecting root would do: they turned around and grew *up*, toward the surface, to where the fertilizer was.

It was weird and distressing. Alarmed at this turn of events, the French winegrowing community finally began seriously reappraising its passion for chemical agents. No sooner had they begun cutting back on them than the bees, the ladybugs and crowds of other indigenous creatures returned to the vines, offering a lesson in just how quickly nature can restore balance if it is left a little bit in peace. Today, *production raisonnée*, a semi-organic approach to viticulture, is progressively reducing reliance on the synthesized wonder chemicals and replacing them with environmentally friendly compounds, and soothing bands of grass between the rows of vines are once more common currency in the Beaujolais. Moreover—as any local booster will insistently remind visitors—Beaujolais vignerons remain much closer to the traditional artisan ways of winemaking than those in most other wine regions, with mechanical harvesters still forbidden in Beaujolais-Villages, the ten *crus* and for the production of *primeur*. While heavy machinery lumbers through vineyards elsewhere, in the Beaujolais it is still largely handwork. Very few consumers, even in France, realize that Beaujolais, this popular wine situated at the economy end of the price scale, shares with Champagne and several of the snootiest, overpriced Bordeaux the requirement to handpick the grapes in order to ensure that they arrive in the vinification sheds virginal and undamaged. It's not for purity of heart—the simple fact is that the gamay grape is delicate and can spoil fast—but it is an element of legitimate local pride nonetheless.

By the end of the fifties, the Beaujolais country might have seemed, in the eyes of that hypothetical casual visitor, to be at a point of stasis. The acreage under cultivation of the vine, about sixteen thousand hectares, was almost exactly the same figure as in 1830, and the density was still unusually high, averaging ten thousand individual vines per hectare. Such high density meant more work, but the figure was not an accident. There is always a tradeoff between too few plants sharing vineyard space (danger of grapes growing too big, and bloated with water) and too many (grapes stunted and puny for lack of nutrients). Over the centuries, peasant empiricism had settled on ten thousand plants as about the right figure. If, then, the postwar vignerons of the Beaujolais were working much as their ancestors had in the 1830s, they saw little reason for anything but satisfaction. As far as they were concerned, what it meant was that they were keeping faith with tradition and doing their job the right way.

But the standstill in which they seemed settled was only apparent. In reality, they were in the stasis of a rocket at the launching pad, venting chilly puffs of liquid oxygen that indicated something was about to happen. That something had been approaching, in fact, for nearly a decade, because in 1951 had occurred a couple of events that proved to be of weighty consequence. First, the French tax authorities rescinded the wartime rules governing release dates of certain types of wines, making it possible for some of them to be sold earlier in the year than had previously been allowed. With that, the phenomenon of *primeur*, or "new" Beaujolais, as the Lyonnais had been enjoying it for a couple of centuries, took its first tentative steps into the formal retail circuit, this time not just in barrels delivered to local bars but bottled, packaged and distributed nationwide.

The second event was considerably more modest: an eighteen-year-old kid from the village of Chaintré, just across the border of the Beaujolais into the Mâcon wine country, got fed up with the way local wholesalers were treating the wine that he and his brother had worked so hard to perfect. On a hunch, he stuck a couple of bottles of his Pouilly-Fuissé into his bike's tote bag and pedaled to the village of Thoissey, over on the other side of the Saône, where the famous chef Paul Blanc had earned two Michelin stars for his admirable restaurant, Le Chapon Fin. Maybe Chef Blanc would be interested in buying a few bottles. The kid on the bike was named Georges Duboeuf.

VI

A BIKE AND TWO BOTTLES OF WINE

THE BIRTH OF A BUSINESS DYNASTY

*T*he Duboeuf family wasn't quite the same as the other vignerons of the Beaujolais. Strictly speaking, in fact, they weren't even Beaujolais at all, but Mâconnais, and their home village, Chaintré, was white wine land planted with the chardonnay grape. Even so, Chaintré's chalky ground lay so close to the invisible border at the northern limit of Beaujolais territory that it was an easy stroll of only a few minutes to pass over into to the much more extensive, granitic vineyards of gamay. Beaujolais-Villages vineyards lay just on the west side of the Duboeuf property, and Saint-Amour to the south. Naturally enough, local identities had always been intimately related to the local products. "I had lots of friends in the red wine," Georges Duboeuf will say, today still, recalling his youth.

But the difference between the Duboeufs and the others was more than simply geography. For a start, this was very old native blood, and much of the history of France could be exemplified by the Duboeufs, or inferred from their family chronicle. Georges' elder brother Roger, who died in 2006, traced the Duboeuf family name back to the ninth century and the Latin *bos, bovis* (bull or steer). Clearly some distant ancestor had been a herdsman, probably in the mountainous country to the east, but the family had been settled into farming and winemaking in the little village of Chaintré (present population about five hundred) since at least A.D. 1500. The roots ran deep.

Largely unremarked over the following centuries within the anonymous multitude of peasantry that constituted the great majority of France's population, the Duboeuf ancestors rose a notch in their station with the French Revolution. The operation that brought the family to a certain prominence was a process of musical chairs with real estate, one that was perhaps typical of those unsettled, fast-changing revolutionary times. Under the ancien régime, the big local landowner had been Pierre-Elisabeth Chesnard, baron of Vinzelles, a nobleman who had a sharecropper on his land named Claude Debeaune, Georges Duboeuf's maternal great-great-grandfather. Vinzelles must have congratulated himself for a smart move when he snapped up the abbey of Saint Vincent de Mâcon, in the riverside village of Crêches-sur-Saône, after the anticlerical revolutionaries booted the monks out in 1791. Only a year later, though, Vinzelles had to skip town himself when his own noble head suddenly looked to be destined for the guillotine. When Claude Debeaune proved to the Mâcon adjudication court that Vinzelles had left a large outstanding debt to him (aptly enough, a transaction involving cattle), the big monastery building, the chapel in its courtyard and the three hectares of attached fields were transferred over to him. With that, the family came into possession of something very much like a manor house and its properties. Added to the farm in Chaintré, three kilometers away, and their total of fifteen hectares of vines, it made a good, substantial holding, well above the norm of local vignerons.

The Debeaune-Berthilier-Duboeuf family — in the lines of maternal succession names changed with each marriage — formed a serious little clan, marked by hard work and sobriety: certainly not wealthy but still of higher condition than most, rather like the kulaks of pre-revolutionary Russia, peasants who were looked upon as rich because they owned a horse or a few more patches of land than their neighbors. In the case of the Duboeufs there were even a couple of "employees," half-fruit winegrowers working their acreage on *vigneronnage* contracts. Roger Duboeuf went so far as to qualify the family as "petite bourgeoisie," people with a penchant for reading and a deep respect for education. Grandfather had been something of a rural intellectual, a *notable*, a man who exchanged philosophical letters with Raymond Poincaré, *président de la République*. He had also become friendly with the famous Lumière brothers, inventors of cinematography, after hitching up his oxen to pull their newfangled motor car out of the mud of the old National 6 highway, then inviting them into his house for lunch.

"We weren't exactly dirt farmers," said Roger matter-of-factly.

Farmers they were all the same, though, and in 1935 Georges and Roger received a harsh lesson on the realities of survival when their father, Jean-Claude Duboeuf, suddenly died of a stroke. Georges could hardly realize anything at all, because he was only two years old at the time, but for Roger it meant assuming the duties of the man of the house at age twelve. From that point on, little Georges was raised at home by his mother and his elder sister Simone, while Roger, still learning himself, became his mentor and instructor in agriculture and the craft of making wine. Uncle Louis Galud, married to their defunct father's sister, came by to advise and help out when he could, but he had his own work and his own family, so for all intents and purposes it was the boys who took the farm and the vineyards onto their shoulders and, over the following years, held their properties together without losing a single hectare. The exceptional work ethic for which the Duboeuf brothers would become famous was in part simply a mirror of the hardscrabble habit of stubbornly plugging along through adversity that thousands of Beaujolais peasants, like Papa Bréchard, had known before them. But with these two boys there was the added motivation of an absolute determination to keep the family patrimony intact: the only thing that a peasant hates more than not getting a piece of land he covets is losing a piece that he already owns. The grave, methodical, almost puritanical manner that within a few years would be guiding the young Georges Duboeuf as he carved out an exemplary career in the wine business, one that was to become a celebrated template of success in French individual enterprise, was only a continuation of this same determination to do well for the family. The boy's early maturity and the man's ability to start work earlier than the others, then keep at it long after everyone else knocked off, clearly had their roots in the tragedy of losing a father he never knew.

There's not much of the peasant farm boy that shows in Georges Duboeuf today. Rich, universally admired and courted by politicians, bankers and hustlers of every nature, he sits in his headquarters in the village of Romanèche-Thorins, almost smack on the border between the two great growths Moulin-à-Vent and Fleurie, at the center of a remarkable little empire of his own making, a private firm that he took from literally nothing to a turnover of well above $100 million a year, as, one by one, he crept up toward, caught up with and overhauled all the great established wine houses of the Beaujolais.

Piat, Mommessin, Thorins, Aujoux and the rest could only watch, dumbfounded, as this insignificant little upstart company called Les Vins Georges Duboeuf appeared from nowhere, steadily ate away at their lead and finally left them all in the dust. He is now far and away the area's biggest and most important wine dealer, inevitably labeled Mr. Beaujolais wherever in the world wine is sold. That's a lot of places, too, because no one ever managed to export the wine of the gamay grape like Georges Duboeuf.

Installed in his modest ground-floor office—cluttered, deliberately unglamorous, overlooking a parking lot—he is surrounded by abundantly tangible evidence of wealth, power and influence: enormous, state-of-the-art bottling lines and storage sheds bearing the steer-head logo he designed as a young man; an ultra-modern vinification plant about the size of a couple of football fields; a university-level laboratory; an amazing wine museum that he conceived, stocked and laid out himself, probably the best and most complete of its sort in the world; an elegant retail shop; a café-restaurant for tourists; and even the high-gabled bulk of the nineteenth-century Romanèche-Thorins railroad station, which he bought from the state to house an extraordinary train exhibit, both full-sized and in spiffy little electric models, demonstrating how wine is transferred and shipped.

There's a disconcerting style to the man, though: he doesn't follow the customary promotional script of the self-made man. A few years ago, when he built his huge new vinification plant, by far the most modern of its kind in France and probably in all of Europe, a computerized behemoth of glass, tile and glistening stainless steel—this is a mega badge of importance if ever there was one—he invited the press to Romanèche for an inauguration ceremony, but it wasn't to get his picture taken posing by this multimillion-dollar investment. Rather, he wanted to show off *Un Jardin en Beaujolais*, the botanical garden and demonstration vineyard that he had laid out on the sloping ground just to the east of it.

Duboeuf the CEO dresses his spare frame elegantly, slings cashmere sweaters casually around his neck and drives a high-powered, silver Audi equipped with enough buttons, switches and automatic controls for a small space station. Like Yves St. Laurent, Christian Dior and Coco Chanel, he has imposed his name as a brand of worldwide recognition in his own lifetime, something that no one else in the French wine business has managed to achieve. (In fact, until he became so famous that even the most distant and benighted member of the trade was aware of the basics of his biography, foreign retailers often assumed that Georges Duboeuf was a marketer's invented name, like Mr. Clean or Betty Crocker.) With all the worldly renown and prestige, though, it was only a few decades ago that he was the skinny kid in Chaintré clinging to a plow that was too big for him, yelling gee and haw (in French it's *hue* and *dia*) at the family Percheron, and it doesn't take much for memories of those years of youthful anonymity to come flooding back, sharp and clear. Duboeuf's madeleine, the morning I saw him in Chiroubles, was the smell of burned horse's hoof.

"Yesterday I was talking with a grower when a blacksmith came into the room," he said in that characteristic whisper of a voice. "He still had his leather apron on, and suddenly the room was filled with that smell, that very particular acrid odor you only get when the smith hammers a hot new shoe onto a horse's hoof. Suddenly I was carried straight back to Chaintré, when I was a boy.

"We had one horse, two cows, two goats and a pig. There had been an earlier time when we had two horses, but I only knew the period when there was one. I milked the cows, but I wasn't allowed to touch the goats—that was Grandmother's job. I don't know why only women were allowed to milk the goats; that's just how it was.

"I was good for the cows and horses, though. Every year we village boys would take our family horses to the main square to show them to the vet, who came through to check on their health and estimate their value. On the morning of the presentation I worked on mine for hours and hours, cleaning him up, brushing him, varnishing his hooves, combing his tail, braiding his mane. We led our horses up to the vet one by one. The mayor was there, the president of this association and that group, four to six serious men with mustaches who came to judge our work. I stood there admiring my horse. I was so proud. It was extraordinary."

I had joined Georges in Chiroubles that morning for the *Concours Victor Pulliat*, a formal, blind tasting to determine the year's best of the ten Beaujolais *crus* (when the prizes were announced a few days later "*la sélection Georges Duboeuf*" dominated the list), and in spite of the fact that we were in a high-perched little French village that scarcely could be quainter—stone houses roofed with round Roman tiles, winding streets, geraniums on windowsills, the occasional wandering cat—the atmosphere was all efficiency, organization and dead-serious business. The cell phones, electronic gadgetry and high-tech vinification chatter were about the same as what you might expect to encounter at a conference in California or Australia. When Georges entered the crowded meeting room and took his seat at his assigned tasting table, he may have been treated with a shade more respect than most, given his eminence and experience, but part of that respect was also for his white hair and the lines of fatigue on his face. He was already old, a man of another time: plenty of his fellow wine experts in the room were about half a century younger than he. Most of them could have no idea of the Beaujolais he had known as a boy, the prewar Beaujolais of Papa Bréchard and his countrymen, who still had one wooden shoe planted in the nineteenth century. In fact, I rather doubt that many of those present in Chiroubles that morning even cared much at all about the old Beaujolais, concerned as they were with scrambling for their share of sales in the globalized wine marketplace. Georges, on the other hand, was stalked as always by the essential ambivalence that defines him: old and modern; nostalgia and ambition; aesthetics and profit; tradition and progress. Within that crowd of dealers, brokers and growers, he was the one who had done the most to bring new wealth and cutting edge technology to the Beaujolais, but he was also the one whose memory was suffused with the smell of burned horse's hoof. Duboeuf's feet straddled a few centuries, and a few contradictions, too.

Over the years, I've poked and prodded at Georges to tell me about the Beaujolais fifty, sixty and seventy years ago. Our conversations have always been on the fly, between meetings, phone calls and business trips, often in his car as he drove to tasting sessions, because this perfection-crazed workaholic almost never has any free time. If my insistence on the past amused him at first, he understood and accepted the fact that Duboeuf the businessman, however much he represented a model of entrepreneurship for the French economy, interested me less at those moments than Duboeuf the descendant of and witness to a particular slice of rural France that has disappeared forever, one that few foreigners and not even so many of the French themselves could conceive of today—but one whose memory ought to be preserved, and maybe even cherished. Unsurprisingly enough, there was always plenty of nostalgia that accompanied these forays into his past, but the single leitmotif that recurred most frequently was work: the steady, obstinate, relentless work of the peasant who stakes his entire livelihood on what he grows, tends and raises, year in and year out.

"When you live in the environment of a wine family, you start very young," he explained. "You follow the work of the vine and vinification through all the seasons, even if it's just at a child's level. I clearly remember turning the handle of the crusher while Roger fed the grapes in from the harvest. I was five or six then. Like all the other children, I lived the period of the harvest intensely every year, carrying the tubs of grapes, then helping with the vinification as I got older. By the time I was fifteen, I was strong enough to participate in all the phases of the harvest at the same level as the adults. The harvest was only ten days or so, though, and once a year. For the rest of the time, it was all the usual work of spraying, pruning and tying up the vines. For me, that meant mostly work on weekends and Thursdays, when school was out.

"Our house in Chaintré was very simple by today's standards. For water we went to the pump at the well in the courtyard, and we used to chill bottles of wine in the well itself. Later we had running water installed in the house, but for a long time there was no hot water supply apart from the big woodstove in the kitchen, that had a built-in water tank. We took our weekly bath in the kitchen, using the hot water of the stove's reserve tank. For all intents and purposes, we lived in the kitchen, like all farm families. It was the warmest room in the house. The other rooms were heated just by fireplaces.

"We had ten hectares of Pouilly-Fuissé, three or four hectares of red wine and three or four of Noah. I used to plow between the vines, of course, but I didn't start at that before I was thirteen or fourteen, because you need a certain amount of strength and dexterity to handle a horse with the reins over your shoulders. Luckily, horses were accustomed to the work. They knew where they were supposed to go. Early in the fifties, we got rid of our Noah. That was handwork, too. We did it with a big wooden lever, almost two meters long, forked at the end. It ripped the vines right out by the roots."

Like most of their neighbors in those days, the Duboeufs were both farmers and vignerons. Wheat and hay were the two most common farm crops, and the harvesting was by a horse and the mechanical sickle bar it pulled. In the awkward spots too tight or too mounded for horse and machine, the handwork took over again: sickle and scythe.

"We ran behind the cutting machine and picked up the wheat to make sheaves, then carried them to the threshing machine. It was driven by a leather belt from the power train of one of those huge Locomobile steam engines with the smokestack and the big flywheel. We put the wheat into a chute on top of the threshing machine, and the straw came out on one side and the grain on the other.

"Once, I remember, when I was eight or nine I grabbed a big bunch of wheat, and there was a bees' nest inside it. I got stung all over my arms. My grandmother came over and said don't worry, it's nothing. She rubbed vinegar all over my arms. An hour later I was back at work.

"In July, there was the haying. That was hot work. You couldn't keep animals if you didn't have hay for them in the winter. After it was cut we had to shake it out and load it onto the cart. Since I was little, they put me up on top of the cart. My job was to take the hay as they passed it up and lay it out. There was a whole art to handling hay. You had to take it into your arms and roll each bunch, then comb it out with your hands. When it was piled up high we tied a rope around the load and took it up to the barn in Chaintré. There were some railroad tracks to cross on the way to Chaintré. Once, when I was twelve or thirteen, I hadn't tied it down well enough, and the whole load fell out, right onto the tracks. I had to act fast to get it off before the next train came.

"When we got to Chaintré, we brought the hay up into the loft above the stables, through a little opening like a window. My job was to take the bunches they pitched up and carry them to the back of the loft. The smell of fresh hay—ah là là, I'll remember that all my life."

Down on the plain by the Saône in Crêches stood the big old family house, the former abbey misguidedly acquired by the bargain-hunting Baron de Vinzelles. In Georges's childhood, it was inhabited by his grandparents Debeaune and Berthilier. The Domain of Arbigny, people called it, and there were two details, two aspects of its situation, that particularly intrigued the boy: the chapel and the flooding. The flooding occurred when the Saône rose and overflowed its banks, as it was wont to do when the late winter rains persisted and the snow melted in the mountains. First the domain became an island, and then, if the rains persisted, the house's ground-floor rooms went under water. Imperturbable, the family simply carried the furniture upstairs and moved into the second floor until the river receded back to its normal bed.

The chapel was a relic from the days of the monks of Saint Vincent de Mâcon, and it brought a touch of exotica that otherwise never would have come to this little corner of the French countryside: gypsies. "The chapel was part of the property, in the courtyard in front of the house," Georges explained. "There was a statue of Mary in front and Martha inside, along with Saint Lazarus and his two sisters. The saints had the reputation of curing *la patte d'oie*, a genetic disease that was prevalent among gypsies, especially those from Hungary, who used to come there on pilgrimage. Sometimes they left rosaries behind, and notes and testimonials for the saints."

In those days saints still counted for the French, too, and the Duboeuf family's attendance at Sunday mass was unthinking and automatic, as much a part of the normal routine of life as tending the vines. Serious and conscientious, young Georges was inevitably drafted into altar boy duty, and he fulfilled his pious chores from age seven to sixteen. Dressed in the surplice, he prepared the altar, the wine and the host, carried cross and candle, rang the bell and murmured the responses along with the rest of the parishioners. The wine for the mass could only have been Beaujolais or Mâconnais red—what else? So it was at home, too, for both children and adults.

"We drank our own wine, sometimes white, but mostly red. Like all the children, I drank mine mixed with water. We ate a lot of bread, and mostly products from the farm—vegetables, milk, cheese. Cheese was the meat of the peasantry. When we had 'real' meat, it was pieces we had salted ourselves. We killed the pig once a year, and of course I participated in that. That was one of the normal rituals of farm life. Grandmother taught me how to kill rabbits with a blow behind the head, and then to skin them and tan the hides for making gloves. Same thing for killing and plucking chickens. When I was about fifteen, I raised ducks in a little shack near Grandmother's place. You could make a pretty good profit with ducks, because they were ready for sale in just three months. I took them live to the open-air market in Chatillon. Supermarkets didn't exist then, of course, so a lot of the merchants came to us. The baker and the butcher came by the house every day or two. They had horse-drawn wagons until the end of the war. Then, slowly, cars and trucks started taking over.

"There was a monsieur who came around with a little cart that he pulled from town to town, the *Caïffa*. '*Caïffa, Caïffa!*' he shouted outside the gate, and we'd all come running out of the house to see him. He wore a splendid green uniform, boots and a postman's cap, and he was selling coffee and spices in little boxes. Then there was the *patti*, too, the junkman. '*A aux pattes!*' he shouted. It was a question: any junk or rabbit skins for sale? He picked up anything imaginable, all the things you didn't want anymore and were ready to throw out. All these people were part of the rhythm of the seasons for us, each thing in its time. Christmas, Easter, haying time, harvest time, time for killing the pig, time to release the wine, time for the distiller to come for making eau-de-vie . . . Everything contributed to a familiar routine that hardly changed from year to year."

If anything, the ancient routines of country life became even more frozen into the tracks of tradition during the war and the German occupation. With no cars on the roads anymore and hardly any civilian trains, the norm for transportation was horse, foot or bicycle. Rationing prevailed throughout the country, but in any case there was hardly anything left in the shops to buy. The Beaujolais fell instinctively into its ancestral habits of farming for survival, and villages shuttered up and drew back into themselves, isolated little units waiting the war out, their populations virtually immobile, as if thrown back into the nineteenth century. Now the city dwellers in Lyon and Mâcon hungrily envied their country cousins, because they knew that whatever happened there would always be fresh food on the farms: milk, cheese, vegetables, eggs, and occasionally meat, too: chicken, rabbits, sometimes game and, most lusciously, fresh pork, blood sausage and andouillettes around pig-killing time. The entire year's production of wine was supposed to be reserved for the German military authorities, but everyone knew that the peasants held back as much of it as they could, and enough of the excellent 1941 and 1943 vintages found a way into commerce to offer solace during the long wait for liberation.

One year before the war erupted, five-year-old Georges had begun his education by trudging up the hill behind the house to the Chaintré elementary school, a single room in the town hall. He carried a basket containing the lunch his mother had prepared for him, and at noon Madame Delancelot, the schoolmistress, ushered him and five or six other urchins into her apartment above the schoolroom and heated their food on her stove. The other children took lunch at home in the village. After elementary school Georges graduated to the secondary *école laïque*, a secular all-boys school, pendant to the *école de filles* into which the girls were segregated. Public morality still largely separated the sexes in those days, both in schooling and in civic responsibilities—French women, remember, were not trusted with the right to vote until Charles de Gaulle's provisional government gave it to them in 1944.

With no cars, no movies, no comic books, no television and of course nothing even remotely resembling all the other transistorized amusements of young people today, Georges spent most of his early years like all the other sons and daughters of the vine: studying at school and working at home. The horizons opened up at war's end. Just entering his teens now, he swam and fished in the Saône, joined a little theater group rehearsing in a room above the bakery in Chaintré under the guidance of the village priest and tested his physical endurance by biking through the Beaujolais hills. Professional bicycle racers were his heroes. He covered the walls of his bedroom with his own caricatures of the top competitors and listened to reports of races on the little crystal set radio that he built himself at the cost of a few francs. (Based on a crystal of galena, a rock that vibrates to radio waves, this granddaddy of all receptors uses neither electricity nor batteries, but requires headphones to be heard.)

By the time he was fifteen and sixteen, his own bike trips had become long-range expeditions with friends—up to two hundred kilometers a day, once to Switzerland and back, another time to Nice, and a round trip to Marseille, carrying their own tents and provisions. He discovered on those trips, without quite realizing it, that he was a leader—or, rather, that if someone had ideas, others would follow. Young Georges wanted to do things and go places.

"I never intended to stay in Chaintré as a vigneron," he told me one afternoon as we drove back from a visit with Roger in the old Duboeuf house at the edge of Chaintré, surrounded in every direction by a sea of vines. "I had this wonderful teacher in the *école laïque*, Mademoiselle Jeanine Frontier, and I told her I wanted to go live in Canada. She found me a Canadian pen pal whom I corresponded with for a while, but then my mother sent me for three years to Catholic boarding school in Mâcon, and there I really got interested in sports. That's when I developed the ambition to make my life as a sports trainer."

Normal schooling was finished at age sixteen. Georges read about a new discipline just then coming into the French educational network, the paramedical practice of *masseur-kinésiethérapeute*, similar to the American chiropractor. There were different options, but what interested him was the specific sports angle, which was taught at a specialized school in the Paris suburb of Maisons-Alfort. Georges studied for the entrance exam, easily passed it and boarded the train to the capital, where a cousin who had an apartment in the Latin Quarter on the Boulevard St. Michel had offered to put him up. Everything seemed to be in place for the beginning of a career in a white blouse with a handful of liniment.

Georges's bright new ambition lasted exactly two months. The country boy hadn't been able to imagine the realities of student life and commuting in the big city. "I spent more than two hours a day on the bus and in the metro. After a while I realized it just wasn't possible, losing all that time going back and forth. It was stifling. The stress was too much. I finally said no. I couldn't live in Paris like that. So I came back to Chaintré, where my professors were my brother and my uncle, and my school was the apprenticeship of winemaking."

In truth, there wasn't much about winemaking that he hadn't already learned over the years since his first turns of the grape crusher's crank, but he and Roger refined their methods and procedures with manic, perfectionist determination. "We turned away from a lot of the old local habits," said Georges. "A lot of growers used to use rusty old buckets or tubs to collect the grapes. Impurities like that could affect the wine, and sometimes give it a metallic taste, so we ordered special wicker baskets instead. We were the first ones to use them. For the harvest, Roger insisted that we had to clean the vinifying room and all the equipment a week early — hose down and scrub the floor, clean the filters, then hose down the press and the vats and wipe them with eau-de-vie. There were just the two of us, but we were very, very meticulous about the work, because we shared the same respect for wine and the same passion for making it right."

For the Duboeuf brothers, the only right Pouilly-Fuissé was a perfect Pouilly-Fuissé: bright gold with glints of green, mellow, richly redolent of ripe fruit, grilled almonds and nuts, but at the same time balanced with enough of the citric touch of acidity to prevent it from turning soft and flabby. Severely trimming back their vines and clipping their buds, the brothers deliberately lowered their yield per hectare, to ensure that their grapes developed harmoniously by drawing the optimum of nourishment from the soil.

As estimable as this policy was, though, it was confounded by the realities of the economic chain of command. Like all the other growers, Georges and Roger were victims of the syndrome of the little window in Villefranche: for selling their wine, they were a tributary to the dealers — *le négoce* — and the dealers set the price, take it or leave it. The price was the same for everyone, low yields or high, passion for perfection or not. So what was the point of limiting the yield, when you could make a lot more money by the ancient dodge known as *faire pisser la vigne?*

And that wasn't the end of it. Once the samples had been tested and the sale agreement signed, the dealers sent their tank trucks around, siphoned off the storage vats, carted the wine away, bottled it at their premises and sold it under their own labels. All the lovely Pouilly-Fuissé that Roger and Georges had worked so devotedly to bring to perfection disappeared into anonymous bulk batches. That hurt almost worse than the money they lost by limiting their yields. It was an insult to their pride as artisans, and it wasn't even smart, because the system only encouraged sloppy winemaking. Georges knew there had to be a better way. In 1951 he set off in search of it. He was in his eighteenth year when he stuck a couple of bottles of Pouilly-Fuissé into the saddlebag of his blue bike and set out in the direction of Thoissey.

The story of Georges Duboeuf's beginning in the wine business has been frequently written, but what is most significant is his prescience: he was the first to see what should have been glaringly obvious to everyone, and he was young enough—not settled into the stultifying ruts of routine—to go out and do something about it. His idea of selling restaurants exceptional wine in bottles, directly from selected producers, rather than relying on the traditional practice of selling whole barrels to bistros, was an inspired anticipation of the changing trends of the modern world, and it had never been done before—not in the Beaujolais, in any event. The days when bistros and restaurants bought wine in bulk and bottled it by hand in their cellars (usually reached via a trapdoor in the floor by the bar, then a vertiginous ladder down into the black hole) were drawing to a close. Professionalism and specialization were entering the modern world; the old folklore was on the way out. And Georges Duboeuf, the kid solemnly leaning on the pedals that afternoon as he left Chaintré, was gifted with an extraordinary lucidity that in following years was to make him the author of a considerable pack of innovations that, put together, constituted something very much like a revolution in the wine trade.

The famous first bike ride to Thoissey was easy, a mere ten kilometers or so down the N. 6, then a hook left across the Saône and a pleasant promenade in the shade of a majestic canopy of towering roadside plane trees to Paul Blanc's famous restaurant, Le Chapon Fin. The great chef received the boy in the bar. The standard version of the story is that Blanc tasted on the spot, but I suspect that he took Georges' samples, put them in his cellar or the fridge to settle and cool off, then contacted him a day or so later. At any event the result was this: "*Petit,*" he growled, "I'll take your white wine. And if you can find me some reds as good as this, I'll take them, too."

He found them, and then some. In coming years the spectacle of this black-haired youth with the soft voice and the inquiring brown eyes, as skinny as a Giacometti statue and hardly any more voluble, single-mindedly nosing through vineyards, cellars and *caves coopératives* in a quest to do as Chef Blanc had said, was to become one of the unfailing constants of Beaujolais life. Sooner or later, everyone who had anything to do with wine would have met or heard about Georges Duboeuf. For the moment, though, all that interested him in 1951 was to squirm free of the dealers' armlock and sell his own Pouilly-Fuissé, under his own label, as he and Roger made it.

That took a little doing. For one thing, he had no proper bottling equipment—almost no individual vignerons did. Bottling in any appreciable quantity had always been the exclusive domain of the dealers; growers had only simple hand devices in their cellars, often no more sophisticated than funnels and a basic corking device, for their use at home or for filling the sample bottles they brought on their yearly treks to the little window in Villefranche. Georges went a notch up from that. Biking north to Mâcon, he picked up a secondhand pump, some piping, filters and a slightly more sophisticated corking device, and arranged with a printer for a supply of labels of his own design. It was still all hand-operated gear, but it was enough to put their own production into bottles.

"We were so confident of the quality of our wine that we dared to go knocking on some more doors after Paul Blanc encouraged us," Georges explained. "I wasn't really a born businessman, but I was proud of my product and I could personally guarantee its quality. I suppose I had more of a feeling for communication than Roger. He stayed in Chaintré watching over the wine and studying archaeology and genealogy, while I went out and did the selling. At the start, it was only our own Pouilly-Fuissé, and we were using the labels that we designed together. I used to sit up at night cutting them out of the printer's sheets, because I didn't have a machine for that.

"Paul Blanc helped us tremendously, because he liked what we were doing and the way we did it. He came and visited us in Chaintré, then talked to his fellow cooks about us. Next thing we knew, we got orders from some very prestigious places: the Hôtel de Paris in Sens, the Grand Monarque in Chartres, the Aigle Noir in Fontainebleau, Chez Pauline in Paris, le Mouscardin in St. Tropez."

Still a teenager, Georges found himself with privileged entry to some of the heavy hitters of French gastronomy. It was a very considerable hand-up for his budding enterprise, but as unexpected as this may seem, it was also something like the norm within the cooking trade. Although frequently factious and disputatious in most normal pursuits, the French can demonstrate extraordinary depths of solidarity within certain professions whose roots lie in the world of medieval artisanry and the cooperative traditions of les Compagnons du Devoir, the ancestors of today's Freemasons. Nowhere is this truer than in haute cuisine, where an improvised, shifting but constantly active tom-tom beat of phone calls, faxes and e-mails keeps top chefs apprised of what the others are doing, how they are doing and why—all the while passing tips, contacts and warnings back and forth. Naturally there are tendencies, leanings, clans, cliques, divisions and schisms within the whole, but the information goes around nonetheless, and at lightning speed: if some farmer grows truly exceptional leeks, beets or turnips, he won't remain anonymous for long. Paul Blanc was only following the traditions he had learned during his own apprenticeship when he passed the word into his network of restaurateur friends that there was some unusually fine Pouilly-Fuissé to be had from the Duboeuf brothers in Chaintré.

And so the tradition continues today. No one who has ever heard a Paul Bocuse, a Guy Savoy or a Pierre Gagnaire on the phone with his own mafia of kitchen confrères can have any doubt about that. And there's a very salient characteristic that by definition accompanies these networks: you don't forget help, and you pay back in kind. Over more than fifty years since that first helping hand in 1951, Georges Duboeuf never forgot Le Chapon Fin, regularly arranging his most important business lunches and catered group meals there long after Paul Blanc's death, right up to the grand old barn's closing in 2005.

Another manner of helping hand appeared in 1951, and it was a big one, too, even if no one recognized at the time the full extent of its importance to the Beaujolais. In March of that year the French administration finally got around to lifting the wartime timetable that governed the release dates of the country's different wines, a spacing out of the supply chain that had been established strictly for the use of the army. Since twelve full years had passed since the start of the war and six since the German defeat, there was no justification for maintaining the timetable any longer, as the growers had been insisting ever since 1945. Administrations grind along slowly, but now at last a new, earlier release date was approved for Beaujolais: December 15 for wines of that same year.

That wasn't good enough for many of the vignerons. Eager to return to the good old days of St. Martin, when they sold their young wines as of November 11, they loudly protested that history and nature were on their side, as proved by all those burping barrels riding the gentle Saône down to Lyon. It was indisputable, they reminded the administration, that the gamay grape possessed the miraculous capacity to produce a pleasant wine extraordinarily early. Low in the aggressively astringent tannins that caused other wines (notably Bordeaux) to be virtually undrinkable in their youth, Beaujolais was already singing of fruit and flowers a mere two months after pressing. The argument was compelling, and on November 13, the administration caved in and authorized the new wine, the one that the growers called *primeur*, to be sold as of zero hour on November 15. With that, the phenomenon known as Beaujolais Nouveau was given its official, statutory life.

Primeur and Georges Duboeuf were destined to be dancing such an intimate tango together in future years that the wine came to be virtually identified with his name, but in the early fifties it was little more than an episodic curiosity, and Georges had nothing at all to do with it, occupied as he was with learning his infant business, doing his twenty-eight months of military service and courting his future wife Rolande Dudet, daughter of the Juliénas baker and the girl in charge of Victor Peyret's *caveau* inside the old church. Luckily, the army stationed him nearby in the Nièvre *département*, where he landed a cushy assignment as his captain's secretary, and he had plenty of leave time.

Georges was prescient; he was smart and he had ideas. Long before that awful word "marketing" existed, he was inventing his own instinctive version of it when he turned the big old basement kitchen of the family's Chaintré house into premises for receiving customers. This was an entirely new idea at the time. A few of the *crus*, like Juliénas, had established municipal *caveaux* for presenting and selling their local wines, but at the start of the fifties the notion that individual vignerons could profitably do the same thing at their own properties was simply not a part of the culture. As their fathers and grandfathers always had done, Beaujolais vignerons limited themselves to growing the grapes and making the wine. But Georges had given the matter a bit of thought: with the private automobile coming into general use, why not try selling to passing motorists?

The old kitchen was just right, a spacious, heavy-beamed, high-ceilinged room with a picturesque open fireplace and antique cabinets. He installed tables, chairs, upright barrels and various odd bits of winemaking equipment for local color, creating an atmosphere that was informal, easygoing and not too blatantly mercantile. Down by the side of the road where the driveway left the property, he stuck a big sign that he had ordered from a friend of Roger's whose business was making posters for movie houses: STOP — COME IN AND TASTE THE DUBOEUF WINES.

It was the first private *caveau de dégustation* in the Beaujolais.

Georges named it Au Cul Sec (Bottoms Up) and painstakingly created a promotional flyer. It was a rather amateurish job, to be sure—commercial *art naïf* —but he had all the right ideas. One side, printed in bright, eye-catching tones of yellow and green, showed a carefully labeled map of the winding roads leading off the N. 6 main highway to Chaintré. On the right fold was a cutout of a huge bottle of Pouilly-Fuissé (vintage 1955), a barrel and a tempting glass of cool, golden-hued wine. On the back side was Georges' painstaking black-and-white sketch of the interior of the *caveau*. "Pouilly-Fuissé Duboeuf Brothers, Winegrowers in Chaintré," it was labeled. "Au Cul Sec, our tasting room, into which we invite you."

Georges was only twenty-two then, but the example he set spread throughout the whole area. Today there are thousands of private *caveaux* in the Beaujolais, and every other house, it seems, has its present-day version of the "Stop, Come In and Taste" sign planted by the driveway. The blandishment is as alluring as it is clever, because every vigneron knows that it is hard to resist the temptation to sample wine for free, and that a glass or two of Beaujolais has the magic capacity of changing the world: cares evaporate, expansive optimism appears out of nowhere, wallets spring open. Twenty percent of Beaujolais stock now goes through direct retail sale by individual vignerons.

Georges was on to something, then, and it was only the start. He never forgot Paul Blanc's admonition to go out and find some good red wines, an admonition insistently repeated by the other restaurateurs on his growing list of Pouilly-Fuissé clients. When he was freed of his army duty, he took the bicycle clip off his right ankle and splurged on the purchase of a motorbike. Mechanized now, he pushed his prospecting trips farther and deeper in expanding circles through the Beaujolais hills, tasting and spitting over and over again as he moved from barrel to barrel and vat to vat, methodically instructing himself on the style of each vigneron, the layout of his vines and the different quality of wine delivered by each different *parcelle* of vineyard. Served by a hypertrophied sensorial memory, one that only improved with repetition over his more than fifty years in the trade, he made himself into something like a living wine almanac. Today there is no one who knows every nook and cranny of the Beaujolais as intimately as Georges Duboeuf, and no one who can taste, judge and select its wines with his speed and precision.

"His talent as a wine taster is stupefying," Papa Bréchard told me a few years before his death. "And he does it at a speed that is just incomparable. In tasting sessions he leaves everyone else behind. And he's got the science of tasting early samples and knowing what the wine will become later on. It's almost an art, his talent."

Even more famous as a winegrower in his time than Papa Bréchard was the late Louis Savoye, admirable vinifier and collector of tasting prizes with his intense, spicy Morgon. He was already eighty-seven when I met him in his *caveau* in Villié-Morgon back in the early nineties, but he retained a vivid memory of his first encounter with the prospecting kid from Chaintré. "He looked terribly young the first time I laid eyes on him," Savoye recalled, "but he made an extraordinary impression on me — on all of us. We saw that we had someone here who was faster and better than any of us. I'm not ashamed to say I learned a lot from Georges Duboeuf. We all did."

The concentric circles of Georges' marathon tastings widened through the years as his graduation from bike to motorbike to automobile allowed him to cover more ground faster, but the basic method never varied: ceaseless, obsessive tastings, barrel to barrel, vat to vat, choosing and eliminating. With thousands of vignerons to visit — each working in his own way to tend vineyard, plot within vineyard and *parcelle* within plot, then vinifying with whatever skill or dedication he possessed — there was a tremendous diversity of wine quality out there, ranging from superb to execrable, and Georges knew of no other way to get the good ones than to taste them all. As a result, he became a numbers man of Stakhanovite proportions.

What sort of numbers? There's an old debate about how many wine samples a competent professional can intelligently judge in any given period of time. The debate has grown especially acute in America since the arrival on the oenological scene of the Marylander Robert Parker, whose sensorial and marketing skills have made him prophet and lord chancellor among wine critics. His eminence is not without its detractors. A while back, in a *New York Times* review of a Parker biography, the writer Tony Hendra called into doubt some famous Parker numbers, notably that he was endowed with the prodigious capacity of sampling between 50 and 125 wines a week, or even more in hurry-up, one-time tasting sessions. "Tasting 100 wines (especially at the rate of one a minute)," Hendra concluded, "and judging No. 100—or No. 50—as accurately as No. 1, is a physiological impossibility."

Georges responded with a little half smile one evening when I told him about the article, shaking his head and raising an arm in a gesture of the futility of attempting to bring noninitiates to an understanding of his business. That day alone, he had sampled somewhat more than three hundred wines.

What he had been chasing that day was the same elusive trophy that he had gone after during his early forays into the hills for Paul Blanc and through all the years since: *le goût Duboeuf* —the Duboeuf taste—his idea of what a good Beaujolais should do for the nose, the palate and the soul. All the Beaujolais he bottles and sells is wine that he has tasted himself, and the wine he loves is a reflection of what the gamay grape gives best when it is handled by a skillful vigneron: a clearly defined rush of fruit reminiscent of fresh-picked red berries, jamlike in the richer *crus*, but still totally dry, marked with the refreshing nip of acidity that adds the necessary body to its soft tannins.

In the universal, eternal trilogy of wine—color, fruit and structure— Georges' eye for one, nose for the other and palate for the last are so unvarying that a diligent Beaujolais drinker with a modicum of experience can almost infallibly identify his wines from year to year by the simple act of lifting a glass, examining its color and inhaling its bouquet. In effect, Georges' early years prospecting for Paul Blanc were the postgraduate studies that earned him his oenological Ph.D. Step by step, from his first taste of the delicious, sweet, freshly pressed juice whose sugar is only beginning to turn to alcohol—the nicely named *paradis* —until the vinification was complete and the final product was ready for bottling, Georges observed, sniffed and tasted thousands of times, eliminating candidates until he had chosen exactly the batches he wanted.

The wine trade is riven by just as many factions and jealousies as any other, but everyone in the Beaujolais, even those who have spent their entire careers among his legion of competitors, acknowledges his uncanny ability to predict, from the earliest run-off juice of newly harvested grapes, what the finished wine of the future will be like. For this, tasting talent alone isn't enough. Choosing from thousands of samples in hundreds of different *caveaux* and *chais*, ordinary mortals tend to get confused and forgetful but, like a top-level chess player, Georges was either born with or developed prodigious powers of memory. Garry Kasparov never forgets a position on the chessboard; Duboeuf never forgets a taste or an aroma.

"His nose!" cried Pierre Siraudin, whose velvety Saint-Amour Georges has been selling for some four decades now. "I wish I had a nose like that. If he hadn't gone into the wine business he could have been a champion perfumer."

I once asked Michel Brun, who worked for more than thirty years as Georges' deputy in Romanèche-Thorins, whether his boss could identify the different Beaujolais growths in a blind tasting—make the pick, for instance, between the neighboring *crus* of Fleurie and Moulin-à-Vent. "Oh, come on," he said impatiently. "That's child's play. I've seen him identify eleven different vineyards within the same *cru.* "

André Poitevin, now retired from working his four and a half hectares of Saint-Amour on a hilltop above the hamlet of Les Thévenins, met Georges at age sixteen, when he joined one of the long-range bike expeditions, and he was one of his friend's earliest suppliers. "I had taken the vines over from my father in 1954, and Georges came to see me on his motorbike a year later," Poitevin recalled. "He was just starting his business in Chaintré, and he was looking for supplies of good reds, so he started with his friends. He tasted and we had a long talk about who else in the area was making good stuff. His customers were still just restaurants then, but he was expanding his list of suppliers fast.

"His business was small, so he could only afford to buy a few barrels here and there, but everyone could already see he was a crack at tasting. And that memory of his! He would come and taste my different batches of wine and then, three or four months later, remind me which barrels in which rows were less good than the others. He's incredible! He taught me everything I know about tasting, and he never slowed down. If I ever called him to say I had an especially good vat, I knew he would be there in an hour or two.

"In the beginning, he took my barrels to Chaintré for bottling. A few years later he came and did his bottling here with his portable equipment. I sold him wine for forty-seven years, but"—Poitevin's grandfatherly features set into a Gallic moue of dissatisfaction—"he dropped us in 2001 and 2003—didn't buy a drop. I was a little bit vexed when he didn't buy, but we still tried to keep on saying nice things to each other. He came back to us in 2004, though."

Poitevin's relief at renewing commercial ties with Les Vins Georges Duboeuf was visible and unconcealed, and time and time again over years of talking with vignerons I have encountered this same sense of triumph and/or trepidation in relation to the company in Romanèche-Thorins, because selling to Duboeuf is the gold standard of the Beaujolais, the signal that your wine has passed the test of a maddeningly difficult and demanding taster who can't be fooled, knows exactly what he wants and recognizes it immediately when it comes into his glass. Being dropped is almost a mark of shame, like being demoted to the minor leagues. And if Duboeuf can drop a childhood friend like Poitevin, he can do it to anyone.

In the early years, the situation was not as portentous as all that, because it was Georges who was hustling and scraping by on a perilous shoestring budget, often obliged to improvise as he went along. One of the first important deals for his fledgling business, thanks to a recommendation from Paul Blanc, was a double order for Pouilly-Fuissé, from the Hôtel de Paris et de la Poste in the ancient cathedral town of Sens, at the northern edge of Burgundy, and Chez Pauline, a still-famous Parisian restaurant on rue Villedo near the Opera. The only problem with the transaction was that he had no way of delivering the wine. That was where a bit of Beaujolais folklore entered the picture.

"I hitched a ride with my plumber friend Constant Charbonnier," Georges remembered. "He was a good friend, Constant, quite a guy—extraordinary guy, really, very clever. His father had been a *patti* who used to go around the countryside fixing and re-tinning pots and pans. He was from the Auvergne, like all of them. Starting from nothing, he worked his way up, became a plumber and roofer, and earned pretty good money. Constant had this old Renault Juva 4 delivery van. He helped me out in those days, and we did lots of deliveries together, all over the place. What a talker he was—he had this unbelievable spiel—he talked and talked and talked. Great guy. We got to know a lot of restaurants together, with our deliveries."

They got to know a few girls, too. Georges' austere features softened into a dreamy half smile as he recalled the theatrical skills of his plumber friend chatting up three girls in the Puy-de-Dôme, which is about as close to nowhere as you can get in France. Assuring them that in spite of their beat-up old delivery van, he and Georges were in fact young men of cosmic distinction and merit—destiny's darlings—he persuaded them that they were worthy of the most tender affections right now. The spectacle of the motormouthed plumber and the grave, silent beanpole vigneron, both of them barely removed from their teens, must have lent a welcome breath of exotica to the young ladies' dreary provincial circumstances, because Georges suggests that Constant's rhetoric was not altogether without success.

Not long after this triumph of bucolic libertinage, a capital encounter occurred that was to shape the entire future of Georges' career: in 1955, while he was at home on leave from the army, a buyer for Alexis Lichine appeared at Chaintré.

Today, many wine devotees may have forgotten the fundamental role that Lichine, a Russian-born American wine expert, entrepreneur and writer, played in introducing the culture of wine to his adopted country. "He taught Americans to drink wine," wrote the eminent *New York Times* wine critic Frank Prial. A genuine and passionate connoisseur, Lichine was a speaker of many languages, a charmer, a romantic and a yarn-spinner with a fabulist's gift for persuasion. Twenty years older than Georges and fairly glittering with polished urbanity, Lichine immediately won the starry-eyed admiration of his near-exact opposite, the quiet, diligent, meditative and monolingual son of the Beaujolais peasantry whose world travels had carried him no farther than Switzerland, Marseille and the Puy-de-Dôme.

"He fascinated me as a personage," Georges told me. "This Slav, this Russian Jew, was someone completely out of the ordinary. He was an excellent taster, he was a fervent wine lover, and he had the gift of words—he could absolutely bewitch people with his eloquence. Everything about him was elegance and charm, and it was never vulgar—always first class. There was a certain noblesse there, a stature, a manner of speaking, a look in his eye, a bearing and a presence. He was a dominator, a *séducteur*. It was spellbinding. He was miles above me. His personality squashed me underfoot."

Listening to Georges telling of the early days of his relationship with Lichine, a parallel springs inescapably to mind: *La Cigale et la Fourmi*, La Fontaine's archetypal tale of the hedonistic, singing grasshopper and the industrious ant—and exactly as the moral of La Fontaine's little poem suggests, it was Georges' steady, unremitting industry that would eventually carry him to even greater heights in the business than his suave mentor. (In truth, there's a good dose of the grasshopper in Duboeuf, too, but he keeps it carefully concealed most of the time.)

Glib and beguiling though he may have been, Lichine also had solid credentials. He had begun in the profession during the Great Depression, as national sales manager for the equally dashing and polyglot American wine merchant and writer Frank Schoonmaker. With Schoonmaker he was the moving force behind establishing the "varietals" system, the practice of identifying American wines by the name of the single variety of grapes from which they were made. The system was neat, handy and simple, a marketing tool that went over well with customers and was destined to spread through South America as well, and then on to Australia and New Zealand. Moreover, this manner of naming wines was perfectly logical, because it broke the bad old habit of identifying American wines analogously, by their resemblance to French counterparts, however vague that resemblance might have been. The jugs of California wines that had been called Burgundy, Chablis or Beaujolais were far more appropriately labeled Pinot, Chardonnay or Gamay. In today's globalized marketplace, when New World wines are making serious inroads into France's near-monopoly of the fine wine trade, the varietal system has proved to be an outstanding sales weapon in the head-to-head competition with INAO's far more complex, often confusing AOC model. The average wine buyer, it turns out, prefers fast and easy to slow and complicated.

Lichine's credentials were impeccable, then, but he was also possessed of an ego of proportionate size, and he and Schoonmaker split up, as inevitably they were doomed to. Opening his own competing import company, Lichine set up in France and found that the choice Château Prieuré in Bordeaux's Margaux district was up for sale at a bargain price. He snapped it up, instantly renamed it Château Prieuré-Lichine and spent a small fortune beautifying grounds and dwelling, while totally making over the vineyard. He presided over his domain like a prince, breaking the routine of commerce by throwing gala parties for the press, local dignitaries and assorted Beautiful People. Soon he went on to half ownership of the even more prestigious Château Lascombes as well, all the while churning out books and articles that further burnished an already enviable international renown. The icing on the cake of his celebrity came in 1964, when he married the retired but still glamorous Hollywood actress Arlene Dahl. If there ever was one person who, in the fifties and sixties, could be labeled Mr. Wine USA, it was Alexis Lichine. The contrast with the peasant winemakers of the Beaujolais could not have been greater. No wonder young Georges Duboeuf was impressed.

On furlough from the army on that fateful afternoon in 1955, Georges was as yet unaware of all these trappings of glory when Lichine's buyer paid a visit to Chaintré. His arrival there was by itself testimony to the efficiency of Paul Blanc's pass-the-word information system: a friend in the restaurant trade had tipped him off about the excellent Pouilly-Fuissé of the brothers Duboeuf. At first, Georges—cagey, perhaps a bit suspicious, reluctant to part with his last remaining bit of stock—gave him the brush-off. Sorry, we're all out, he said. But Roger had apparently intuited something about the buyer that Georges hadn't, and he pointedly reminded his brother that they had stashed a couple of barrels in a cousin's cellar in Crêches. With that, he had no choice but to sell, and the deal was on. He brought the barrels back, bottled the wine, and a few days later the buyer shipped it away. Had it not been for Roger's timely intervention, Georges might have missed the first great defining stage of his career. The association with Lichine was to take him beyond France and introduce him to the world at large.

While that momentous professional step forward was still lying over the horizon, Georges made his first serious material acquisition, a boxy, gray, pig-snouted, old Citroën "Tube" delivery van with a sliding side door, four antiquated, roaring cylinders, a crash gearbox and natural air-conditioning via seams in the corrugated bodywork. The days of hitching rides with Constant Charbonnier were over.

It was this capacious, all-purpose sherpa of a truck that allowed Georges to break new ground once again when, in 1956, he became France's first custom bottler. Like his idea of setting up his own wine-tasting *caveau*, this was something that no one had ever thought of before. His scouting trips had located dozens of vignerons making wonderful wine, much too good to disappear into the anonymity of the big *négociants'* common vats, but they had neither the skills nor the equipment for bottling it. The eureka idea hit Georges at age twenty-three—why not come and do it for them, at their vineyards?

In the noble vineyards of the Côte d'Or, and especially in the rich, swanking world of the Bordeaux châteaux where Lichine was swimming like a fish in home waters, the winegrowers commonly bottled their own production because they could—they were wealthy enough to afford good professional equipment. Estate bottling, the operation was called. (The French phrase is *mise en bouteille au château*.) The vignerons of the Beaujolais, on the other hand, were neither noble nor rich, and definitely could *not* afford the equipment. And there were hardly any "estates" in the Beaujolais; mostly it was just peasant properties. When Georges went to the business registry office in Mâcon to get a commercial license for his new venture, he discovered that there was no category for him to sign up for. He didn't even know what to call his new line of business. I guess we'll say *façonnier embouteilleur*, then, if that's all right with you, suggested the bureaucrat: "custom bottler." Fine, said Georges with a shrug.

Georges was the first of this new category and, at the time, the only one in France. His roving status allowed him to break free of Chaintré and deliver his pumps, pipes, filters and bottles to where the wine awaited him. It proved to be a masterstroke. The vignerons whose wines he had already selected—men like Siraudin, Poitevin, Savoye and all the others—were flattered by the personal attention, allured by the prospect of a new sales outlet and proud to see their wines receiving individual care, then leaving the property under their own labels.

No matter how much mechanization and industrial technology may mark its creation elsewhere, wine cannot be just another product for men of this sort. Wine is special in France, weighted as it is with centuries of tradition and mystic symbolism that not even the aggressively secular Enlightenment could shake off. Nowhere is this truer than in the Beaujolais. No one who has spent any time with the best of its smallhold craftsmen can doubt the sincere, almost paternal pride that they invest in the artifact whose birth they spend their lives attending through the endlessly repeated yearly cycle of seasons, always the same and yet, with each vintage, always different.

The analogy to parenthood is axiomatic, but it is no less true, and you see it again and again. Take Paulo Cinquin, for instance. He is a sixtyish, tough-talking, illusionless reformed hippie, distinguished by a huge shock of graying black hair, piercing ice blue eyes and the impatient, no-nonsense manner of a CEO who would fire his own mother for the good of the company—but he insists on growing the seedlings himself for his vines in Régnié, and every year at harvest time he sleeps for ten to twelve nights in his cellar to keep constant watch over the baby wine bubbling away in his vats.

And then there was Saint Joseph. Joseph Boulon he was by the administrative records, but his intemperate, some might have said dissolute ways—he enjoyed a touch of the grape—had gained him the angelic sobriquet. His place of business was a remarkably unkempt farm-vineyard in Corcelles-en-Beaujolais, complete with the wooden shoes, the picture-postcard slothful cat and the imperialistic rooster strutting at liberty. In spite of or because of the disorder, Saint Joseph had the talent for producing, year in and year out, a perfect Beaujolais that caused envy kilometers around. When I first plunged into the penumbra of his *caveau*, I discovered a meager, gaunt little man in a sweaty undershirt with a Gauloise dangling from his lip, seated next to a gas-fed space heater whose orange glow was directed against the wall of a big storage vat containing an important part of his newly fermented wine.

"*Il a la fièvre*," Boulon said. He's got a fever.

I never did get the news about how well or how quickly Baby 1978 recovered from its infant catarrh, but if anyone could have pulled that batch back to health, I am confident that it would have been Joseph Boulon. It was people like him who constituted the first basic address book—a few dozen names—that underpinned the young Duboeuf's early steps in the business of buying and selling the wines of the Beaujolais. There would be a lot more of them in the future, along with a modicum of twists, turns and detours on the path to success, and it was not until he had reached the age of thirty-one that the company called Les Vins Georges Duboeuf came into official existence.

That did not mean, though, that he wasn't keeping himself busy— au contraire, he never stopped. But he did slow down a bit in 1957, just long enough to persuade Rolande, the pretty, dynamic baker's daughter in Juliénas, that she would be better off as his wife. Rolande knew plenty about wine because her mother's family were vignerons who produced their own Juliénas. When her father wasn't baking baguettes and croissants, he tended his own little vineyard, too. And there was something else, something unusual about her character: she was the only person in the world who was willing to work as hard and as long as Georges Duboeuf. Well, almost as hard and long.

VII

ONE OF US

A Champion for the Beaujolais

he Beaujolais harvest was small in 1957, a mere 240,000 hectoliters (the vines had suffered from the hail and deep frosts of the previous year), but the quality was excellent. Things were coming along nicely that year for young Georges Duboeuf, too.

At twenty-four he was just out of the army and freshly married to Rolande. He and his bride had set up in a wing of the family house in Chaintré, and the Duboeuf Frères Pouilly-Fuissé was selling well. His head was full of addresses for splendid wines both red and white, and thanks to Paul Blanc, he was becoming more and more widely known in French restaurant circles as a *courtier* (wine scout or broker) of unusual talent. He had already been selling to Lichine for a couple of years when he and Rolande loaded the Citroën Tube with six hundred bottles of Pouilly-Fuissé and a mattress and clattered off across the Massif Central to make his first personal delivery to Bordeaux. The great man wanted to meet him at home in his fiefdom.

Georges had no idea what to expect when he was ushered into Lichine's office, and so, logically enough, he began by speaking about his Pouilly-Fuissé. Lichine said no, let's not bother with that. I'm busy with journalists and distributors this afternoon, but we have to talk. This evening you'll come to dinner at the Prieuré, and you'll spend the night at Château Lascombes. I've got a nice room for you. The scene was like a general interviewing a newly arrived private. Refusal was out of the question for Georges, all the more so since he and Rolande had been expecting to spend the night in the back of the Tube after liberating it of its bottles. That was why they had packed the mattress.

Lichine was no dummy. He already knew all about the excellence of the Pouilly-Fuissé from Chaintré, and he had been hearing a lot about the talents of this Duboeuf boy. Now, sizing him up in person at dinner, he listened intently as Georges described his custom bottling operation. Even for an illusionless old pro like Lichine, hearing Duboeuf expatiate about wine was an impressive and edifying experience. "Georges," he exclaimed, "that's exactly what I'm looking for! You're going to handle the Beaujolais and Mâconnais for me. You go to the domains, bottle the stuff and send it to me in Bordeaux. I'll put the labels on and sell it. I only want domain wines—Moulin-à-Vent and Fleurie to start with, along with Pouilly-Fuissé. After that, we'll see."

The delivery of those six hundred bottles turned into a two-day sojourn in Margaux, during which Georges took the full atomic blast of Lichine's hospitality, charm and salesmanship. Bordeaux—the money, the sophistication, the power—was dazzlingly different, miles above the little peasant world of the Beaujolais-Mâconnais. For Georges, that first visit was a commercial *coup de foudre* (love at first sight), as if destiny had meant him to work with Lichine. An entire new universe of business prospects was dancing in his head when he and Rolande took their leave of Prieuré-Lichine.

That night, the Duboeufs parked the Tube in a village in the Massif Central and bedded down on the mattress. When Georges awoke the next morning and, scratching and yawning, slid open the Citroën's door, he found that they were installed smack in the middle of the town's open-air market, making an embarrassing new attraction of themselves for early morning shoppers, between a butcher and a fishmonger. It was

a salutary humbling after the glitter and luxury of Margaux, and a reminder: there was a lot of work to be done.

Over the next years Georges scouted so perspicaciously in the
Beaujolais that a second promotion arrived: Lichine asked him to expand the operation and do the same throughout the whole of Burgundy. This unlikely collaboration of contrasting Franco-American
temperaments was to last for a couple of decades, enriching both men
and bonding the two in a solid friendship that lasted until Lichine's
death in 1989. Most importantly for Georges, it established a first-class
reputation for him among wine distribution professionals. Although
he remained virtually anonymous to the wine-buying public in America during most of that period (while the labels were all Lichine's), the
people who ordered and sold Burgundy and Beaujolais knew where it
was coming from. When Lichine reoriented his operation to concentrate on Bordeaux wines alone, the distributors were already primed for
Georges to step right in and take his place with Beaujolais wines, now
under the Duboeuf label.

As yet, though, all that was in the future. For the moment, as he
and Rolande motored homeward, east-northeast over the twisting roads
of Central France, Georges' business was still a shoestring operation,
about as small as one could be: himself as wine prospector and bottler,
Rolande as wife, assistant and all-purpose factotum. When Georges ran
the bottling machinery, it was Rolande in her blue workman's blouse
who watched over the bottle-washing apparatus. When Georges was off
scouting and tasting, she handled the phone, accounting and billing;
and when they began hiring, it was Rolande who washed the employees'
work clothes and cracked the whip to encourage them to work as hard as
Georges and herself. Or maybe just half as hard; that would be enough.

The French were still drinking about 150 bottles of wine a year per
capita in those days, and it was a comfortable seller's market—a good
time to be in the wine business, then, but that didn't mean it couldn't be
improved. Georges had an idea, one that he had been caressing for several years. It centered on the *pot Beaujolais*, the graceful, thick-bottomed

glass carafe containing exactly forty-six centiliters of gamay wine, mandatory accompaniment to the exertions of *boules* players, source of inspiration for countless hacks, poets and dreamers in bars in and around Lyon, the very one that the abbé Augustin Ponosse always emptied like an honest man as he made his parochial rounds in Clochemerle. Why not, Georges reasoned, sell Beaujolais in a bottle shaped like the *pot*? His innate sense of commerce told him that the novelty would be a hit with the wine-buying public, and events were to prove him entirely right. In 1957, though, there was a problem: no such bottle existed, and it would cost a lot of money to have one made.

The amount Georges needed to get the bottle made was 500,000 old francs, or somewhat less than $2,000. For any well-established company, or just a normally prosperous private citizen, raising that amount of money would have posed no particular problem, but even so, $2,000 was not a negligible sum in 1957. Considering inflation and the inevitable debasement of currencies over the years, its value would be at least ten times greater than today. It would have covered, for instance, a year's tuition at an Ivy League college of the time, or bought a quite respectable new car.

Georges drew a sketch of his ideal bottle, compromising with the realities of commerce by bringing its capacity up from forty-six centiliters to half a liter, and took it to several of the glass manufacturers who had plants around the wine area. All of them but one, a little company in Chalon-sur-Saône, turned him away with more or less polite expressions of refusal: not worth it, no market for it. The company in Chalon at least took him seriously enough to quote him the 500,000 franc figure, but the matter was pretty much academic, because Georges didn't have anything close to that amount of cash. He *did* have enough money, though, to pay a local craftsman to turn him a wooden demo model of the bottle on his lathe. That was step one. Step two was obviously to round up the funds, but the banks weren't lenders in those tight-credit days before free-flowing commerce. There was another way—the old way, the same informal, clannish Beaujolais solidarity system that had allowed him to make his early deliveries with Constant Charbonnier's Juva 4. Georges went to see Le Père Vermorel.

Fittingly enough, Old Man Vermorel lived in Vaux—Clochemerle itself. I've heard Georges tell the story of Père Vermorel more than once, and each time, unfailingly, his voice takes on a dreamy, tender tone as he remembers the time and the man, because everything he loves about his native land is reflected in the duality of person and place as it was that afternoon: the steep, snaking climb up Vaux's rue Gabriel Cheval-lier, the church with its massive square clock tower and Romanesque portal, the *boulodrome*, the little bistro Chez la Jeanne, between the bakery and the château—and, of course, Old Man Vermorel. If anyone could advise him on how to get his bottle done, he would be the one.

"He was extraordinary: a perfect vigneron's face, round, red-cheeked and mustachioed, a straw boater on his head and a cellar master's apron over his belly. He had a house up on the ridge overlooking Vaux, and his wife was a former schoolteacher. Monsieur Vermorel was the village sage, like the unofficial priest or mayor. People used to come and consult him for advice on family matters, inheritances and the like. He would receive them up on his terrace, and then after having a talk you would always go down and drink a *canon* with him at La Jeanne's place.

"So we talked and I had my drink with him and we talked some more, and that was all there was to it. A few weeks later I got a letter from him with his check for 500,000 francs. 'Get your bottle made,' he wrote. 'Pay me back whenever you can.' And that's how I started my business."

With that, the Duboeuf couple left Chaintré for new quarters in the village of Romanèche-Thorins, squeezed between the slopes of Moulin-à-Vent and the N. 6 main highway. Georges had his bottle made, pat-ented the design and ordered the first consignment. It was then, late in 1957, that he had an uncharacteristically bad idea—or, rather, a very nice idea that proved disastrously impossible to carry out.

L'Écrin Mâconnais-Beaujolais, he called it—the Mâcon-Beaujolais Showcase. Reasoning that his years of prospecting had acquainted him with the best that the region had to offer, he persuaded forty-five top vignerons to join him in a hybrid joint venture (essentially a winegrowers' union, the first ever in the Beaujolais) for commercializing their wines. On paper, it looked perfect: the best vignerons, the best wines and a dynamic young man—a peasant and vigneron himself, not a bourgeois like the dealers whose arrogant ways had humiliated their caste for so long—to sell them. Georges would put the skill of his nose and palate to the task of selecting the best of each man's vats, come around with his equipment to bottle them, then label and sell them with the individual vigneron's name, under the Showcase logo.

The promise of the name on the label signified a recognition and legitimation of a sort that had never occurred before in the Beaujolais, certainly not for the smallholders that Georges had discovered in his wanderings. My wine, my name—my identity. Vigneron pride of personal accomplishment had never been taken into account before, but Georges saw it day after day as he sniffed, tasted, spat and entered into erudite discussions of yeasts, temperatures, fermentations, fungi, phases of the moon, rainfall, the north wind and all the other countless imponderables that each winegrower juggled in his own way to give birth to the expression of his talent and care that came once a year and once only—his sole professional chance to say: this is me. Considering how systematically and for how long the gamay grape and Beaujolais wines had been held in contempt by their wealthy confrères to the north and west, their sense of affronted dignity was all that much stronger. From his first juvenile turns of the grape crusher's crank, the winemaking experience had taught Georges to never underestimate the motivating power of peasant pride. For the vignerons who signed up with *L'Écrin*, the personalized labels meant respect long overdue; and the prospect of their wines being sold to the widening list of restaurants clamoring for the Duboeuf super-selection was very much like a consecration.

"In a way, you could say that the dealers in the old days acted like medieval lords," Georges reflected some years back as he thought back on his early days in the trade. "The peasant winegrowers were in a hopeless situation with them. As a winegrower myself, I revolted, and I was right to do it."

Georges always keeps a little supply of jotting paper or index cards in his shirt pocket to note down ideas and reminders, and his progress on the climb from zero to becoming the region's top dealer and most widely respected wine expert can be traced directly back to these little slips of paper. One that he jotted down for himself was a personal code of conduct. It offers a revealing peek at the altar boy scruples that never quite abandoned him in adulthod. Eventually he had it printed out in black-and-white:

> —*Never trick or deceive a vigneron, especially if he is naïve.*
> —*Never humiliate him, especially if he is of modest means.*
> —*Always give him the respect that he and his wines deserve.*

Words of that sort that can sound dangerously hokey or meretricious in the cut-and-thrust world of modern business—after all, the eternal rule of all business everywhere is to buy low and sell high, and entire advertising and PR staffs are hired to disguise or sugar that central fact—but Duboeuf is dead serious. He speaks with such grave sincerity that it would require a misanthrope of Olympic-level cynicism to doubt him. The forty-five vignerons of *Écrin* sensed the same thing as Paul Blanc, Lichine and all the others who dealt with him over any length of time. It was the George Washington syndrome: Georges Duboeuf could not tell a lie.

The vignerons believed him, and they believed *in* him, in spite of his youth. His energy and dedication were impressive, he was a straight talker, and he had good ideas: his new bottle, the *pot*, was a beauty, already widely praised by the restaurant trade. In short, everything augured well for the new association when it got under way. That was the theory, anyway. Unfortunately, practice didn't follow theory, and the *Écrin* proved to be a quixotic bust. No sooner had Georges swung his little troop into action than he got that sinking feeling and began to realize what experience ought to have taught him already: each one of the forty-five vignerons was in love with his own wine and expected it to be promoted with the utmost vigor, sold first and in greater quantity than the others. Manager of the operation, Georges took the blame when it didn't happen.

For three exhausting years he plugged along in the three separate functions that he had assumed for himself: selecting his wines batch by batch; bottling them at the property; then trying to sell them equitably, giving each member of the association equal time and attention and paying each producer individually according to the number of his bottles sold. His brainstorm was going nicely, too—by the third year of activity he'd reached the magic plateau of a million bottles of Écrin wine sold. That should have made everybody happy, but it didn't. The multiple, cross-referenced system that Georges had invented was complicated to begin with, but the hurt feelings, the jealousies and the suggestions of favoritism that it generated increased the complications exponentially.

"Vignerons will be vignerons," said Georges with a fatalistic shrug. "They quarreled then the way they quarrel now. Nothing's changed. Everyone wanted to be first. Chiroubles thought I was favoring Morgon, and Morgon didn't like what I was doing for Fleurie. And so on and so on."

Finally it was all too much. The unanticipated fourth function of playing nanny to a querulous pack of Gallic *artistes* of winemaking overwhelmed his patience and gifts for diplomacy. He threw up his hands and resigned. By 1961 the Écrin was finished.

It was time for a serious reappraisal. At age twenty-seven, his worldly advantages were several: a dwelling house and a grime-sided old workshop building with adjacent storage sheds in Romanèche-Thorins, purchased three years earlier for the Écrin; a devoted, industrious wife, baby daughter Fabienne and newborn son Franck; the beat-up Citroën Tube; a fat address book for top-level wines; the Lichine connection; the unanimous respect of Beaujolais and Mâconnais vignerons; and the placement of his wines in an enviably high number of prestigious restaurants throughout France. A nice little niche. A man could live comfortably enough with that.

Circumstances, though, were not shaping up for Georges Duboeuf to remain in a little niche. For one thing, Paul Bocuse had come into his life. The future emperor of French cuisine had not even earned his first Michelin star yet—that was to come in 1962, followed a year later by a second one and then, in 1965, by the third—but it was inevitable that Paul Blanc's grapevine would finally lead Georges to the Lyon suburb of Collonges-au-Mont-d'Or, home of this force of nature seven years his senior and infinitely more schooled by natural inclination in the art of public relations, publicity and the care and handling of the press.

Paul Bocuse had always carried a lot of space around with him: big personality, big aura. Apart from his unsurpassed native talent for the preparation and presentation of food, he also possessed a sunny, sybaritic disposition, prodigious reserves of energy and an easy, unforced charisma. In many ways he was Duboeuf's opposite: a robust, spontaneous, frequently brash extrovert and something of a heller where Georges was careful, meticulous, reserved, reined-in. But each man sensed the uncommon human and professional qualities of the other, and the comradeship that developed between them was virtually instantaneous. Best friends, they would soon be roaming the world together with their wives, on vacations that were partly professional inspection and comparison tours (restaurants, vineyards), partly establishing business contacts and partly the simple pleasures of ground-level ethnology among the mysterious inhabitants in enormous automobiles and wooden houses on the other side of the Atlantic: Bocuse fastidiously peeling a hot dog with his Opinel pocketknife; Duboeuf sticking his learned nose into a glass of foxy New York State wine and keeping a straight face.

Naturally, Bocuse stocked his wine cellar with a range of Duboeuf Beaujolais and maintained it there right through and into his ascension to the gastronomic firmament of three Michelin stars. This was relatively unusual. Many three-star restaurants considered the prestige level (and the profit potential) of the wine of the gamay grape to be below their lofty standards. The old prejudices hang on hard.

Where Bocuse led, others followed. His enthusiastic endorsement spread Duboeuf wines beyond Paul Blanc's network into his own more extensive one, the elite world of France's haute cuisine establishment, then around Europe, and eventually America and Japan, too, because this was a man of singular influence. More and more frequently now, Duboeuf's name was appearing on wine lists of serious restaurants everywhere. Clients liked the prices, liked the look of the elegant oval labels Georges had designed and, most of all, liked what they were drinking. The news got around.

But there was more: it was one thing when Bocuse passed the word to his fellow chefs—the likes of Jean and Pierre Troisgros, Roger Vergé, Michel Guérard, Paul Haeberlin—but quite another when he corralled and oriented the herds of international journalists who flocked to Collonges-au-Mont-d'Or, eager to meet this chef whom everyone was talking about and who, before long, would be known as one of the principal founders of the movement called nouvelle cuisine. Majestic in his brilliant white, floor-length apron, his high starched toque (chef's hat) and his imperial manner, Bocuse force-fed them *poulet en vessie* and *loup en croûte*, poured Brouilly down their throats until they gagged with pleasure, then sent them on to Romanèche-Thorins to meet the man he was already describing as *le roi du Beaujolais* (the king of Beaujolais).

"Formidable!" Paul would exclaim. *"Extraordinaire!"* Off the scriveners went, and for the first time there was an opportunity for them to write about the personality Georges Duboeuf himself and not just the wines he sold. A short exposure to the man made it obvious that Bocuse's recommendation was not a line of bogus goods, but they found it too frustratingly difficult to make good striking copy from this Duboeuf guy. At the time, he was a mere *courtier*, a small operator compared to the major *négociants*, so there was no particular money angle to write about. He wasn't funny and outrageous like Bocuse, so the eccentricity angle didn't work, either. Deprived of easy outs, the press usually fell

back on the wines. Some of the more discerning ones even picked up on an interesting phenomenon lying just over the horizon: the growing popularity of the new wine, the one that the growers called *primeur*. But the real story of Georges Duboeuf—his intelligence, his encyclopedic knowledge of wine, his passionate love for the Beaujolais countryside, his quiet determination, the sense of ethics and esthetics that gripped him, his essential role as advisor to vignerons, his prodigious capacity for work, the almost painful sincerity that drove him—remained largely undiscovered.

When the journalists left, Georges turned back to work, as usual. The more he had, the more new work developed. He began hiring his first personnel well before age thirty—a few warehousemen, drivers and freight handlers, others to man the bottling line—but the specializations were very much open-ended. As often with young enterprises, everyone did a bit of everything, including the boss, and what they didn't know they learned by improvising.

"He took me on even though I didn't have any qualifications," said Jean Bererd, a seventy-five-year-old retired vigneron from Le Perréon who in 1962 became one of Georges' earliest employees after he threw his back out defying gravity as he clung to his winch plow on the steep slopes of the climb up to Vaux-en-Beaujolais. I met Bererd in company with his son Bruno, forty, in the handsome salon-style *caveau* of his house, a few dozen yards behind the church in Le Perréon. As usual—as always with the vignerons of the Beaujolais—one of the first subjects to arise was Duboeuf's legendary capacity for work.

"He was always in the office before anybody else, of course, and stayed much later, too—really an exceptional worker. When the bottling line broke down, we went to see him and he came and fixed it himself—took off his jacket, fixed it, then went back to the office for more paperwork, or out to the vineyards to taste more wine. He was like that all the time. Never stopped.

"He was young, but he was born to lead, not follow. That's why he left the *Écrin*. You could see it immediately—a very big personality. We liked him a lot. He knew how to motivate people without ever raising his voice. Rolande, she did raise her voice sometimes, but she kept on us. She was everywhere. Strong, tough woman. She worked almost as hard as he did."

"Aw, Duboeuf's just a normal guy," cracked Bruno. "He's twice as old as me, so he works twice as hard."

From the very first day of his career—that seminal meeting with Paul Blanc in Thoissey—Georges had recognized a special kinship with restaurant professionals, particularly chefs. Almost unfailingly, the natural complementarity of wine and food was reflected in the relations between the men and women who had built their lives around either discipline; the kitchen and the cellar understood and respected each other immediately and instinctively, without need for the conventional diplomatic niceties and mannerisms that are de rigueur in most sectors of French society. With the Michelin red restaurant guide his indispensable companion as he delivered bottles and took away empties, Georges frequented a good number of the elite of the French culinary establishment and bonded effortlessly with them: fellow artisans on their way up in the world. None of them gave him more work in those early days than Jean Ducloux, owner and chef of the wonderful two-star restaurant Greuze in the riverside city of Tournus, twenty miles north of Mâcon.

He was a case, this Ducloux, an authentic character of the Beaujolais-Burgundy region, a brusque, no-nonsense, hustling entrepreneur of the old school who had been everywhere and done everything in a cooking career that had begun on the day he turned thirteen. He had a voice like a foghorn, a pugnacious in-your-face manner, a command of slang like a French version of a Damon Runyon character, and a jet-black wig covering the pate that had gone bald overnight after he lived through the terror of discovering himself in the middle of the impact zone of an American bombardment of Lyon in 1944. Ducloux had built up a thriving catering business that he ran simultaneously with his very traditional Escoffier-style restaurant, and his specialty was feeding gourmet meals to large—often very large—numbers of diners. Wherever a lot of people wanted to sit down and eat together, Ducloux was prepared to go there and feed them. Equipped with an army surplus field kitchen left over from World War I, a jeep to pull it and a small fleet of accompanying trucks, he led gastronomic caravans that crept at 25 mph through the Burgundy countryside like a circus, trailing fragrances of onion soup, roast veal and snails in garlic, butter and parsley. In young Georges Duboeuf he found his preferred purveyor of wine, because Georges' Beaujolais and Pouilly-Fuissé were authentic gems of the region, reasonably priced and always available. They were always available because Georges never said no to a Ducloux order, even if he had to deliver it himself—which he chose to do rather frequently, because joining Ducloux's circus was like briefly playing hooky from the routine of normal work and entering another reality, one that had a touch of magic to it. There was more than a bit of theater to the lunch and dinner celebrations that Ducloux organized, and the soft-spoken, impassive young wine scout harbored a secret passion—his carefully concealed grasshopper side—for the world of spectacles. In time, he would be doing some serious organizing of them himself.

"Ah, là là," he said, recalling these heroic days of his professional youth. "I did dozens of events with Jean, and it was always an adventure. Once he did a dinner for two thousand people in Montceau-les-Mines. I opened two thousand bottles of Beaujolais that day all by myself, one by one. Jean was an important client for me, and a friend, too. So I took good care of him."

One bottle of wine for each person at the table was just about the minimum in those days. Neither traffic cops, Breathalyzers nor the systematic pursuit of boozy drivers had yet come into practice, and the Renaults, Peugeots, Talbots, Simcas and the ridiculous little 2CV, the Citroën Deux Chevaux, the engineering aberration with the sewing machine engine, the corrugated sheet metal body and baby carriage suspension, rocked and rolled around French highways with an ethylic abandon that would be unthinkable today.

The country was booming in the sixties, the first decade of the great postwar expansion that was to see Paris leading Europe into its future as one of the world's most muscular economic powerhouses. France had been chased out of its North African colonies, had happily passed the hot potato of Vietnam over to the Americans and, under the astonishingly theatrical leadership of Charles de Gaulle, was insistently assuring the world that it had reassumed its rightful place as a great power, exploding an atomic bomb here, then a hydrogen bomb there, building missiles, launching nuclear subs, walking out of NATO in high dudgeon and thumbing its nose simultaneously at Washington and London, all the while gesticulating on the global stage, in the grandiloquent manner that would be imitated half a century later by Kim Jong Il of North Korea. In short, it was a time for thinking big.

Down in Romanèche-Thorins, far removed from the seat of world events, Georges Duboeuf took the cue. He saw opportunity beckon when he learned that Pierre Crozet, the local *négociant*, had decided to put his business up for sale and retire. He decided to go for it. Crozet's operation was only a relatively small-time affair compared to powerful *négociants* like Piat, Mommessin or Thorin, but even so the purchase of a wholesale wine dealership was a heavy investment, vastly more so than anything he had undertaken before, and well beyond the folklore of Beaujolais self-help or the ministrations of Old Man Vermorel. As matters resolved themselves, though, there was a nice little historical pirouette, because the solution he found for raising his seed money did hark back to Vaux and Père Vermorel, after all. Georges knew that he had a trump card in his possession, one that was seriously coveted: his *pot Beaujolais*—his *patented pot Beaujolais*.

The graceful little bottle had shown itself to be extremely popular with his bread-and-butter clients of the restaurant trade, and it was going well in the United States, too, under the Lichine label. It was no secret in the trade that Charles Piat, the most important *négociant* of the Beaujolais, was dying to get his hands on it. Piat was convinced that it had potential for sales of greater scope than either Lichine or the little *courtier* Duboeuf had been achieving, and he had elaborated a plan to market it with a new wine, different from anything else he had done before. Georges got together with Piat, and they struck a deal: for 6 million old francs, he ceded all proprietary rights to the *pot*.

Charles Piat had guessed right. Filled with the wine he named Piat d'Or, an ingratiating, easy to drink, slightly sweet, gold-colored concoction created specifically for the foreign market in this new packaging, the *pot* was hugely successful. Critics and wine sophisticates almost unanimously panned Piat d'Or as a wine, often gracing it with adjectives like "ghastly," but for first-time drinkers its soft, uncomplicated fruitiness was all seduction, and the *pot* went on to sell upward of 35 million bottles a year. The basic white Piat d'Or was later joined by a red variety, and the profits of this marketing coup made a hefty contribution to the erection of a monument to Charles Piat's perspicacity, the new company building that dominated the scenery on the main N. 6 highway just south of Mâcon, a giant, gray, windowless cube that fairly shouted out to passing motorists that Piat was the big dog, number one in the Beaujolais.

Had Piat been able to peer a bit more deeply into the future, though, it is not so certain that he would have made the deal for the *pot*, because there was something of the kiss of death about the transaction. Today the giant gray cube is nothing better than an anonymous warehouse and the Piat company doesn't exist anymore, having been absorbed into an English conglomerate. It is Duboeuf who is number one now. From time to time, he rents space in the warehouse.

The company officially known as Les Vins Georges Duboeuf came into existence in 1964, when Georges changed his status and professional card from *courtier* to *négociant-éleveur*, a fully fledged wholesale dealer, assembler and preparer of wines. In spite of the rather grand title, he was only a minor curiosity within the club of Beaujolais and Burgundy dealers, a niche player specializing in direct sales to the high-end restaurant trade. But the move from independent wine scout to an officially registered dealership at last made Duboeuf respectable, moving the banking establishment to deem his company worthy of being trusted with small-business loans: there would be no more trips to Vaux for raising cash. With his account boosted by an infusion of funds from the Crédit Agricole bank, Georges set about increasing his reach. One of his first acquisitions was a big old Renault truck with opening side panels, recently retired as government surplus after years of service as a traveling X-ray and blood-donor unit. Georges had it cleaned up and fixed up, installed a portable bottling chain in the back, painted it Good Humor Ice Cream white, added his name in big red letters and hitched a white trailer behind it for carrying all the miscellaneous gear that this operation required. With that, he was in possession of the best and most modern mobile equipment for estate-bottling in France.

As much as anything else, it might have been this nifty bottling truck—the red flag—that focused the minds of the region's established dealers. They watched in alarm as Georges branched out from his niche clientele to wine retailers throughout the country, around Europe and finally worldwide, while simultaneously developing an innovative mail-order business. For the previous ten years or so, he had been the polite young man from Chaintré and Romanèche who quietly went about his quiet little business. Now he wasn't playing that game anymore, and he had that lean and hungry look.

"They tried to take away his clients, of course," Papa Bréchard told me with a chuckle. "They made some pretty heavy threats to a few of the vignerons; they sent flyers around and they put pressure on some of the *courtiers* who worked with him, but eventually all that just petered out. Trying to undersell Duboeuf didn't work because Georges wasn't interested in the low end of the market. What the other dealers didn't realize back then was that it was already becoming an honor to sell your wine to Duboeuf, because everyone knew how good he was, and how tough about quality. He only took the best. And he was one of us."

That "one of us" is a mantra that returns again and again in the Beaujolais whenever a visitor takes the trouble to go to the smallholder vignerons and talk with them about their life, their land and their craft. The contrast between their homey little *caveaux* and the palatial tasting rooms and presentation cellars of the big-money Bordeaux châteaux could scarcely be greater, and the personalities invariably follow suit: hands unsullied by physical labor, natty and stylish as an English toff, the typical Bordeaux owner reflects the lofty, world-weary ennui of his wealthy cousins on the other side of the Channel, while the Beaujolais peasant is a pure representative of *la France profonde* — muddy shoes, *bleus de travail* (work overalls) and calloused hands. The fact that Georges Duboeuf had been born to exactly that same world and had sweated at the same vineyard chores raised his prestige among winegrowers far above any status that the *négociant* establishment could hope to achieve. Knowing as well that he tasted wine twice as fast and twice as accurately as anyone else only added to their esteem for him.

"There's an amazing bond of loyalty between him and vignerons," reflected Marcel Laplanche at his vineyard in Blacé, at the limit of Beaujolais-Villages country. "He always takes the trouble to come see them in person, and they respect him for being so difficult about quality. He bargains hard on prices, but he's fair, and there's a tremendous prestige attached to selling to him. What it means is that he's chosen you, you see? When Duboeuf buys your wine, it's the sign that you're in with the best. It's like winning a medal. Sometimes people criticize him, but you know why? They're jealous."

Few winegrowers of the Beaujolais are as intelligent, energetic or articulate as Nicole Descombes Savoye in Villié-Morgon — yet another of those strong, admirable women that the region seems to breed. Blonde, dainty and remarkably attractive, she does not look one bit like a person who spent most of her girlhood at hard physical labor, but such was her destiny as daughter of the late Jean Ernest Descombes, another rare personnage of the Beaujolais, a man renowned as much for his floral, surprisingly delicate Morgon as for the roguish ribaldry of the *caveau* that he lovingly decorated himself. Descombes was one of Georges' earliest discoveries, and from the moment he became a *négociant* he bought Descombes' entire yearly production. Nicole maintains the tradition today and is enormously proud to see Papa's name continuing to feature prominently on the label. She happily admits that both she and the wine she makes are "Duboeufalized."

"Whatever anybody says, it is Georges Duboeuf who made Beaujolais what it is today, and who gave it a worldwide reputation," she proclaimed roundly, popping the cork on a bottle of her delicious 2003 Morgon and pouring me a glass without so much as a by-your-leave. "He is very, very close to the vignerons—he's devoted his life to them. If there's something that isn't quite right with our wines, he lets us know right away. At harvest time when we begin vinifying, I bring samples of the *moût* (must, the young juice turning to wine) to him in Romanèche every day, and I check in with his lab two or three times a day. Georges is always watching over how our wines are developing. Not many people outside the Beaujolais realize how important his advice is for us. Plenty of times he has saved a vigneron's year. He *knows*."

Smiling with filial affection, Nicole surveyed the unmistakably masculine décor of the *caveau* that her father had bequeathed her for receiving visitors—the gravel floor, the lineup of lacquered barrels, each one marked with the name of a *parcelle* of his vineyard, the walls covered with photos of Papa and Grandfather, of Duboeuf, of Bocuse and other great chefs, the pile of naughty business cards with the corny old "happy feet" drawings (his toes pointed down, hers up) that might have drawn an "*ooh, là là*" in the fifties—and conceded that she had asserted her feminine prerogatives firmly enough to have taken down the somewhat more explicitly naughty illustrations with which Jean Ernest had been pleased to decorate his walls. Even with Nicole's editing of the décor, though, every inch of the *caveau* still bespoke a man in love with his trade, his place in the world and the work of his hands. With his daughter, it was no different.

"Look," Nicole went on. "I know wine. At age fourteen my father told me I had to drop out of school and come work with him in the vines. The school director came looking for him, saying I was a good student and that I should continue in school. At the time, my ambition had been to become an airline stewardess—that was very fashionable then—but my father refused. 'She's the only child we have,' he said. 'She has to work with us in the vineyard.' So I did it. I worked between the vines with a pick and a hoe; I grafted the vines, and in the winter I pruned them. When I told Mother my feet were cold, she told me to put straw in my boots. We worked all the time, right through Saturday, when my girlfriends were out having fun. It was hard work. Too much. I vowed I would never marry a vigneron—but that's exactly what I ended up doing.

"With all that experience, though, Monsieur Duboeuf knows my wine better than I do, and he works harder, too. The other day he called me at half past noon. He had just gotten back from Tokyo at 4 A.M. that morning, but he was in the office. There aren't many people who can do that. He's much harder on himself than he is with anyone else. He created his company from nothing, and he runs it like an act of love. It makes him sick to see vignerons in trouble. He gets letters every day asking him if he wants to buy their wine or even their vineyards. He's basically a very straightforward, uncomplicated person who works for the good of the Beaujolais. So, yes, I admit that I'm *Duboeufalisée*. And, yes, I put him on a pedestal. We all do."

Nicole's blue eyes positively flashed defiance, as if daring any person present in flesh or spirit to deny the least syllable of her addition of the Duboeuf qualities. Nor was her tribute all that exceptional: hero worship of the man is pandemic in the Beaujolais. It is a curious and very unusual situation, certainly one that I have never encountered before, not where businessmen are concerned, at any rate. Capitalists anywhere may be respected for the jobs they create, the boost they inject into an economy, the skill with which they manage a company, or their civic actions, but even so they remain basically distant stick figures, more symbolic than real: the boss, the CEO, the owner, the guy who manufactures widgets and rides in a corporate jet. Who ever could feel a direct human bond with a Henry Ford or a Bill Gates? But Duboeuf is a good deal more than just the leading VIP of the region where he was born and raised, because in his person he incorporates and represents the projection of what his fellow citizens like to see as the best qualities and virtues of their microculture. The standing he enjoys in the Beaujolais is more akin to the admiration usually reserved for sports heroes who have led particularly brilliant and unblemished careers, like a Pelé, a Jackie Robinson or a Cal Ripken. It has not yet been demonstrated that Georges Duboeuf can walk on water, but there's more than a hint of Robin Hood in his story. *Il est des nôtres* (he's one of us).

In the forty or so years that I have been frequenting the area, I have met no more than two or three persons between Mâcon and Villefranche, his competitors included, who ever had anything but praise for Duboeuf, and usually of the extravagant sort that Nicole Savoye pronounced. (The reproaches of the rare grousers were so lacking in specifics that it was easy to discount them as examples of envy or simple cussedness, like those salon gourmets who will tell you they had a bad meal at Paul Bocuse's restaurant.) Beyond the limits of the Beaujolais, though, in Paris, Lyon or Lille, plenty of individuals who have never met Georges Duboeuf will express deep suspicions of him. The instinct to pillory anyone at the top of the game seems to be almost engrained in the national character here. That gets Michel Rougier's dander up, but good.

"The French hate success," he spat. "They can't stand it. If someone reaches a certain position, rather than being inspired to emulate him, all they want to do is bring him down to their level. Americans admire success, but the French are jealous of it. They're envious and petty."

As well known as they are for criticizing other nations, the French can do a pretty fine job when they turn it on themselves, too. At this exercise, Rougier was something of an *artiste*. As director of InterBeaujolais, he ran the organization that represents the combined interests of growers and dealers. Born and raised in Lyon, he was a purely urban type who parachuted directly from the world of business to manage the little Beaujolais bureaucracy in Villefranche, and his appearance was about as un-*folklorique* as a wine professional could possibly be: the same earnest manner, rimless glasses, gray suit and conservative tie whether he was arguing with government emissaries, hosting a Beaujolais visit by Hillary Clinton or drinking a *canon* with vignerons in the bowels of a *cave coopérative*. But Rougier's administrative experience and unsentimental eye brought him to some pitiless conclusions to explain the seemingly irresistible rise of young Georges Duboeuf's company.

"Today there are only five *négociants* left in the Beaujolais," he explained. "There were twelve or fifteen of them when I started work here twenty years ago. What happened to the others? I'll tell you what. They went under because the guys used to wrap up their work day at nine o'clock in the morning. They knocked off and went to the local bistro and sat around all day long drinking *canons* and bragging to each other about what great businessmen they were. They were taking it easy. But Duboeuf was working."

There it was again. The work leitmotif returns unfailingly in conversations about Duboeuf, again and again. Sooner or later, it seems, every wine professional in the Beaujolais is confronted in one way or another with Duboeuf's nonstop zeal. Michel Brun got it on his very first day on the job. Brun is an energetic and remarkably good-natured jack-of-all-trades who knocked around Les Vins Georges Duboeuf for more than thirty years in a variety of jobs ranging from bottling technician to sales director, but his original assignment was *chef de chai* (cellar master).

"August 25, 1966," he said. "I'll never forget it. I was supposed to start work at eight in the morning, but since I was new I thought I'd make a good impression by showing up half an hour early. I got there at seven-thirty, but the boss was in his office and he had already unlocked the cellar door. So next day I got there at seven o'clock. Same thing. Next day I tried six-thirty—same thing again. I gave up after that. A man's got to sleep sometime."

A few days on the job were enough for Brun to learn what most winegrowers of the Beaujolais already knew: if you wanted to reach the boss himself, all you had to do was dial the company number at five in the morning. Duboeuf the CEO kept peasant hours.

The wine trade was then entering an odd, hectic and often rather messy period. Simply put, the French had had it too easy for too long. Coasting along for years with little serious competition, growers and dealers became accustomed to selling their wines more or less automatically, and that made plenty of temptation to cut corners. Around Villefranche and Belleville the bistro braggart *négociants* of the sort that Michel Rougier decried could content themselves with buying and bottling the mediocre as well as the good, because sales of Beaujolais were on the rise in France, next door in Switzerland and Germany and across the Channel in the British Isles. Presently they would be ranging out across the pond to America, then in the other direction, on to Japan. Beaujolais appeared to have squared the commercial circle: a first-rate wine that wasn't expensive, wasn't pretentious and didn't seek to intimidate new buyers with a complex pedigree. Even its name was a salesman's dream: euphonious, musical and easy to pronounce, it had a lilt that evoked images of lighthearted fun. Magic: everyone everywhere in the world could enunciate the three syllables of bo-jo-lay. And it was *good*, too.

Or rather, most of it was good. A serious image and quality problem was developing for French wines in general, because in the seventies a wave of scandals swept over the country, implicating not only fly-by-night hustlers but also a few reputable dealers who could not resist the opportunity of repairing bad years and turning a quick profit via the simple expedient of transforming their worst wines, acidic and low in alcohol, by mixing them into batches of cheap, potent *vins médecins* (doctor wines) from the Midi, Sicily, Spain or Algeria. Over the years several documented cases of chicanery appeared in Chablis, Muscadet and Bordeaux, but few were as blatant as the Burgundy dealer who was caught flogging to gullible Americans some sixty-four thousand bottles of *grands crus* (great growths) that were nothing but plonk bought for cheap in other regions and tarted up with sweeteners to appeal to Yankee tastes.

Of course Beaujolais had its doses of cheating, too. At different times, both Duboeuf and Papa Bréchard, the two men most trusted to represent Beaujolais integrity, guardedly told me—"guardedly" because

Left: A café in Vaux-en-Beaujolais, likely photographed in the thirties. Vaux is the real-life town on which the fictional village of Clochemerle was patterned. After mass and lunch on Sundays, vignerons ritually gathered in their local cafés to play *belote*, the traditional *pot* of Beaujolais handily within reach.

Above: Vigneron Jean Demures pours himself a refreshing glass of Beaujolais Nouveau.

Above: René Besson, "Bobosse," *charcutier* to princes and peasants alike, maker of the world's best andouillettes, *saucisson* and *cervelas*, shows off some of his wares next to a Duboeuf Beaujolais Nouveau poster.

Right: Marcel Pariaud, vigneron in Lancié, hitches up Hermine for a trot around town in his old buggy.

Below: A typical church of the
Beaujolais-Mâconnais area

Above: The village churc
of Ville-sur-Jarniou

The famous chapel of the Madonna above Fleurie

This page: Harvest time in Beaujolais, where the grapes are still picked by hand, and where a small army of forty thousand *vendangeurs*, most of them young, arrives every year to labor by day and party by night

Left: Vigneron Guy Dufour of Saint-Julien helps a harvester empty his *hotte* (back basket) into the wagon that will bring the grapes to the macerating vats.

Right: Duboeuf's original bottling truck at the property of François Condemine, the Château de Juliénas

Below: Bottling at the Château de la Chaize at Brouilly

Left: Duboeuf's new vinification plant in Romanèche-Thorins

Right: Duboeuf Beaujolais Nouveau being loaded onto a plane, most likely headed to Tokyo

Below: Barrels of the best *crus*, ageing in new oak in the vast cave under the vinification plant

Above: Huge vats for vinifying
Duboeuf's Moulin-à-Vent

Below: Duboeuf's main
warehouse in Romanèche

Above: Georges and Franck
Duboeuf several years ago at
the Cave Reppelin, posing by a
fermenting vat of Régnié

Right: Georges and his son
Franck toast another
successful year.

D. BARRIER LYON-FRANCE

Above: Georges and
Franck at one of
their ritual twice-
daily tastings, in the
Duboeuf laboratory
in Romanèche

Right: Georges turns
on the sophisticated
aroma-seeking
device he carries on
the front of his face.

COLLECTION DUBOEUF

COLLECTION DUBOEUF

Left: Michel Brun, longtime
assistant to Duboeuf (now
retired), in his costume of the
Compagnons du Beaujolais

Above: Dinner for Duboeuf's top wine suppliers, in Paul Bocuse's world-famous restaurant in the Lyon suburb of Collonges-au-Mont-d'Or. The young woman standing with Bocuse, holding the bottle of Duboeuf Beaujolais, is Georges' daughter Fabienne.

Above: Duboeuf inspecting the ripening grapes in 2005

Right: Duboeuf's Château des Capitans in Juliénas

one doesn't spit in the soup, and they were careful to avoid naming names—of dealers who in the past had obviously imported doctor wines to beef up their sickly local stuff or who had brazenly stuck fantasy Beaujolais labels on the doctor wines without even bothering to mix in a bit of Beaujolais. Crooks will be crooks, and the games were not exclusively French. Duboeuf pointed out that before the UK joined the Common Market there had been little to prevent unscrupulous English entrepreneurs, unbound by European regulations, from brewing up lakes of phony Beaujolais that they hawked at unbeatable bargain prices on their domestic market. Their innocent customers, treating themselves to a glass or two of wine to accompany their baked bean sandwiches and bangers and mash, may well have wondered how it was that so many people could say Beaujolais was such a lovely wine.

There was a particularly painful irony implicit in these swindles. As much as any other factor, it was Duboeuf's tireless scouting for the best batches of wine from the best vignerons that created the burgeoning new popularity of the wines of the Beaujolais, but it was precisely this popularity that allowed the con men to thrive with their mischievous brews. The irony even doubled back on itself: the more Duboeuf demonstrated just how good a high-quality Beaujolais could be, the better would be the chances to sell poor or phony Beaujolais like the English brews that became known as "Château Ipswich."

When an item sells, inevitably more items will appear on the market. Now companies and private entrepreneurs joined growers already in place to make extensive new plantings of vines throughout the French wine regions. In the Beaujolais, acreage under vines eventually rose from about 18,000 to 22,500 hectares. In the enormous winegrowing regions of the Midi and Bordeaux, the increment was vastly greater. Production shot up in consequence, but at the risk of reproducing the same old feast-or-famine story that had bedeviled France's wine industry for centuries. In years when undersupply led to oversupply, prices fell, unsold wine backed up in storage vats needed for the next harvest, and furious vignerons demanded that the government bail them out, all the while keeping their eyes peeled for tank trucks carrying wine from competing Italian or Spanish winemakers. The lucky competitors only had their contents spilled out onto the highway; those who resisted were rewarded with a beating as well.

The mess of the recurrent economic seesaw was compounded by the fact that much of the newly planted vine stock was being raised in poorly suited "grain terrain" where wheat or sugar beet would have been a more rational choice of crop. And whether his vines were rooted in sugar beet soil or perfect old granitic *terroirs*, the typical Beaujolais vigneron always faced the seductive possibility of pushing his yields—*faire pisser la vigne* —above the authorized limits. More wine = more money, and everyone knew that INAO did not have anything like enough inspectors to control who was doing what.

How many of them were doing it, and how high did they go? The subject is delicate. Suspicious by nature, some French critics viewed Beaujolais' popularity and ubiquity as de facto evidence of cheating and made wild pronouncements about the extent of the overrun, condemning anywhere from 10 percent to half of Beaujolais as undrinkable. In any case, it's safe to say that a lot, if not most, of the increased production from the new plantings was mediocre stuff. If the price was right, though, there would always be one dealer or another willing to put it into bottles and unload it on markets where low cost was enough to make it sell—Germany, for instance. Germans are notoriously thrifty, and German intermediaries are so skilled at squeezing prices to the bone that even Wal-Mart, the *Tyrannosaurus rex* of American commerce, was obliged in 2006 to give up its eighty-five stores and slink away back to America with its retail between its legs. German shoppers are both a joy and a despair. There are a lot of them, and they have a lot of money, but they stubbornly tend to seek out bargain prices above other considerations. This was disastrous for the long-term image of Beaujolais, because this tendency filled the shelves of German stores mostly with cut-rate wines that were almost invariably acidic and thin. If this poor stuff was Beaujolais, the local consumers logically concluded, then all Beaujolais was acid and thin.

"There was and there still is too much irregularity in quality," admitted Michel Bosse-Platière, president of the Beaujolais Interprofessional Committee. "The French system is based on controlled, or certified, origin. It's a very good concept, but it's not working—the origin is controlled, all right, but not the quality. The system of *agrément* [tasting and approving wines before authorizing them to go out to market] is out of kilter. Today, only about 1 percent of French wines are refused *agrément*. I'll be frank with you: this is a joke. Why? Because when really good, serious controls are carried out, the percentage of refusals is closer to 10 or 15 percent. So of course all that bad wine perverts the image of the product. For a long time people thought that the AOC system offered them a guarantee of quality, but it doesn't. The result is that we all lose credit with the consumer."

Michel Bettane, author of a guide to French wines and one of the country's top tasters and experts, was rather more succinct when I asked him what he thought about the quality protection offered by the old AOC system. Entirely agreeing with Bosse-Platière's indictment, he felt constrained to add that it was not only foreigners who allowed themselves to be victimized. "The whole French wine industry," he drawled, "should be eternally grateful that we have so many citizens in this country who are patriotic enough to drink *de la merde.*"

So there it was: there will always be a certain amount of shabby stuff in any wine country, noble or peasant, whether from traditional producers or newcomers, and it's up to the buyer to beware. In the Beaujolais, Georges Duboeuf had his own Stakhanovite nose and palate—finicky arbiters carrying out their own *agrément* several hundred times a day—to back up and substitute for INAO's quality control. But of course not everyone had that same level of expertise and dedication, and hardly more than 20 percent of the Beaujolais wine production would ever be sold through Duboeuf's operation. That left plenty of room for the mediocre, the dubious and the fake to slip out into the channels of world commerce.

Clearly, the French wine industry had not yet cleaned up its act when Georges Duboeuf appeared on the scene and rapidly showed himself to be a major new force for innovation. For Michel Brun, the old act will forever be exemplified by the great storage depots at Bercy, the former center of wine commerce on the right bank of the Seine in Paris. Anyone who dealt in wine would always have reason to go to Bercy at one time or another, and for Brun his first visit there was like a vision of vinous apocalypse. "It was so filthy that you had to wear boots to wade through the mud and protect yourself from the rats," he told me. "When I went to work for Duboeuf, I found a place that was so clean I could have eaten off the floor."

The old depots are gone now; grubby old Bercy has been reconverted into one of the most modern business and administrative quarters of Paris, and the wine industry has generally hoisted itself up to a level of hygiene that can almost be compared to Duboeuf's sparkly installations in Romanèche. This greater, industry-wide transformation was not directly Duboeuf's doing, of course, but his nose is as sharp for new ideas and trends as it is for judging wines, and it has always tended to set him at the forefront of anything that is smart, interesting and new. Early in 1970, he came up with the idea that was to define Les Vins Georges Duboeuf for the wine-buying public thereafter, would set the company apart from all others and would go on to exert a considerable and lasting influence on the presentation of wine everywhere in the world: the famous Duboeuf floral labels.

It was quite obvious, really. All it took was someone to think of it, and Duboeuf thought of it. For as long as anyone could remember, wine labels had been boring—businesslike, administrative and boring, offering enough information to fulfill INAO's requirements and little more. About the closest any of them came to fantasy or artistry in layout was to present the domain's name on faux medieval scrolls or parchments. But who ever said they had to be so tiresome? As early as 1967 Georges had been designing labels with floral trim—vines and grape bunches around the edges—but in 1970 his eye caught a bouquet of flowers. The lightbulb lit up over his head.

He was in London for a wine fair, staying in a country hotel in the suburbs, one of those cozy, homey, fluffy places, a touch old-fashioned, that only the English seem to be able to carry off without appearing ridiculous. And there, on a windowside table, was a bouquet of violets, daisies, poppies and blue cornflowers. *Mais voilà!* The idea struck him immediately. Georges bought himself a set of colored pencils and began making some sketches. On his return to Romanèche, he turned his sketches over to a professional illustrator, and within a few months an entirely new genre of wine labels was born, one that has been endlessly copied throughout the world. Eye-catching illustrative labels of every imaginative sort are now commonplace in the wine business, but they all have a common parenthood in that bouquet in Duboeuf's English country hotel.

Ever since his creation as a dynamic teenager of the first private *caveau* in the Beaujolais, it had been obvious that Georges Duboeuf did not intend to remain just one more obscure peasant among others. His STOP — COME IN AND TASTE THE DUBOEUF WINES was the first indication of a native sense of customer relations that would mark every step of his fast-developing career. In travels to the United States and Japan with Bocuse, Georges saw time and again the capital role that advertising, marketing and public relations of all sorts played in the economies. The floral labels were only the latest indication of his ability to project himself beyond his wines into the minds of his future customers.

"*Le bon dieu est bien connu, mais ça n'empêche pas le curé de sonner les cloches,*" Bocuse was always saying. (God is well known, but the pastor still rings the church bells.) Georges heeded his friend well, then went on to undertake some clangorous pulling of the bell rope himself. One of the most striking and effective efforts, also inaugurated in that year 1970, was the first installment of an ongoing series of publications that, taken together, constitute something like a Duboeuf oratorio — praise to his company, certainly, but beyond that to what he loves and cherishes more than anything else: the land, the people and the wines of the Beaujolais. His initial offering, a booklet of fifty-six heavily illustrated pages, was a bit awkward and amateurish compared to the slick professional stuff that would follow in later years, but there was an indubitable ring of sincerity to every page. One by one, Georges presented the region's wines, beginning with ordinary Beaujolais, moving on to Beaujolais-Villages and the *crus* and ending with a final salvo of accolades to Mâcon Blanc and Pouilly-Fuissé. Each wine had its own little illustrated section with photos and text blocks, in prose that was both didactic and sentimental. Pure Duboeuf: the reader had to be edified, seduced and instructed at the same time.

Over the next years Georges would go on to systematize his promotional literature into a regularly scheduled succession of annual publications of considerable expense and sophistication. Choosing a central theme, he hired professional photographers, writers and layout people to produce lavish representations of his wines and the beauties of the Beaujolais. The principal publication was and is always a large, magazine-sized brochure of thirty pages or so, a kind of Beaujolais yearbook on glossy paper, where a profusion of gorgeous color photographs of the region's endlessly varied landscape is backed up with black-and-white historical snapshots and illustrations from centuries past. Four lesser booklets, *La Trinquée*, smaller in size but also heavily illustrated, go out in the mail to his regular customers winter, spring, summer and fall, discreetly accompanied by a price list and order sheet. Georges himself writes the critique of the *millésime*, the year's vintage. He never tells a lie, but he has the wine dealer's indispensable talent for presenting even a lousy year as one whose bottles any self-respecting oenophile needs to order for his cellar right now.

Georges is clearly proud of this literature, and he gives it his closest attention. Unquestionably, the man has an eye. Art director manqué, he spreads print and graphics over such fine-quality paper that one is reluctant to throw them away, in spite of their clear commercial nature. The closest I have ever seen Georges come to boasting was when he told me, with barely disguised satisfaction, that in certain circles his brochures have become collectors' items. Few people would ever be tempted to collect used cardboard boxes, but the cartons in which he ships his wines from Romanèche are so prettily printed—luminous floral motifs on virginal white backgrounds, as classy and tasteful as a Dior wrapping—that the foot stomps them with regret and the hand hesitates to burn them. Duboeuf never leaves you quite alone.

That year 1970 proved to be pivotal in several ways for Georges and for the Beaujolais in general. The harvest had been healthy, and with a wine that was good, frank and straightforward, overall production rose to the nice round figure of a million hectoliters. More significant, though, was the fact that for the first time ever, fully one hundred thousand of these were vinified as *primeur*. Beaujolais Nouveau was taking off. Now it was a hit with Parisians, thanks to those refugee journalists who had spent besotted war years philosophizing in the back rooms of Lyon bars and *bouchons*, and demand was on the rise everywhere else. The progression was telling. In 1955, somewhat less than fifteen thousand hectoliters of *primeur* had left the Beaujolais in November, and most of that had made the traditional ride down the river to Lyon. By 1960 the early wine had become much better known, but even so only forty thousand hectoliters of wine had been sold as Beaujolais Nouveau. Now, with the new decade, the figure had reached a hundred thousand—10 percent of production!—and everyone was wondering if the phenomenon had peaked and might be heading downhill after that.

They needn't have worried. Beaujolais Nouveau was only at the start of an explosive international career, and no one was to accompany that success around the world like Georges Duboeuf.

VIII

LE BEAUJOLAIS NOUVEAU
EST ARRIVÉ

*S*trange thing, fashion. Suddenly entire nations go berserk for a book, a plastic cube, a homely doll or a certain manner of dressing and grooming. Someone tries something a bit new or a bit different, another picks it up, word gets around, a few articles appear and maybe some TV, more hear about it, and the swell gathers. Before you quite know how or why, the famous tipping point arrives: the swell becomes a craze, and a new fashion is born. Say what you will about New York, London or Tokyo, but the hub and the nub of fashion — *la mode, la vogue, le style, le chic* — is and probably always will be Paris, because no one seems to sniff out trends the way the French do. It was in mid-November of 1970 that the trend for drinking Beaujolais, and more specifically the year's new wine, the *primeur*, gained the status of a true fashion in France. The spark that officialized it was a mere slip of paper, a little yellow handbill, or banner, containing just five words: *Le Beaujolais Nouveau Est Arrivé.* The new Beaujolais has arrived.

Suddenly the plate glass windows of cafés all over Paris were plastered with yellow and red stickers, partially obstructing the view through to the bar, where the knots of smokers were arguing above the din of the inevitable pinball machine, that American invention that the French adopted with almost unseemly enthusiasm. In the more high-tone restaurants, small inserts, table tent cards or handwritten addenda appeared on the menus to announce the same happy event. No one knows exactly who coined that simple but oddly compelling little slogan (there are several versions of its paternity), but it was just right, and the Comité Interprofessionnel in Villefranche was happy to print up stickers by the thousands and provide them free with shipments of the new wine.

It was just right because it finally indicated a bit of good news for the cold, wet and disgruntled Parisians. Good news because in Paris everybody was fed up and bad-tempered by mid-November: the long summer vacation was a distant memory, the tans had disappeared, the weather was lousy—the damp, the chill, the slush—and the Christmas holiday was still six weeks away. In America, Thanksgiving can always be counted on to bust up the autumnal blues, but there was nothing like that in Paris, only more rain, more political quarrels and probably more strikes, too. The arrival of the year's new wine on November 15 broke into the routine like a sunburst, offering a change, a diversion and an excuse to push the door of a bar and down a *ballon* of optimism juice. It wasn't a profound wine—it was never meant to be—but it was pleasant, tasty, invigorating and fun, and it could be drunk without delay or afterthought. By the mid-seventies, tasting the new wine had become very much like a social ritual, and there was scarcely an early winter business lunch in Paris that was not washed down with a bottle of *primeur*.

What the Parisians were discovering was what the Lyonnais had always known, of course, and they threw themselves at it with a joy of discovery that looked suspiciously proprietary: our thing. Wine-wise Lyonnais, seeing "their" tradition being kidnapped, grumped that this rapture of possession was excessive and typical of the imperialistic manner of the capital city. What the Lyonnais felt didn't matter, though, because commerce and fashion had taken the game over, and there was an eternal rule in play: if Paris liked something today, the rest of France would like it tomorrow, Europe the day after tomorrow and the whole world right after that.

And that's exactly what happened. Through the next decades, as the vogue for Beaujolais Nouveau rippled out in concentric circles from

Paris and demand grew more insistent everywhere, production of the new wine followed an upward curve to satisfy that demand as naturally as day follows night. By 1975 production of *primeur* had risen to 139,000 hectoliters, by 1982 to 400,000 and 1985 to 516,000—more than half of the region's entire output. By the mid-nineties, more than 60 percent of the entire annual output of the basic Beaujolais crop and half of Beaujolais-Villages was leaving the vinifying sheds as *primeur*. (The difference between normal, traditional Beaujolais and *primeur* is essentially a matter of the time the grapes spend macerating in fermentation vats before being pressed: about four to five days instead of seven to eight. The ten *crus* are not concerned one way or another; by common consent backed by INAO regulations, these bigger, more complex wines are never vinified as *primeur*.)

Over the years since that 1970 benchmark of one hundred thousand hectoliters, Beaujolais Nouveau has gone from the status of little-known but congenial regional curiosity to worldwide smash hit, one of France's best performing export items since the invention of Catherine Deneuve and Brigitte Bardot. Faced with this totally unexpected triumph, the peasant vignerons who made the wine could only wonder at their good fortune, shake their heads and repeat the observation that one anonymous member of their caste had spoken with blunt clarity back in the late sixties: "*Le vin est bu, payé et pissé dans les vingt-quatre heures.*" The wine is drunk, paid for and pissed within twenty-four hours.

The period was unusually propitious for this gratifying situation. The three decades of *les trente glorieuses* were bringing what appeared to be a permanently growing rush of wealth to France and her partners of the European Union; the liberal democracies of the West—big alcohol consumers, all of them—were mostly at peace and eager for novelty; the nascent phenomenon now known as globalization was spreading goods, services and profits with unprecedented speed and ease in every direction; and entire populations were learning to enjoy the superfluous necessities that are the basis of The Good Life. And now they had the money to pay for them, too.

Things came together. In Paris, two smart young journalists named Henri Gault and Christian Millau, working for a now-defunct Parisian daily paper, made a hit with readers by writing lively, often funny and sometimes outrageous restaurant reviews that broke with the solemn, respectful style of traditional critics. They quit the paper, founded their own gastronomic magazine and put out a yearly restaurant guide bearing their own names. Hanging around bright young chefs like Paul Bocuse, Michel Guérard, Alain Chapel and the Troisgros brothers, they invented a slogan that proved to be a pure stroke of promotional genius: nouvelle cuisine, they called the cooking they liked.

What was nouvelle cuisine? No one quite knew, but it influenced— no, it didn't just influence, it *evangelized*—a whole generation of chefs. Creativity was one of its tenets, of course (it always is), along with artistic presentation (huge plates, food arranged as precious little ornaments) and originality (unusual, frequently gimmicky combinations of ingredients), but above all nouvelle cuisine had to be fresh, done at the last minute and light. Light was the most important buzzword of all, because Gault and Millau personally tested as many restaurants as they could, and they were sated with the surfeit of delicacies that ambitious cooks hurled at them. So if nouvelle cuisine was light, it was also fun and it was new—just like the Beaujolais Nouveau that had appeared on the Parisian scene at almost exactly the same moment. They complemented each other perfectly—a match made in heaven. New cuisine and New Beaujolais held hands, liked each other, got gastronomically married and flew around the world in an idyllic commercial honeymoon.

The best part was that it was almost a free ride for the winemakers and distributors—no massive ad campaigns were needed, no expensive promotions and no endorsements from high-priced public figures. The Comité Interprofessionnel in Villefranche rarely faced investments weightier than printing up their red and yellow flyers and equipping the Compagnons du Beaujolais with a few train or plane tickets for ad hoc appearances, along with an adequate supply of bottles, which they got free from the dealers and *caves coopératives* in any case. Unlike

Burgundy's more famous, richer and infinitely more hoity-toity Chevaliers du Tastevin in Beaune, the foot soldiers of the Compagnons were mostly simple vignerons with real vineyard mud on their shoes, who took time off from their chores to promote Beaujolais by making quasiethnographic exhibits of themselves, dressed in their folklore suits: black jacket with wine red buttons, green cellar master's apron, black porkpie hat with green ribbon, and a profusion of pins and logos. Peasant amateurs of street-level showbiz, they appeared singly or in groups at railroad stations, airports, department stores or any other venue guaranteed to attract plenty of passing people, sang their drinking songs, handed out free samples and generally created an atmosphere of country bonhomie that proved to be far more effective than the smooth, professionally smiling hostesses that PR agencies trotted out for most giveaway promotions. And the atmosphere wasn't entirely make-believe, either. The vignerons really did enjoy visiting the big city, and their joviality was unfeigned after a matutinal nip or two of their own goods. Only the most intractably irascible of Parisians could have failed to be cheered by the amiable bucolic spectacle, the free drinks that the Compagnons provided, and the rich, chewy syllables and rolling peasant r's of their pronunciation, deliberately exaggerated for the city slickers. When the vogue of *primeur* really got into gear and the demand spread from Europe to America, Japan and, later, China, a few of the luckier Compagnons got free rides to the faraway places that their forebears of only one generation earlier could never have dreamed of visiting. The tickets cost the Comité Interprofessionnel a few thousand francs or euros, but the outlay was peanuts compared to what a full-blown professional advertising and promotional campaign would have cost.

"People always think that Beaujolais has a huge budget for promotion," said Michel Rougier. "But it's not true. Of all the world's great wines, we're the ones who have done the least marketing for our product. We don't have that kind of money. It was the press that made Beaujolais known throughout the world. We just accompanied the phenomenon. You know, it all comes down to that early release in November—it made a good story. Take away that early release, and there's no Beaujolais Nouveau."

Back in the late seventies, at the height of the *primeur* craze, I briefly met with the export director at Piat, still a bigger, more important dealer than Duboeuf at the time. His tone of bemusement bespoke the breadth of the historical bonanza that had befallen him and the wares he was charged with putting into the commercial circuit. "It just sort of sells automatically," he said, the happy man.

It couldn't go on that way forever, of course, but while the iron was hot it would have been foolish not to strike, and down in Romanèche Georges Duboeuf recognized the trend for the potential world-beater that it was. Now, once again, things came together just right: there was a perfect match between one man's inclinations and the hoops that Mother Nature could be persuaded to jump through in the Beaujolais vineyards. Because that is what all agriculture is about, after all, whether it be soybeans, barley or grapes—hoops. Bending nature to jump the way you want her to go.

From the very beginning of his career Georges had insisted that a certain kind of Beaujolais represented the most true and faithful expression of the gamay grape: a wine that was friendly, candid and unpretentious, fragrant with hints of field flowers and the fruit native to the region: blackberries, cherries, currants, strawberries, raspberries. *Un vin de soif* (a wine of thirst), it was easy to drink, but was also buttressed by a structural bite of acidity, lacking which it would merely be an agreeable but undistinguished alcoholized drink. This was what wine professionals would soon be calling *le goût Duboeuf* (the Duboeuf taste), the one he doggedly sought out in those relentless treks of his to peasant domains and *caves coopératives*. What was most significant for the Beaujolais was this: the Duboeuf taste corresponded perfectly to the qualities of a good *primeur*.

That taste alone—the personal preference—was not enough, however, to shake up the Beaujolais as thoroughly as Georges Duboeuf's arrival on the scene did. There was something else, too, this one rather

more technical. Call it the Duboeuf touch. It was not exactly a professional secret, because the option had been there all along, but rather a
different approach to the genius and potential of the gamay grape, one
that he gradually persuaded many of the region's best winemakers to
share with him. His own experience as vigneron and then *courtier* had
convinced him that the best way to capture the charm of the gamay in
the final product was to vinify quickly and bottle early. When, still young
in the business, he began bottling the *crus* in mid-December—always
starting with Chiroubles, because its vines were the highest in altitude,
closest to the sun and the quickest to ripen—Beaujolais traditionalists
cried heresy and madness. Reigning wisdom dictated that the *crus* had
to have "done their Easter" before they could leave the vats and be im-
prisoned in glass. But it was Duboeuf who best captured the fruit and
the flower of the gamay by rushing his wines into bottles in the prime of
their youth.

If early bottling worked well for the noble *crus*, it was all that much
more suited to the less complex Beaujolais and Beaujolais-Villages,
which were precocious by nature, and it was these that gave birth to
primeur, that extraordinary exception to winemaking's usual rules. When
Georges spotted the Beaujolais Nouveau fashion and correctly guessed
that it had not only not peaked but was set to bloom into a worldwide
phenomenon, he was right in his comfort zone, because he knew that
the new wine would give a foretaste of the later releases of mature, fully
finished Beaujolais, and everything he loved in the gamay would already
be there, in cheery adolescent form. Whenever someone asks Georges
for a description of his ideal Beaujolais he invariably falls back on two
key words, the virtually untranslatable French adjectives *friand* and *espiègle*. Roughly, this means delicious but at the same time roguish and
perky, like a slightly risqué old song by Maurice Chevalier, grinning
rakishly, cap canted down over one eye. *Bonbon anglais*, he will say,
too—English rock candy, the equivalent of American sourballs, meta-
phors for the touch of acidity indispensable to any respectable wine.

As soon as the first juice began flowing from the freshly picked grapes of each new harvest, Georges turned on the sophisticated aroma-seeking device he carried on the front of his face and set off to track down, batch by batch, the wines—or rather the future wines—that nose and palate assured him would develop into *le goût Duboeuf.* Hound dogs have nothing on Duboeuf when he is on the prowl.

"He calls me every morning at six-thirty," Pierre Siraudin explained to me in Saint-Amour. "He knows everyone's cellar vat by vat, and he never forgets them—all the barrels and tuns and vats, every single one. If there's a vat he doesn't like in a cellar, you can't slip it past him. Even if they change the number, he'll find it. No one else can do that. He can't stand it if a vigneron holds anything back from him, even if it's just information—he has to know everything about the cellar, even the vats that aren't for sale. Other dealers make wine to the taste of their clients—more fruit, more tannin and so forth—but he only chooses for *le goût Duboeuf.* Always, always, always. And he is the only one in the Beaujolais who is capable of buying wine after only four or five days, when it is still bubbling in fermentation. He already knows which vats will be the good ones."

Siraudin is something of an exception among Beaujolais vignerons. Although deeply attached to his land—ten hectares of Saint-Amour and eight of Saint Véran—he is not of peasant stock, but rather a bourgeois who inherited a lovely little mansion, *le Château de Saint-Amour,* and did university studies of agronomy. His time with the books may or may not be partly responsible for the quality of his wine, but his stuff is wonderfully delicious. Now a somewhat elderly gent (and coquettish about his age), he received me like a true chatelain—gray suit, conservative tie, knickknack-cluttered sitting room—at ten o'clock on a bright June morning. At precisely 11:00, Madame Siraudin appeared with a frosty bottle of Champagne and poured us all a tingling pre-lunch libation. It was, he explained, part of his regular morning ritual—*"mon péché mignon."* My little treat. The wine business has done well by Pierre Siraudin.

The functional, concrete-walled office where I met with Jean-Pierre Thomas, boss of the Liergues *cave coopérative,* was considerably less elegant than Siraudin's mansion, but the tone of the talk about Duboeuf was exactly the same. Liergues is true, classical Beaujolais territory in the south, and its warm, sandy soil produces an early-ripening grape that is perfect for *primeur*. Duboeuf has been sniffing out its best vats for as long as anyone can remember. Like Siraudin, what impresses Thomas the most is the constancy, the straight, beeline, unvarying constancy, as predictable as the tides.

"Other dealers come here, taste maybe ten vats, and then, as often as not, they choose two wines of completely different character," he said. "And they change from year to year, too. But Georges never varies. He always chooses the same style of wine—elegant, aromatic and perfumed. And he does it fast, fast. Others will hesitate and drag out their choices. Not Duboeuf. He knows what he wants, he gets right to it, and he's adamant about getting just that and nothing else."

Thomas winced with a rueful little smile and went off on a tangent to tell a story on himself about the Duboeuf intransigence. "I've only ever had one run-in with him. It happened in 1985. You know, this is a big place. We've got two hundred different storage vats here. That time, we had picked out thirty of them for him to taste, and he chose twenty. Each one was twenty thousand or thirty thousand liters, so it was a lot of wine. I thought maybe he wouldn't notice if I sold one of the vats—just one—to another buyer. But, sure enough, he noticed when he tasted those twenty samples again back at his place later. All of them corresponded to the quality he wanted—all except one. Well, of course he wanted it back. He was very firm about it. Almost angry. He got his vat back. You can't hide anything from him. He is rigorous, and he imposes that rigor on all of us."

Today, after more than half a century of roaming through the countryside and rummaging in the most obscure little backwater cellars, Georges carries in his head an unparalleled mental map of the Beaujolais vineyards and a minutely detailed assessment of each one's possibilities and performance: who's having a good year, who isn't and why. With each new vintage he updates the assessment, of course, but he knows he can trust this extraordinary memory only so far, so he is careful to back it up with blind tests: each vat he pre-chooses will get six, seven or eight tastings as it evolves, before he makes the final purchase and brings it back to Romanèche.

There is a dismayingly great amount of it. Working as he does with twenty-four *caves coopératives* and four-hundred-plus individual vignernons, he faces a Niagara of samples: every working day without fail he tastes for at least two hours, in company with his two top laboratory technicians. The basic daily slots are 12 noon to 1 P.M. and then 6 to 7 P.M., but this shoots up to considerably more time during the wild, manic few weeks every year when he has to choose fast for his *primeur*—three to four hundred samples to be appraised daily, putting his money and his reputation on the line with each one, because what he chooses will appear later in shops and restaurants with the Duboeuf label. There are few, if any, wine professionals in the world who are capable of holding such a pace with such accuracy. I certainly have not met or heard of any who can do it, but in any case it underlines an essential point of his success: the *goût Duboeuf* is not so much made as *found*.

It was in one of the regular laboratory tasting sessions, in December or January, after the mad *primeur* days had passed, that Georges' erudite nose and palate picked up on a far more egregious diddle than Jean-Pierre Thomas's attempt to do a favor for a friend with one vat out of twenty. It is one of Michel Brun's favorite stories.

"It happened in the mid-eighties. I was tasting with Monsieur Duboeuf at a vigneron's place in the Pierres Dorées (golden stone) area, and there were two vats side by side at the far end of his cellar, each one 7,200 liters. He sampled both of them and chose the vat on the left, shook hands on it, and we left to continue tasting at other domains. Three months later, when the tank truck brought the contents of the vat to Romanèche, he tasted it and said: '*Merde!* They've given us the vat on the right. Get over there quick.'

"I drove down and went straight to the guy's *cave*. When I walked in, there he was—pumping out the vat on the left and transferring it over into the vat on the right." The poor devil was trying to hide the evidence of sin. With that, he lost his position as a Duboeuf supplier.

Georges' gustatory prowess, his memory and his ironclad work ethic made him the undisputed world champion of Beaujolais Nouveau, and he has sold more of it than any other single *négociant*. This has not, however, always conduced to his advantage. In later years, after the Parisian passion of the seventies and eighties had begun to cool and Beaujolais Nouveau was no longer the acme of fashion, it became common to hear critics—a great many of them winemakers from other regions, wracked with jealousy at the insolent success of this despised upstart—dismissing *primeur* with any number of derogatory epithets: half-made wine, fake wine, alcoholized fruit juice. Often the criticisms were worse, sometimes downright slanderous, and the 747s en route to New York, Chicago, Tokyo or Toronto in November, their holds stuffed with new wine, offered an easy whipping boy symbol for cynics and the disenchanted who had adored Beaujolais Nouveau when it was fashionable. In short, they reacted like the Lyonnais of a few years earlier: if the Americans and Japanese were drinking the stuff, it wasn't authentic anymore. It was precisely the same psychological situation as two divas arriving at a reception in the same dress.

The French didn't turn their backs entirely on *primeur*, to be sure, and its annual release continues to be celebrated around the country, but the thrill of discovery and trendiness has now pretty much become quotidian routine. Further, a couple of perfectly senisible rule changes by INAO contributed mightily to destroying the mystique of that traditional old release date. Reasoning that November 15 could in certain years fall on a Sunday, causing all sorts of logistical problems, the institute allowed the far more practical option of the third Thursday in November. The second rule change simplified life for shippers. So long as the Beaujolais Nouveau was not *released* until the third Thursday, INAO decreed, it could be shipped earlier to sealed warehouses and held there until the famous third Thursday. The wine industry's operations were eased, and the new regulations meant that drinkers the world over would be able to pop their bottles of *primeur* on the very same day—but all this commercial utilitarianism seriously sapped the aura of spontaneity, novelty and romance that had been attached to those barrels burping through straws as they coasted down the Saône toward Lyon. Eliminating November 15 was a bit like officially declaring the nonexistence of Santa Claus.

Inevitably, critics of Beaujolais Nouveau carped especially at Duboeuf, because he was the one who had bet most heavily on *primeur* and whose efforts had, far and away, paid off in the most spectacular manner. There could be no doubt that Duboeuf was guilty, because he had chosen those batches of wine, he had blended them, bottled them, packaged them and sold them with whatever marketing blandishments his native talents inspired. Certainly he could take comfort from the fact that his guilt was shared by the millions who lifted a glass of Beaujolais Nouveau every year in all innocence because they found the ritual congenial and the wine tasted good. But wine snobs—especially French wine snobs—tend to get cross with reasoning as straightforward and simple as that. A brooding Beethoven of a wine will always be accorded reverent respect, but a sprightly Vivaldi reaps scorn—doubly so if it is selling well.

Whatever the opinion of the chattering classes, Georges' efforts were rewarded many times over, and the phenomenal success of his Beaujolais Nouveau was the most conspicuous signal that the polite, soft-voiced young man from Chaintré had arrived as a new powerhouse in the French wine business. A few other companies on the national scene were (and today still are) bigger and richer, but none had the flair or the personal prestige of Duboeuf. The secondhand truck with the pumps and filters in the back was soon relegated to the status of museum piece, and a series of enormous modern structures for stocking, bottling and shipping sprang up behind Monsieur Crozet's old headquarters. Pure white with neat red trim, surmounted with the steer's head logo that he had designed years earlier, the new buildings loomed like the statement of an inescapable economic fact: Georges Duboeuf had arrived, and Romanèche-Thorins was Duboeuf City. The artisan was beginning to look very much like an industrialist. For many, this was clearly bad. Today still, large segments of French public opinion, influenced by journalists and other opinion-makers heavily in debt to the vague Marxist noodlings that no amount of reality ever seems to be able to chase from the intellectual discourse here, remain deeply mistrustful of entrepreneurial success in capitalism, while yearning instead for some ideal, mythic socioeconomic system where the country could live in joyous communal fraternity like the comic strip inhabitants of the Gallic village of Astérix and Obélix.

Of course that past perfect never did and never will exist, and Georges' modern installations were in all ways cleaner, more precise and more efficient than the single-family peasant operations to which he had been born himself, but the stigma of success and profit clung to him like a burr. What most critics could not grasp was that in spite of all the impressive logistics of the modern shipping industry—the computers, the pallets and containers, the wine-heavy trailer trucks on the roads and the 747 cargo planes winging to Tokyo and beyond—his Beaujolais Nouveau was not an anonymous industrial product but a real wine with its own personality, one whose birth he had midwifed from first juice to bottling, seeking it out and blending it himself for *le goût Duboeuf.* Clearly, a lot of people around the world agreed with the Duboeuf taste, because in a good year he sold more than 5 million bottles of *primeur.*

Getting that taste was and will always be a matter of the *terroir* first of all, that and the care of the grapes growing on it, but once the grapes are in, everything hinges on the crucial next step: vinification. Turning grape juice into finished wine is a bafflingly complex process, half-science and half-art, one in which an obscure peasant who quit school as a stripling, all instinct and folk wisdom, can easily surpass the best efforts of a battery of technicians and Ph.D. microbiologists. Vinification tricks and manipulations are in constant evolution, but the fundamental idea is simple enough: to bend nature by persuading her to turn the fermenting juice into wine rather than vinegar. The great Louis Pasteur discovered that it was yeasts rather than the hand of God (as most peasants had assumed) that caused fermentation, and that thousands of these micro-organisms occurred naturally on grape skins. But trusting nature to choose exactly the right yeasts from this rich cocktail is a bit like throwing a pack of cards in the air and hoping that the one you want will land faceup and the others facedown. In consequence, winemakers around the world, with the exception of a handful of inveterate risk-takers, prefer to vinify by starting their fermentations by inoculating their must (fermenting grape juice and pulp) with selected yeasts that have been carefully isolated from grape skins, then grown and cloned in oenological laboratories.

Inoculating different yeasts will make different styles of wine, and for a few years in the seventies and eighties many winemakers of the Beaujolais, Duboeuf included, succumbed to the seductive fruitiness produced by the one known in professional circles as 71B, isolated by a researcher in the Narbonne laboratory of INRA, the National Institute of Agronomic Research. There was a curious property to 71B's fruitiness, though. The enzymes it produced caused one particular aroma to stand out prominently: banana. During the 71B years, then, much of the Beaujolais production, especially *primeur*, exhaled a characteristic fruit and floral bouquet dominated by a pleasant but nevertheless strangely anomalous chord of a fruit that had never been seen to grow between Mâcon and Villefranche. The fascination with this quirky little yeast could not last long, and it didn't. You're not likely to find 71B in the Beaujolais today, but the episode underlines a salient point: in winemaking as in everything else, fashions come and go.

The saga of Beaujolais *primeur* had a considerable impact in France and, indeed, around the world, because it signaled the presence of an unsuspected market that could be developed on a far wider scale than anyone had supposed. What had been a tiny niche—those barrels on barges riding the Saône down to Lyon, straws through their bungholes lest they explode—swelled into a new and gloriously profitable commercial opportunity. Eager to exploit that market themselves, other winemakers quickly revised their practices and rushed to get into the act that Duboeuf and his fellow *négociants* of the Beaujolais had pioneered. One of the first to appear was Gaillac Bourru, a fruity, cloudy, tingling and slightly sweet white wine from the southwest near the cathedral city of Albi. It enjoyed a nice little ride on *primeur*'s coattails for a few years in the seventies, but the magic wasn't there. It was strictly a one-glass-at-the-bar drink that could not reasonably accompany a meal, and it soon faded from Parisian bars.

There are other white *primeur* wines that may be sold as of November 15, Muscadet for instance, but the true tradition and romance of the genre corresponds to reds alone. Several newcomers hit the market to join the new red wines of Beaujolais and Beaujolais-Villages. Inevitably the Loire Valley reds of Touraine and Anjou, also produced from the gamay grape, were among them, as were Côtes du Roussillon, Coteaux du Languedoc and Côtes du Ventoux, but the main competition came from the Côtes du Rhône, familiar old neighbor and rival from south of Lyon. Although sales of these me-too wines never approached the stunning success of Beaujolais *primeur* of the glory years, their simple presence on the market underlined how acute Duboeuf's instinct had been. More than anyone else, he taught the world to take a taste of new wine at least once a year. It is surely an exaggeration to say, as Gérard Canard, Michel Rougier's predecessor at InterBeaujolais, did in a paroxysm of admiration few years ago, that Duboeuf "invented" Beaujolais Nouveau (any more than to affirm that Dom Pérignon "invented" Champagne) but in the context of modern commerce Canard was not so far off the mark. The man in Romanèche is the one who imposed his conception of the wine's character and the one who marketed it more intelligently than anyone else. If the arrival of Beaujolais Nouveau is a yearly event to be celebrated in Chicago, Moscow, Beijing and Tokyo, it is mostly because of Georges Duboeuf.

Within a decade of taking his card as a *négociant*, Georges was already a major force of the Beaujolais trade, and his position was improving every day. Bocuse's "King of Beaujolais" label had stuck fast, and the tremendous popularity of *primeur* was elevating him and his wines to a certain level of media stardom. Duboeuf was new, he was different from all the other *négociants*, and his ideas and energy were generating an excitement that revivified the sleepy old tradition-bound trade. A true precursor, he alone among all French wine professionals anticipated the marketing, graphics and packaging of modern commerce, the touches of salesmanship that in later years would be employed with stunning effectiveness—and to French discomfort—by wines from the United States, Latin America, South Africa and the antipodes.

By the beginning of the eighties he had risen to number three among Beaujolais *négociants*, surpassed only by Mommessin and Loron. Within a few years he would be leaving them, too, in his wake, but for the moment he was still referring to his company as a family affair, with Rolande managing the seventy employees (about half the company's size today), their raven-haired, radiantly good-looking daughter Fabienne in charge of public relations, and son Franck still deep in his studies before coming to join Papa in Romanèche two years later. Big brother Roger, the sage, assured an unbroken continuity of ancient family tradition back in the house in Chaintré, while overseeing the Duboeufs' own vines and carrying on as confidant and advisor, the role he had played in Georges' life ever since early childhood. Every Sunday the brothers met, ritually, for an hour of talk. As for Georges' part in the business, he remained what he still is today: the point man, the one who goes out and finds the wine.

I'm not sure whether the planetary popularity of *primeur* had ever been for Duboeuf the divine surprise that it was for the peasant growers and *caves coopératives* in whose vats he systematically tracked the stuff down—after all, he had worked hard for just that purpose. But certainly the boy on the bike with his Pouilly-Fuissé in the saddlebag could never have imagined a future day when his wines would be served in the *Palais de l'Elysée*, the French presidential mansion in Paris, or when he would be riding a supersonic jetliner to New York with Paul Bocuse to further the cause of the greater glory of French wining and dining (a glory that won him the *Légion d'Honneur* along the way), but his years of collaboration with Lichine had given him a good glimpse of the world beyond the Beaujolais and shown him just how far a capacity for selecting superior wines could carry a business. All of this could only add to the exceptionally powerful motivation he was born with. And so, being by nature both perfectionistic and conscientious, the more he worked, the more work he found to do. I have had several occasions over the years to observe Duboeuf at work at different periods of his seasonal routine, but never is this exercise more characteristic than in the crucial September-October-November months when the tasting is the most hectic and he is nailing down his choices of vats of wine to buy.

It's a curious occupation, the hunting and gathering of wine. On the surface, it would appear to be an extraordinarily pleasant way to make a living, in that it entails long rambles through France's most beautiful and scenic vineyards, halts in picturesque stone villages and sincerely warm welcomes in any of the thousands of winegrowers' *caveaux* that proliferate in this nature-blessed landscape. Pleasant and instructive it was for me to tag along behind Georges as he made his rounds, but I certainly could not have lasted more than three or four days at his pace without collapsing in fatigue and despair: too much of everything. The best and most illustrative of these expeditions remains the very first time I went to Romanèche to join him on one of those expeditions. With minor variations, it can stand as the template for any of the years since, because the routine is fixed and unchanging. The adventure began on a chilly mid-October morning in 1981.

Compared to Georges I had it easy, of course. I didn't have to put any money on the line, and I could stop persecuting my mouth with the acidity of young wine whenever I chose. I was lodged that day in the little Hôtel Les Maritonnes in Romanèche, where they made a very nice chicken fricassee with morel mushrooms, and where the frogs' legs were fresh and delicious. I also enjoyed the luxury of sleeping as late as seven-thirty in the morning, because my appointment didn't begin until an hour after that. I was taking my ease at a wrought-iron table under the thick auburn foliage of a plane tree when, at 8:30 precisely, Georges drew up in his gray, mud-spattered Citroën CX Prestige GTI with the high, swaying radio antenna of those years before cell phones.

"*Ça va?*" he asked, one hand on the wheel and the other holding his bulky car phone, and almost before I could utter the ritual *ça va* myself, he crunched out of the gravel courtyard and headed south and then west: direction Beaujeu. Shortly another call came in, and with a nod of his head, Georges indicated that I might help out by shifting gears for him. It seemed like a prudent idea, since once again both his hands were otherwise occupied. Now, as we barreled down the N. 6 at 90 mph (no speed traps or traffic cops in those days, either), I saw he had lodged the tool of his trade next to the hand brake: a large *dégustation* (tasting) glass, shimmering with the purplish patina of a thousand tastings.

"The price doesn't matter," Georges was insisting to a *courtier* at the other end of the line. "Just get me the best." It sounded too good to be true, like some hokey TV ad, but there it was, he actually said it. (And of course the price *did* matter, as it always does in business, but the urgency of his imperative set the uncompromising tone that never leaves him.) He slammed the phone back down on its cradle with a sigh. "Ah, *là là*," he muttered, "this is no way to live. I got four hours of sleep last night and five the night before. You've got to be everywhere at once, because all the others are out there buying, too. You know, a chef gets to do his marketing every day, but we've got to do ours for the whole year right now. So everyone's a little bit tense."

Well, since he brought it up, what about this sleep deprivation? I asked. Two alarms, he said mechanically, choosing to answer the how to rather than the what about. First the wristwatch at 4:30 and then, ten minutes later, just in case, a Japanese electronic clock with a loud voice, across on the other side of the bedroom. After a quick cup of tea—always tea, because coffee blunts the taste buds—he would arrive in the office shortly after 5:00 to fight the piles of papers and make phone calls. But that's of no interest to you, he said, coming back, as he always does, to matters of wine. The 1981 vintage was going to be good—much better than 1979 or 1980, and almost as good as 1978—but it was going to be expensive, because it was a short harvest and everyone had jacked up prices by more than 20 percent. He threw up an arm in a gesture of impotence. The law of supply and demand was implacable, and now everyone wanted good Beaujolais.

Above Beaujeu in the hamlet of Saint Didier, Georges pulled up next to an unprepossessing stone and stucco house behind which stood a much larger, older and lovelier stone barn, roofed with half-round Roman tiles. The master of the domain was Louis Tête, a rival *négociant* but nevertheless good friend. He was eagerly awaiting the arrival of the gray Citröen, because he had set up a *dégustation* of new wines.

Tête, who died in 2004 at a ripe old age—Beaujolais preserves, they always say—was another true regional character. Possessed of, and by, an almost juvenile enthusiasm for wine that belied the fifty-plus years he then was carrying, he was one of the rare professionals who tasted nearly as often and as copiously as Georges—loving it, endlessly repeating it, keeping his nose and taste buds exercised to maintain their acuity. The testimony to this lifelong passion was an iridescent, rubicund complexion, sparse white hair, a portentous tummy carried low and weighty with dignity, and the intelligent, darting eyes of a brain fine-honed by decades of bargaining over prices. He was comfortably dressed in what most people would describe as rags: ancient, baggy corduroys and a tattered, moth-eaten green sweater that the Salvation Army would surely have rejected.

"In Beaujeu they call him Croesus, he's so rich," Georges said, poker-faced, but deliberately loud enough for anyone to hear it. Tête rolled his eyes and sighed.

Leaving the Citröen's door open so he could hear if the phone rang, Georges followed Tête into the barn's beautiful, double-arched stone cellar, where a long plank on sawhorses held twenty-two sample bottles, unidentifiable except by numbers chalked on the plank in front of each. Tête had aligned them with military precision, and a single large tasting glass stood in front of each. This was no fancy *dégustation* for show; everyone would be sharing the same glass in turn. The wine was the color of young raspberries. Several more cases were stacked under the table, to be opened when the first batch had been finished. In all, sixty different samples were to be tried.

"*Voilà, messieurs*, everything's ready," Tête said. "I've told the maid to bring in the sausage and bread."

"Kind of cold, isn't it?" Georges observed, rubbing his hands in the morning chill. He could see his breath. Two *courtiers*, men who scouted wine for both Duboeuf and Tête, waited respectfully for the big guns to start first. Big Gun Tête was eager to get going. Everyone always wanted to see how Duboeuf would react.

"*Goûte!*" Tête roared. Taste! A young woman entered the room carrying a tray laden with a big round loaf of country bread cut into rough chunks, along with a platter of steaming hot garlic sausage. Outside in the yard a rooster crowed.

"*Goûte!*" Tête thundered again. Georges cocked an ear and heard his car phone beeping. He sprinted out to take the call. Tête tapped his foot impatiently.

At length Georges returned and the *dégustation* got under way. He started at the right end of the table, and the immutable professional routine began: the small portion of wine splashed into the glass, the long, thoughtful analysis via the nasal passages, plunged as far as they could go below the rim, the careful sip, the sucking, slurping and chewing, then the few paces to the sawdust-filled bucket to spit it out and move on to the next sample. In scarcely more than a minute the year's work of some unknown producer was judged, undiplomatically and irreversibly.

"*Goût métallique*," Georges said. Metallic taste. Now, as the samples succeeded one another, the room echoed with the watery sibilants and the smacking and clacking of wine entering mouths, being assessed and then departing in admirably precise crimson streams to the sawdust bucket, followed by sotto voce murmurings of judgments being passed. Much opinion was exchanged about *la malo*, the secondary fermentation that may or may not have happened.

"Not my style at all," said Georges, rejecting number two. "Too harsh."

Some minutes later, Tête remarked that he had liked number ten quite a lot. Without a word, Georges pointed to the chalk mark he had already made in front of it.

"*Ooh, là là,*" he exclaimed now, jerking his nose free of a succeeding sample. "This one I won't even taste."

Shortly after that he had an even more dramatic experience. After a dubitative sniff of a sample, he decided to give it a second chance and took a taste. Suddenly his poker face convulsed into a mask of astonished indignation, as if he had been goosed in church. He pumped his forearms up and down, his whole body shuddering with revulsion. In three quick strides he was over to the bucket to rid himself of the execrable intrusion. He spat and re-spat with emphasis, fastidiously wiping his lips with his handkerchief and casting a mournful glance of reproach at Tête.

"*Pas bon, hein?*" asked Tête. Not good, eh? He was enjoying the spectacle.

"*Ah, là là*" Georges replied. "That one makes me cold in the back."

Within less than an hour he had tasted all sixty samples and concluded that the lot were generally mediocre. That was all right—there would be plenty of others. But he was already behind schedule. He grabbed a chunk of bread and a slice of still-warm sausage and hightailed it out to the car. Speeding off southward, he held his hasty breakfast with two fingers of his left hand and steered with the other three. He was expected at the *cave coopérative* in the village of Quincié-en-Beaujolais.

"Last year there was about 10 percent of very good wine," he was saying. "This year, 90 percent is good, and of that 90 percent, 10 percent will be extraordinary. It's a serious wine, more body and character than last year. Some of the ones I've tasted are so intense that you'd think there was pinot in them—powerful, well-constructed stuff—but this isn't my kind of wine. I'm having trouble finding ones that are light and elegant, but yesterday I tasted an extraordinary sample from a vigneron I'd never bought from before. I don't know why it was so good. Maybe he harvested at exactly the right moment. There are so many imponderables, and sometimes you just get lucky. But his wine was extraordinary."

He didn't say *le goût Duboeuf,* but out came the magic adjectives *friand* and *espiègle* again. In Quincié he alighted from the Citroën glass in hand and marched up to greet the *chef de cave.* With his lean frame and resolute gait, his alert brown eyes and purposeful expression, he could have passed for a perfectly reasonable Hollywood cowboy if that were a shootin' arm rather than a *dégustation* glass dangling in his right hand. No fancy stuff here, either: the Quincié storage field was purely utilitarian, a yard of impeccable white gravel punctuated by a series of what appeared to be manhole covers. The *chef de cave* heaved up one of the steel covers, removed a stopper and dipped a yard-long aluminum pipette into the mysterious depths. The silver cylinder emerged glistening with streams of crimson. Georges held out his glass.

"Good," he said, swirling and sniffing. The vat under our feet contained twenty-seven hundred hectoliters of young wine, a subterranean swimming pool of Beaujolais-Villages. "Three weeks ago this was still grapes," Georges said with unconcealed satisfaction. "In five more days they'll bottle it as Beaujolais Nouveau. There's no other place anywhere in the world where you can do wine like that."

He told the *chef de cave* to reserve him 250 hectoliters, took a couple of sample bottles for analysis in his lab (percentage of alcohol, malic acid and volatile acidity, iron, copper and at least a dozen other components) and returned to the road for a long haul south past Villefranche and then westward into the steeply escarped hills of the Pierres Dorées, where the sun, just then glancing through the cloud cover, suddenly illuminated a scattering of villages huddled in clefts among the yellow, amber and russet of the autumnal vine leaves. Houses, walls and church steeples glowed like honey.

"*C'est pas beau, ça?*" Isn't that beautiful? Georges had slowed to a crawl and now gazed amorously over the countryside, unable to restrain his pride and the urgent need to share his feelings. The view was indeed gorgeous, as perfect as a tintype illustration of *la douce France* (sweet France), the soft, rich, benevolent countryside that all the French carry in their hearts as proof and justification of their long centuries of tending, taming and civilizing nature into harmony with mankind's wants and needs. Time and time again on rambles like these, Georges would pull over to contemplate a view, indicate a local curiosity, offer up an anecdote from his childhood or maybe take a picture. The landscape of the Beaujolais exalts him the way the Lake District did Wordsworth or the Vermont woodlands Robert Frost.

But then it was straight back to business. Georges' next appointment was at the *cave coopérative* of Létra, dramatically sited on a hill at the extreme western limit of Beaujolais territory, where the pine forests began over on the other side of the Azergues River. Monsieur Coquard, the co-op's president, incongruously dressed in a blue, white-striped training suit (the trappings of globalization had come to Létra, too), was there in person to greet Duboeuf, and the two men plunged into the obscurity of the winery, Georges with his tasting glass, Monsieur Coquard with his racing stripes.

Their conversation followed the same dual track that it always does with wine professionals: weather and prices. Monsieur Coquard agreed that it was a pity that both Juliénas and Chiroubles had suffered from frost and then explained that it was only *logique*, given the circumstances of the market, that Létra's price would be going up 22 percent that year. Georges replied with a dubious shrug. He was the one who would have to pass on the increase to his customers, and the last thing he wanted was for Beaujolais to become a pricey wine — danger lay in that direction.

This glum speculation was erased by the majestic arrival of Paul Bocuse in his Mercedes 300 TD station wagon. The emperor was in fine form, as usual, and the imperatives of his business — he was off to Tokyo the next day, then on to Hong Kong — called for no time to be wasted. "*Allez, Jojo*," he said. "Let's get to it."

Apart from the wines of his own vineyard, Bocuse was eager to taste the super cuvée, the special selection of Létra Beaujolais that Duboeuf would be choosing for the Japanese market, to be sold under the Paul Bocuse label. From tank to tank they marched for the best part of an hour, each with his own glass, tasting and spitting into the concrete gutter and exchanging scholarly opinions like Jesuits in a cloister.

"The one I liked best is the one all the way over on the right on the second floor," Georges concluded when they had returned to the glass cubicle that served as the *cave's* lab and office. "Now, how about price?"

There ensued the long, painful silence that always leads off bargaining encounters, each party waiting for the other to name a first figure, which naturally will be judged outrageous. No one had yet spoken when an insistent beeping drifted down from the Citroën's open door. "*Merde*," said Georges, and sprinted out to the parking lot.

"He's really equipped, isn't he?" observed the *chef de cave*.

"He's the James Bond of the Beaujolais," said Bocuse.

The meeting finally adjourned without any firm commitment one way or the other, but at least it was clear which wine was the one Duboeuf wanted. Bocuse cruised off to Collonges-au-Mont d'Or to oversee preparations for lunch, which reminded Georges that it was coming up time to have some ourselves. In a country bistro hard by a gushing river we were joined by Patrick Léon, Alexis Lichine's purchasing director. Over salad and steak the two men analyzed pricing trends against the year's yields of the different *crus*. At one point of the conversation Léon named a *courtier* of his acquaintance and wondered whether Georges happened to know him. Negative, but when Léon went on to describe the fellow's behavior at a recent tasting, Georges' face froze in disbelief.

"*Il boit?*" he asked—you mean he *drinks*?

Georges was scandalized. Oh, come on, I said, perhaps a bit too lightly and hastily, surely that's a normal occupational hazard, isn't it? Georges swiftly corrected me. No, he said, that was not tolerable in a professional. Already in deep water, I compounded my faux pas with yet another barbarism: but everyone gets drunk from time to time. He ought to be able to understand that a colleague could occasionally slip from monastic rectitude. Which I followed up with a predictable question, purely rhetorical, I thought: why, you've been drunk a few times yourself, haven't you?

Again that look of disbelief. "No. Of course not."

Never?

"Never."

After that I shut up. Some years later, I experienced a remarkably similar occasion for shutting up when I asked Garry Kasparov, reigning chess champion and strongest player of all time, if he had ever experimented with drugs, as most young people of his age bracket had so liberally done.

"What for?" he shot back, fixing me with the same stony, uncomprehending gaze that Georges had shot at me just then.

I was insistently reminded of both these exchanges in succeeding years as I spent time around Georges in different situations, especially meals and *vins d'honneur*. The *vin d'honneur* is a specifically French institution, practiced at all levels of society and at any occasion that calls for people to gather and "honor" some event, anniversary or person with a glass of wine. Whether it be fine Champagne for a gathering of wealthy bourgeois in Paris or a glass of local plonk from a keg at the annual meeting of the *pétanque* club of an obscure village, the practice is ancient and immutable. Duboeuf is invited to innumerable *vins d'honneur*, of course, and his routine never varies. He accepts the proffered glass, takes a real or a pretend sip, mingles with the crowd, and then discreetly deposits the glass in an opportune corner at an opportune moment. At meals he does drink—I have seen him empty a glass—but it is always in tiny, precautionary sips, savoring each little mouthful. (While diligently avoiding water, of course. One is not Beaujolais for nothing.)

"Wine is for health and pleasure, not drunkenness," he says gravely. Even when admitting the eventuality of a certain inebriation, though, he draws a fine semantic line between the routes of excess that may bring a guilty party to fault. "The whiskey drinker is a drunk; the wine drinker is an alcoholic."

Duboeuf's asceticism, so unlike the cheerfully indulgent nature of most Beaujolais natives, is well known throughout the region, of course, and often earns him monkish or priestly comparisons, but it is generally forgiven as an inherited family trait, like a genetic aberration.

Braced by the lunch, palates cleared by careful doses of mineral water (not too much, though), Duboeuf and Léon moved on to the next scheduled tasting, this one at the *cave coopérative* of Saint-Laurent-d'Oingt, a picture-postcard town in the very heart of the Golden Stone area, halfway between the sublime little villages of Ternand and Oingt, itself hard by the felicitously named hamlet of Paradis. Like Juliénas and Chiroubles, this high-lying district had been badly hurt by the spring frosts, and this year there would be only thirty-one vats to taste, whereas in 1973, a year of superabundance throughout French vineyards and of Saint-Laurent's greatest production, there had been no less than eighty-one of them. No matter: Monsieur Papillon (Butterfly), the co-op's president, assured the visitors that the quality was much better than 1973, and that quantity did not necessarily mean quality. With this undisputable folk wisdom established, Georges and Léon set to work.

They had the tasting room all to themselves. Teeming with tourists in the summer months, the spacious room—picture windows overlooking the vines, neatly aligned tables and a bar constructed of old wine barrels—was deserted except for Monsieur Papillon and a pleasant lady rinsing *dégustation* glasses at the bar. She lugged a sawdust-filled spitting bucket to tableside, and the two friends set to work, jotting their conclusions in notebooks.

"Not bad," said Georges of the first sample. "Possibly a *primeur.*" Léon agreed. Presently Georges was surprised to see that a vat he had disliked a few days earlier now struck him as excellent—the wine had evolved favorably. He upgraded the old mark he had given it. Next to Léon's fine, meticulous handwriting, his notes looked like monkey scribbles. On and on the assessments went. Monsieur Papillon hovered.

"Supple, but murky."

"Bizarre, this one. Very rich. It will keep."

"Good nose, good character. A little bit of tannin."

"Heavy, but opens up well."

"Good nose. Almost like English rock candy. Sweet character."

"Still has some sugar in it. To be tasted again later."

"This one got wet. Rot from harvest storms."

Monsieur Papillon stood stolidly behind them, hands in his pockets, beret screwed tightly down onto his head. His demeanor was impassive, but with this last announcement he betrayed his emotion. "Make us compliments, Monsieur Duboeuf," he implored and then muttered an aside: "He's always so tough."

When it was all over, Georges pronounced Saint-Laurent's production uniformly good, with only a few minor exceptions. Nothing to worry about, he assured Monsieur Papillon. He was still beaming as Georges drove off to pick up the main road northward. Next stop, Fleurie.

"Mint?" asked Léon, taking a package from his pocket and popping one into his mouth. "They're very light."

"*Quelle horreur*," said Georges, making a face. For him, mints or chocolate were every bit as noxious to the taste buds as coffee. What if you get a cold? I asked.

"*Le désastre.* I load myself up with medicine—antibiotics, anything I can lay my hands on. I've got to get cured quick."

The rest of the waning afternoon offered nothing but good news. In Fleurie, every vat of the *cave coopérative* was well balanced and impeccably vinified. Crouched next to the steel cover of yet another swimming pool of wine, Georges tasted and re-tasted with obvious pleasure. The wine was in good hands.

"I'm almost tempted to swallow," he said. No compliment could have been higher.

Nor could the contrast be greater between Fleurie's spacious, modern installation and the next stop in Corcelles, a village south of Romanèche lying in the shadow of a huge, dark, turreted château dating from the eleventh century. The farmhouse/winery where Georges parked had the bedraggled air of centuries of cohabitation between man and beast, both species having reached a relaxed compromise about the importance of neatness. Under inspection by chicken and goat, Georges penetrated into the combination *caveau* and vinification shed, where a thin old man with a cigarette on his lip was tending the eight modest vats that held his production of Beaujolais and Morgon. I recognized Joseph Boulon, "Saint Joseph," the farmer-vigneron I had met three years earlier, tending a sick batch of wine with a glowing space heater. His was a negligible operation in the greater scheme of things—a true micro-production—but Boulon was well known as an instinctive genius of vinification, and Georges had to see what he had come up with.

"*Putain!*" he exclaimed when he tasted. "Damn, that's good! Typical Duboeuf." The young wine exhaled a sweet breath of violets and black currant, and sure enough, out leaped the raspberries and the *bonbon anglais* in the mouth, fresh and lively. It was the best wine he had tasted all day.

"That's worth a Beaujolais-Villages, isn't it," said Boulon, a question that was more like an affirmation. Not demurring, Georges went on to taste the other seven vats. When he had finished, it was clear that Boulon had been touched with oenological grace that year. Georges took virtually his entire production.

"It's spoken, then," he said. "I'll send the paper later."

They shook hands, and Georges hurried back to the office to drop off the day's samples at the lab and make more phone calls. Within an hour the low autumn sun had sunk behind the hills of Moulin-à-Vent and Fleurie, and it was already night when Georges struck out for Régnié, where he knew the Rampon brothers were sitting on a harvest of quality. It was urgent to reach them before any competing dealer might have nailed down their best batches. An enormous orange harvest moon was just beginning to rise over the treetops when he pulled the Citroën into their courtyard. Accompanied by the yapping of a distant mutt, he strode toward the dim light over the doorway to the vinfying and storage shed.

Louis Tête, comradely with Georges like no other dealer, was already there, standing impatiently by the alignment of high, fiberglass-lined concrete vats, *tastevin* cup in his hand. The eldest of the three Rampon brothers scrambled up a ladder, dipped his pipette into the top of the vat, then descended to pour out samples. This was going to be very good wine, Georges and Tête agreed: *sérieux*. The Rampon brothers were pleased with their work, and it showed. When all the vats had been tasted, they knew they had a winner. Now the time had come to talk money. They were not disposed to be as *arrangeant* (easygoing, cooperative) as Joseph Boulon.

"What's your price?" asked Georges.

Silence. No one looked at anyone else. Some studied their feet; others found the ceiling intensely interesting. Finally one of the Rampons spoke.

"*Dites voir?*" What's your offer?

"*Non, non, non.* You're the sellers, not us."

More silence, and considerably longer this time. Finally a few words. Evasive, noncommittal. This was not going to be easy. For nearly an hour the parley drew on, a piece of rustic theater that hesitated between drama and comedy, complete with false exits, protestations of poverty, whispered huddles and even a small masterpiece of feigned outrage punctuated by a Soviet-style walkout by Louis Tête, until at length, at great, laborious length, a price with a little extra tacked on above the going rate was finally accepted with agonizing reluctance—almost adversarial now—by both sides: 1,860 francs for each *pièce* (equivalent of a barrel) of 215 liters. Tight-lipped, all business now, Duboeuf produced a sales agreement, the equivalent of a formal contract, and all parties signed it in triplicate.

"They're hard to deal with," he said in the car on the road back to Romanèche. "Their father didn't used to be that way."

The work out in the field was drawing to a close on a note of exasperation. Things were changing in the Beaujolais, and once again Georges was caught in the web of ambiguities that his own success had largely helped to create. With the rush of prosperity that was flowing into the region, the old days and the old ways were already beginning to fade, and before long the forms in triplicate—a whole world of symbolism lay in the legalese of those documents—would be replacing the customary handshake, artisan to artisan, in every vineyard he visited. Certainly many of the changes were welcome and entirely positive. A decade or so earlier, old-timers like Papa Bréchard could never have imagined the new schoolhouses, municipal tennis courts, gymnasiums and other public facilities that would be coming to the Beaujolais thanks to increased tax revenues derived from all those sales, but the sparkly new equipment would also be paid for with altered attitudes and lifestyle: chillier, faster, choppier, more individualistic and disconnected from tradition. The old village solidarities were eroding as money, cars, consumer goods and television—the great leveler—exercised a surprisingly powerful ascendancy, constantly singing a siren call to consumption, self-interest and acquisitiveness. Georges could hardly criticize self-interest or the profit motive—as a businessman he was deep into its dynamics himself—but even so the loss of the comforting old bonds and human certainties of his youth was regretful. When he was a boy, it had been common for villagers to plan their harvests together and help one another out when extra manpower was needed. If a neighbor was haying and the rumble of an approaching thunderstorm gave an alert, vignerons would spontaneously drop their work in the vines and rush to help get the hay in before the rain. Hard to imagine that today.

Georges dropped me off at the hotel in time for a late dinner. He would grab a bite at home, then head back to the office for more paperwork until close on to midnight. Nothing tempers nostalgia like a heavy workload, especially when that work is bringing present success. And the Beaujolais was enjoying success just then—big time. Those were the days when Michel Brun, Georges' right-hand man and jack of all wine trades, was not afraid to proclaim that *primeur* was "the only food product that is so widely distributed in a single day," and that was probably not too far from the truth, in view of the worldwide infatuation with the new wine and that magic November 15 date.

Duboeuf being Duboeuf, it was inevitable that he would think up something special to do with that date, and he did: he threw a party. The original idea was for a relatively straightforward going away blast—*la Fête du Départ*—to begin on the evening of November 14 and to climax at zero hour of the fifteenth, when the trucks laden with his pretty floral cases of Beaujolais Nouveau would be legally permitted to leave Romanèche and hit the road of commerce, ensuring that the wine would be available in cafés throughout France by breakfast time. Fittingly enough, it was in that pivotal year 1970—the year of his first floral labels, the first time *primeur* production broke through the bar of one hundred thousand hectoliters—that Georges organized the first *Fête du Départ*. He squeezed a hundred or so vignerons, restaurant owners, chefs and journalists into his personal *caveau*, gave them generous tastes of the new wine and a bit of dinner, then led them out at midnight to salute the enormous caterpillar of wine-laden semis as they rumbled off into the night.

But, naturally, Duboeuf couldn't leave it at that. An incurable tinkerer, he was constantly revising, adding, improving. Within a few years the *Fête du Départ* had migrated from his *caveau* to the cavernous confines of his main warehouse and had grown into one of the most lavish and sought-after bashes anywhere in the wine trade. By the nineties it had become an all-day affair for more than eight hundred guests, the Parisians riding in style down to Romanèche in specially chartered first-class cars of the high-speed TGV bullet train, coddled along the way with coffee, croissants and Champagne, and then delivered for a gastronomic lunch at—where else?—the Chapon Fin in Thoissey, the place where Georges had made his first-ever sale of wine to Paul Blanc. Duboeuf doesn't forget friends.

After visits to the massive bottling plant, wine tastings and perhaps a quick zizz back at the hotel, Georges' guests filed back into the warehouse for the main event, a formal sit-down banquet at elegantly laid round tables where vignerons and the cream of French gastronomy—chefs, maîtres d'hôtel, sommeliers, restaurant owners—joined distributors, food industry professionals, journalists, politicians and a scattering of Georges' old friends for a multicourse dinner of astonishingly high quality, catered by Jean-Paul Lacombe, chef and owner of the wonderful restaurant Léon de Lyon in downtown Lyon, possessor of two Michelin stars. (Lacombe also happened to be Georges' son-in-law, having had the excellent idea of marrying Fabienne Duboeuf.)

Lacombe's menus always featured five wines of Georges' selection, beginning with Champagne and moving on to Saint Véran, Beaujolais Nouveau, Moulin-à-Vent and finally a "mystery" wine as a challenge for the guests to identify. Guests rarely left the table hungry or thirsty. A typical menu (this one from 1985) included: pumpkin soup with croutons; Burgundy ham terrine; hare filets *en gelée*; endive salad with walnuts; hot Lyon sausage cooked in red wine; potato salad; duckling terrine with conserved onions; guinea hen with braised cabbage; cheeses from the internationally acclaimed Mère Richard in Lyon; desserts and coffee.

Along the warehouse's back wall was a wide stage equipped with a professional sound system and lighting, where jugglers, singers, dancers and acrobats did their numbers, replicating in the twentieth century the entertainment that medieval lords had provided for their banquet guests hundreds of years earlier, while a magician circulated from table to table picking pockets, removing watches from wrists and pulling large banknotes out of hairdos. Through it all, Georges indulged his secret grasshopper side. MC now, he took over the show, radio mike in hand, to introduce acts, encourage applause and describe the year's growing conditions and the resulting wine.

"He's reserved and he doesn't make much noise, but secretly he's always been *un homme de spectacle*," Michel Brun said. "A showman. It's obvious when you look at his marketing. He loves to organize and preside over these things."

Georges was still wet behind the ears and a beginner to the trade when he had organized his very first event in Romanèche. *La Tasse d'Or* (the Gold Cup) he had named it, and its point was to honor his best winemaker suppliers, with the winner walking away with a gold *tastevin* cup. It was a relatively modest affair, but it was the ancestor of the grandiose *Fête du Départ* in its central purpose: to pay respect to the vignerons. At both the *Tasse d'Or* and the big party, the key to the evening was the moment when Georges called individual growers to the stage for prizes and certificates in reflection of the tasting medals their wines had won in the year. But this was not the end of his tributes. There were also trips to Disney World for vigneron families and, every February, an outing reserved for vignerons alone without intrusion from press, politicians or other such lowlife. It was rather special, this one: an invitation to more than a hundred of his best suppliers to join him in Collonges-au-Mont-d'Or for a three-star meal with his friend Paul Bocuse.

The occasional cynic—the breed isn't lacking in the wine business—might have impugned Duboeuf's sincerity by dismissing these events and recompenses as exercises in public relations and/or paternalism, but the truth of the matter was simpler: they all harked straight back to the little window in Villefranche and the humiliations that the peasant vignerons of the Beaujolais had endured at the hands of the entrenched *négociant* cartel. Georges knew the story all too well, and the very considerable expenses he picked up for these festivities were the best reminder that he had been there himself. The ironies of life had decided that the young vigneron who had begun his career in revolt against *négociants* had become the most powerful *négociant* of all, but he was deadly determined not to abuse that position. The best way he could show that determination was by giving something back.

"*Compliments,*" Georges ritually repeated up on stage at the *Fête du Départ* each time he awarded one of his suppliers a prize, and he meant it, too. When he handed the prize over and shook hands, the essence of the gesture was as much vigneron to vigneron as it was dealer to grower.

IX

THE BEAUJOLAIS NOUVEAU RUN

Now Let Us Praise Drunken Brits

*I*n 1970, Georges' first *Fête du Départ* happened to be snubbed by two worthy Englishmen who had preferred to organize their own dinner with the dignity befitting their status at a private table in the nearby Hotel Maritonnes, where the food was excellent, the ambiance was calm and the Beaujolais was by Duboeuf.

On the menu that evening for Joseph Berkmann and Clement Freud was coq au vin, a rooster stewed, unsurprisingly enough, in Beaujolais. Owner of eight London restaurants at the time, Berkmann also ran his own wine distribution company, was Duboeuf's agent for the UK and wrote a weekly wine column for the London *Sunday Times*. His gallusophagous companion Freud was both a friend and a rival, a man of many talents who at one time or another had been a writer, broadcaster, chef, director of the London Playboy Club and even a respectable member of Parliament. In this instance, he was in Romanèche in his capacity as wine correspondent for the London *Sun*. What neither man could know, as they tied their napkins around their necks that evening and set to destroying the bird that had been sacrificed in their honor, was that they were about to make history.

With all of Duboeuf's energy and marketing talents, neither he nor any highly paid PR genius could have planned or predicted the media event that Berkmann and Freud invented at that meal, helped along as they were with three bottles of Beaujolais wine: one of Beaujolais-Villages, one of Fleurie and one of Moulin-à-Vent, each one more delicious and thirst-inducing than the last. It went on to become the greatest public relations stunt that ever happened to the Beaujolais, one that catapulted its three lilting syllables around the world effortlessly and free of charge. Sometimes things just fall into your lap. It was called the Beaujolais Nouveau Run.

Only the Brits, that admirably odd people, could have given birth to the monument, the *cathedral* of nonsense that these two gents constructed from a tiny spark of an idea, or carried it off with such surrealistic virtuosity. It is such a fetching little chapter of the story of Beaujolais that it would be a pity not to relate a bit of it here.

The best part of the joke is that neither man was a true Brit, not in the usually accepted sense of ancient lineage on the island, at any rate. Berkmann had been born and raised in the Tyrol and Freud was the grandson of a Viennese shrink named Sigmund. But, warmed-over Austrians as they were, both had so thoroughly imbibed of the atmosphere and standards of behavior of their adopted island that they spontaneously came up with an undertaking that possessed to the highest degree every quality that makes an Englishman's heart throb with joy: it was arduous, exotic, expensive, moderately exhibitionist, potentially very dangerous and—best of all—totally futile.

As bottle succeeded bottle that night and as midnight drew nigh, Berkmann and Freud found themselves becoming keener of insight, bolder, more intelligent and more certain of their own virtues and capacities. The germ of an idea took shape; jovial boast became affirmation; affirmation became insistence; and insistence became challenge. The glove was hurled: I can get my cartons of *primeur* to London before you can. Some time after midnight, each man roared away from Romanèche with several cartons of 1970 Beaujolais Nouveau in the back of his car, muttering Central European imprecations

at the other and vowing to write nasty things about his rival's oenological ineptitude.

That year and the next, the race was purely a private affair between
Berkmann and Freud, and both times Berkmann won, not by any ex-
ploits of great speed (both men caught the same morning ferry from
Calais to Dover), but because of Berkmann's superior knowledge of how
to deal with London's rush hour traffic. Little by little, amplified by appropriate tauntings in their respective wine columns, word got around
town that something interesting (that is, arduous, expensive, exhibitionist, dangerous and futile) was going on, and others rushed to join in.

By 1972, it was already serious stuff. Smarting from his two successive defeats, Freud attacked the Run with grim seriousness and a brand-
new Range Rover, which he counted upon to get him to the Channel in
comfort, elegance and high speed, by cross-country with its four-wheel
drive, if need be.

"He cheated, naturally," Berkmann said piously. "He left ten minutes before midnight, but he didn't have a chance, anyway. I had a three-
liter BMW, and I figured out that I could make it up the *autoroute* to
Dunkirk in time for the ferry that left at 4:20 in the morning. So I belted
on up there, passed Freud on the way, and just missed the ferry by a
couple of minutes." (Driving legally, within the 130 kph speed limit of
the *autoroute* system, Berkmann would have spent something like six
hours en route to Dunkirk. As it was, even arriving late for the ferry, he
established an *average* speed of just under 170 kph from Romanèche to
the Channel. This imperialistic attitude toward the French traffic code
was a constant of the New Beaujolais Run in the seventies. It became
impossible only years later, when the gendarmes wised up, got fast chase
cars and decided to crack down an anyone driving more than 130 kph.)

"So I hurried on down to Calais," Berkmann continued, "but at 5
A.M. there was no ferry in sight. Then someone told me about a vegetable ship leaving from Boulogne a little bit later. I drove like mad and just
made it—and Freud was there. He had known about the ship all along,
but of course he had hidden it from me. When I walked into the lounge

he was sitting there telling everybody how he had beaten me. His face fell apart when he saw me. After that, all he had up his sleeve was to give me directions for the wrong turn up to London, but I didn't fall for that. So I won again, in spite of his cheating."

The halo of sanctity was almost visible over Berkmann's head as he recounted tale after tale of the villainy of his rivals and his own irreproachable rectitude. Having attained the supreme consecration of three consecutive victories, he decided to retire the nonexistent cup and voluntarily removed himself from the high-speed category in 1973 in order to "give the Run a bit of class" by covering the route sedately in his new Rolls-Royce and allowing Freud to fight with the newcomers against the chronometer. In 1973 the organization of the Run was in such chaos that no outright winner could be declared, but everything changed the following year when Alan Hall, gossip columnist for the *Sunday Times*, published an article about the race and offered a bottle of Champagne to the first person to bring a bottle of Beaujolais Nouveau to him at his office.

This threw the floodgates open. What had been a semiconfidential competition between rival dealers was suddenly broached to the public and given a precise goal: one bottle of the year's *primeur*, to be delivered to the *Times*, Gray's Inn Road, London WC1, as soon as possible after the stroke of midnight of November 14 to 15. Since Hall didn't specify the means of transportation, it was clear that the winner would be among those dedicated seriously enough to professionalism in inconsequentiality to make the Run not on the French roads but high above them.

Sure enough, the winner of this first "official" race was an enterprising, twenty-eight-year-old Londoner named John Patterson who ran a computerized dating service and who conveniently had opened a wine bar a few hundred yards from Buckingham Palace. Entirely innocent of expertise in the subtleties of Beaujolais procurement beyond the fact that he sold the stuff for a tidy markup in his bar, Patterson simply hopped into his Cessna 310, flew a beeline to the tiny airport at Mâcon, asked the man at the control tower where he could buy a case of *primeur* and took a taxi to the first address indicated. After a relaxed French dinner (he swore he drank only mineral water), he returned to the airport at five to midnight—and there he saw a Piper Navajo, props already turning, into which a crew from the Peter Dominic Wine Club was loading cases of *primeur*. Scorning police, customs and other such normal formalities, Patterson sprinted out to his Cessna with his carton under his arm, taxied away on one engine as he labored to fire up the second one and made an emergency takeoff, heading north-northwest.

For the next two and a half hours the two aircraft were in constant radio contact, lying to each other about their positions. Patterson chose to land at Gatwick, the Dominic crew at Heathrow, and their wheels touched ground at almost exactly the same moment. It was finally the cars that decided the race. Patterson had presciently parked his Mercedes 350 SL in a good getaway position, and motored back to London through fog and rain at 150 kph, leaving a fog light, front license plate and part of a fender at a poorly marked corner. He arrived at the *Times* front entrance just as the luckless Dominic crew was rattling the rear door, which, Hall had assured competitors, would be left open, but wasn't. Patterson persuaded a cleaning lady to let him through and nipped up to Hall's office to be declared winner over the indignant vociferations of his rivals.

Throughout that night and well into the next day, dozens of other contestants straggled in, driving everything from Ferraris to motorcycles to open-top vintage cars. Scarcely anyone in London paid them any attention, but for twenty-four hours or so the racers had been the media darlings of France, reinforcing the unshakeable Gallic conviction that all inhabitants of the British Isles were as mad as hares, spent their entire lives getting drunk and walking about in the rain saying "lovely weather."

The organization in 1975 improved considerably after Hall decreed that there would thenceforth be three categories: aircraft, automobiles and a third one, incomprehensible to anyone but a Brit: "any other form of transport imaginable." Patterson and Berkmann—back in the road race now—were favored in the plane and car classes, and for good reason: both had laid meticulous plans and had greased the right palms. Patterson's new Twin Aztec was a good deal quicker than his Cessna and for the final sprint home he had hired a former police driver with a three-liter BMW and a motorcycle escort out of Heathrow.

"No one even came close," he recalled, savoring his victory. "I made it door to door in two hours and fifty-five minutes."

Berkmann was less lucky. Having covered the route from Romanèche to London innumerable times over years of dedication to drinking, he was determined to show all the contemptible upstarts that no one knew the Run like its inventor and prophet. This time he chose to race in a blood red Jaguar XJS, an even more terrifying automobile than his former three-liter BMW. He knew that there was one absolute requirement: to arrive in Calais in time to catch that 4:20 A.M. ferry. Which was why he had bribed the harbormaster to hold the boat for his arrival.

Berkmann set off from Romanèche that night under a driving rain that offered a visibility only slightly better than zero. Around 2 A.M., his speedometer was registering 225 kph and the tachometer needle was hovering near the 6,500 rpm red line when the trouble happened. A tractor-trailer rig, lumbering along on some anonymous delivery, strayed across the separator line into the *autoroute's* fast lane, all but invisible behind the cloud of mist and spray churned up in its wake. At the instant the truck's taillight sprang out at him from the gloom, Berkmann jerked the wheel over, but he was a second too late. With a ripping crash the truck's protruding bumper sliced open the left half of the Jag's roof, and the car bounced off the trailer's right rear tires, heading for the guardrail. Berkmann was saved only because his car, being English, had right-hand drive: the incision in the roof was exactly where his head would have been in a normal car. Fishtailing and countersteering, he skillfully regained control, but now his car was thoroughly air-conditioned and humidified. He turned the heater up to maximum and plowed on, wondering why he was doing it but doing it even so.

He made the ferry, too, with about five minutes' help from the harbormaster, only to have victory snatched from his hands when the crew suddenly decided to go on strike just as the white cliffs of Dover were coming into view. For the next five hours he sat impotently, buttoned up tight in Folkstone harbor, making useless attempts at further bribes as the other competitors caught up with him. He could only watch in helpless rage as car after car laden with *primeur* was discharged from the other ferry. There and then, he vowed never to engage in the race again, limiting himself to watching over the normal arrivals of wine from Duboeuf, making sure it got delivered on time, and enjoying the profits.

"On the day of release," he told me, "there was more *primeur* in London than there was in Paris. I used to sell twelve thousand cases in the first week alone. If a restaurant didn't get its supply by lunchtime on the fifteenth, I lost a client. The whole bloody town went mad."

"It is difficult to assemble a convincing explanation of why the British should apply themselves so assiduously to a race to get Beaujolais Nouveau," wrote a bemused Hall just before the start of the 1976 campaign, and then he went on to enumerate a new high of three hundred entrants, most of them satisfyingly silly. There was a coach party from Westcliff-on-Sea who, he was certain, would consume their supply of *primeur* long before arriving back in London. There was also, he assured his readers, the entire town of Boston, Lincolnshire. (Which sounded plausible enough until I checked on its population: 35,400. Apparently Westcliff dwellers weren't the only ones into the Beaujolais.) Hall further promised a hot air balloonist, an American health nut who promised to jog up the *autoroute* with a case strapped to his back, a major from the Sandhurst Military Academy and a team from Berkshire called Les Nouveaux Pauvres who proposed to go down and back by hitchhiking.

Sniffing a free publicity bonanza, other non-Brits horned in on the act, making the Run into an international event. Most notable were a Danish Formula One driver who ran a load at top speed from Saint-Amour to the premises of a Copenhagen wine merchant, and a Dutch team promoting Holland cigars by moseying down to the Beaujolais country in a horse-drawn wagon, handing out free smokes along the way.

The foreigners were mere amateurs of absurdity compared to the Brits, though. A team from Milton Keynes invaded first Belgium and then France with a load of British wine called Hambledon. (The Belgian part went all right, but at the French border two hours of palavers and the intervention of a senior French diplomatic official were required to let them through.) Another team, my favorite, whose origins and purpose were obscure, made the Run in a white Bentley Continental with a flashing blue police light mounted on the roof, while wearing gorilla suits.

Most bookmakers gave as pre-race favorites the Ford GT-40 driven by London businessman Robert Horne, but his red, white and blue monster, of the same breed that had won the Le Mans race a few years earlier, shredded a tire near Paris and limped home at half speed. All was not lost, though: the GT-40 team had the distinction of being the only one to present the judges with a case of Beaujolais still piping hot from its proximity to the enormously powerful central engine.

A Ferrari 365 GTC-4 inherited the lead from the crippled Ford and went on to win by catching that famous 4:20 A.M. ferry. The record also showed that four athletes on BMW 900s won the motorcycle class, that the husband-and-wife team of David and Anne Ricketts, flying a pressurized Piper Navajo, finally beat Patterson's airborne record by ninety seconds and that the winning truck was a thirty-two-ton, twelve-liter Seddon-Atkinson with a forty-foot trailer. But the true moral winners (in the nonexistent category of history and decorum) were London businessmen Derek Atkinson and Tony Cattle, who flew to Gatwick, took a train to London and then switched to a coach and four and rolled up to the finish line dressed as Louis XIV and the Duke of Orléans. They were unanimously voted the nonexistent Judges' Cup.

Everyone remembered 1976 as a great year, for the exceptionally hot summer, for the wonderful quality of the Beaujolais, and for the silliness of the racing. Berkmann recalled the story of the truck driver who went AWOL by detouring his wine-laden semi into Paris to engage in some cultural exchange with the ladies of Place Pigalle. Being short of currency to pay his debts to them, he found himself denounced to the police and obliged to spend the night on-site until the banks opened the next morning. His load arrived late, and Berkmann lost a few clients.

Other truckers slipped up differently. Two of Berkmann's crack drivers crashed the buffet that Duboeuf had laid on for press and VIPs, and ate and drank their fill before driving off at midnight. They covered about a kilometer before pulling over to the side of the road and sleeping through the rest of the night. A few years earlier the same scenario had bedeviled Franz Keller, owner of the Schwarzer Adler Inn in the Black Forest town of Oberbergen, whose German drivers arrived three hours behind schedule because of the generosity of Duboeuf's buffet.

"Franz called to bawl me out," Duboeuf recalled. "He was shouting so hard in German and French that I could barely understand what it was all about. He said the delay was a catastrophe that made him lose face."

That great wine year of 1976 proved to be the swan song of the Beaujolais race, *ancien style*, because two things happened to change the picture. First Alan Hall at the *Times* received a visit from a Scotland Yard inspector who crisply informed him that his newspaper articles were tantamount to encouraging racing on Her Majesty's roads, an offense for which both he and the competitors could be liable for severe penalties. Faced with the iron arm of the law, Hall wrote a column amending the rules to turn the race away from pure speed into a rally for the least number of kilometers covered. Second, and even more disastrous for the spirit of competition, the modality for releasing *primeur* was dramatically altered in response to pressure from foreign wholesalers. INAO's new ruling decreed that although *primeur* could not be sold before November 15, it could be shipped anywhere in France as of the twelfth — and to Belgium, Holland, Luxembourg, Sweden, Canada and Japan as well — all of whom offered ironclad guarantees against cheating — and held for release until the fifteenth. The ruling changed the face of the New Beaujolais Run entirely. For the English, it meant that would-be racers had only to pop across the Channel and pick up their stock at a Calais warehouse.

"Who wants to race from Calais to London?" asked Stirling Moss, the great English Formula One driver, who nevertheless signed on a couple of times to do just that, as part of some dealer's PR campaign.

In 1977 the early shipping date rule came into effect, guaranteeing that almost anyone this side of the Solomon Islands could have a glass of *primeur* by lunchtime on the fifteenth. Efficiency was served, but folklore suffered. In 1979 Duboeuf persuaded Air France, Pan American and UTA to serve his *primeur* with inflight meals, and the Comité Interprofessionnel rushed four hundred bottles to the dining room of the Assemblée Nationale in Paris. Three days later they were obliged to supply four hundred more. Lawmaking is thirsty business.

After a pause to think it over, the British resurrected the race by the simple expedient of pretending that the early shipping ruling was not there and, once again, the roads around Romanèche were invaded by a motley army of *Rosbifs* (Roastbeefs), as the English are universally known in France, demanding Beaujolais in loud pidgin French. Off they clattered once again, sometimes on the road and sometimes into neighboring fields, while the natives smiled benevolently and counted their money. In 1981 the long-promised hot air balloon finally materialized when an English aviator named Ian Williams ascended majestically from the village of Saint-Georges-de-Reneins, his wicker basket ballasted with a consignment of *primeur*. As luck had it, the winds were from the north that day, and Williams soared away in the direction of the Mediterranean rather than the Channel, finally putting down north of Lyon to avoid the ignominy of having to deliver his wine to Marseille or Mallorca.

In 1982—not a very good vintage—Duboeuf was offering assorted hot sausages, coq au vin with fresh noodles, cheeses, dessert and the usual five sorts of wine at his send-off banquet, and arranged for racing drivers Jean-Pierre Beltoise and Jacky Ickx to thunder dramatically away from Romanèche. Like balloonist Williams they went only a few kilometers and then came back to the party, but onlookers had enjoyed the spectacle. Action on the international scene was highlighted in Chicago when Mayor Jane Byrne issued an official proclamation declaring the period of November 15 to 22 Beaujolais Nouveau Week. In Germany, a Munich restaurant dramatically brought a load into city center by helicopter, and in Oberbergen Franz Keller finally had his tasting on schedule at eight in the morning.

From a place called Peakirk to a place called Northborough (England, of course), someone delivered a very small load by motorized hang glider, while down in London the Red Devils, the British Army's crack parachute team, spilled out of helicopters hovering over the city and splashed down in the Thames, bottles of *primeur* strapped to their thighs. One of the bottles went astray, tumbled off out of sight and finished its flight a quarter of a mile away, exploding at the feet of Mrs. Susan Weston, a forty-year-old Hampshire lady who had a stall in the Covent Garden Market. *The Guinness Book of Records* thereby missed its first entry for "Death by Falling Beaujolais."

The Run itself, now a rally devoted almost exclusively to vintage cars, was won by Keith Butti, a driver from Brentwood in a 1927 Bugatti Grand Prix racer. With neither mudguards nor headlights to help him along, Butti drove through the night in torrential rain- and hailstorms with two flashlights tied to the front of his vehicle, following the taillights of a fellow competitor. He arrived in London with a heavy cold. I say: jolly good show.

Among the competitors whom Butti defeated were one man in a 1929 Bentley fire engine, one in an armored car and one in a red double-decker London bus. Its navigators carried a survival kit consisting of a French-English dictionary, bars of chocolate, headache pills, a jungle survival book and suntan cream. Another crew, in kilts (wearing nothing underneath, naturally) offered the citizens of Villefranche an impromptu bagpipe concert.

"There's no other nation but the British for this," reflected Stirling Moss, looking back over the history of the Run in the comfort of his souvenir-filled London flat. "Only the English would do something as stupid as this year after year."

Those were wonderful years for the Beaujolais. With *primeur* as the locomotive pulling the rest along with it, the whole world appeared to have had signed on to the habit of drinking the wine of the gamay grape. Sales grew healthily through the eighties, and by 1998 fully 64 percent of normal Beaujolais and 62 percent of Beaujolais-Villages was being vinifed as new wine for November consumption—well over half of the region's entire production.

The party couldn't go on forever, though. Like a favorite song played a few times too many, the Run finally petered out, leaving fond memories and a determination within the British national bosom to go aquesting for other sources of fun: lobbying for tiddlywinks to be accepted as an Olympic sport, for instance, or the baffling pleasures of week-long cricket matches. Meanwhile, North Americans and Latin Americans alike were making more and more wine of better and better quality, Aussies and New Zealanders and South Africans were doing the same, Italians, Spaniards and Eastern Europeans were improving their vineyards and increasing production, the Chinese were rolling up their sleeves, and just about everywhere else in the world where there was plenty of sun and a grudging, rocky soil, investors were either already planting vines or surveying for the best spots to do it. Serious new competition was on the way. The days of easy glory for the Beaujolais had been surprisingly short-lived. Harder times were creeping up.

X

LABOR AND HONOR

A Peasant's Life in the Vines

"*V*oilà," Marcel cried, "you're seeing the birth of wine."

Not many Beaujolais vignerons jump in and trample their grapes anymore, but Marcel Pariaud is a man who likes to do things traditionally, and he vinifies the old way, the same way his father and grandfather did. Decorously dressed in clean shorts and rubber boots, glistening crimson from the mashed grapes massaging his thighs and flowing over his arms, he stood inside his big cylindrical press stomping vigorously while directing a stream of fermenting fruit from a wide flexible tube fed by an Archimedes' screw. Winemakers have many moments in their eternally repeated yearly rituals that might be labeled as crucial, but this one—pressing time—was something like the climax. Now everything was happening at once, and Marcel had only himself and Guillaume, a local lad paid by the hour, to make sure that this, his last batch of Morgon, came out right. Completely hidden from view within the upright oaken vat wherein he was laboring, and similarly stripped to shorts and boots, Guillaume shoveled the mass of grapes that had been macerating there for more than a week up into the mouth of the Archimedes' screw, sending it cascading down to the press below, while Marcel stomped and stomped. The heavy, intoxicating odor of fermentation filled the entire room. Deep red, sweet as a soft drink and treacherously delicious, the juice dripping through the slats at the bottom of the press into the pan below already contained a few degrees of alcohol and bore a name that could not be more fitting: *Paradis*.

The vinifying shed that Marcel had designed and built himself was not exactly a high-tech model of modern efficiency. Certainly he had configured it to be as labor-saving as possible by using the force of gravity from start to finish: outside, an inclined plane led to a high ramp for his tractor, from which he dumped the freshly harvested grapes down to a second level for macerating in vats, then a third for pressing and finally a fourth for storage. Even so, his radically limited budget had always obliged him to use mostly secondhand gear, arranged as best as he could make it. His big, 750-hectoliter oak vats were more than seventy-five years old and looked positively quaint in an era when stainless steel and fiberglass prevailed just about everywhere else, but he had gotten them secondhand at a good price from a co-op in Roanne and, everything considered, was very pleased to have them. The vats absorbed certain ethers that stainless steel could not, he insisted, so modern plants have to use expensive micro-oxygenation systems to do what his wood does naturally. Old equipment and secondhand gear did not bother Marcel in the least. It meant a lot of handwork—shoveling, shifting, pumping, connecting and disconnecting, lugging heavy equipment and loads from one location to another—but so what? He saw nothing wrong with that.

"You know," he said, wine red of leg and arm as he hopped nimbly down from his perch in the press and set to work reconnecting his labyrinth of hoses before clamping the press closed and hitting the switch to set it into action, "there's always a bit of difficulty. Things never go exactly right, but it's not work if things go right all the time, is it? I always want to have some difficulty."

The man is maddening, because there is this about him: he really means it. Nothing, it seems, can defeat the good nature coded into his genes. Whether out harvesting with Choucroute, Zorro and the others, vinifying his grapes with his collection of archaic equipment or snatching a half-consumed chicken leg from the plate of a skinny German youth of his harvesting crew (waste not, want not), his incorrigibly positive attitude exudes such an air of optimism and goodwill that spending a few hours in his presence is enough to make you think that winemaking is a cinch.

It isn't. If a third of the region's vignerons have given up and walked away from their vines since the glory days of the seventies and eighties, if thousands of hectoliters of unsold wine have passed ignominiously to the distillation plants, if reports of suicides are more and more frequent and if several hundred of the Beaujolais yeomanry have petitioned local authorities to go on the dole, it's not because the wine trade is easy. And yet a trade it is, and it can support—even support well—those who are more enterprising and more energetic than the average. Georges Duboeuf built a world-straddling commercial empire without any studies beyond age sixteen, never darkening the door of the least business school; and Marcel Pariaud, who left school at fourteen to help his father in the vines and struck out on his own at sixteen (hired laborer, 8 francs a day, or slightly more than $1.50), rose to become mayor of his village, Lancié, at age twenty-seven, served for twenty-four years straight while tending his vines and making his wine at the same time and finally entered his sixth decade comfortably well off and looking forward to a moderately prosperous retirement. All things being equal, each man had succeeded similarly in his own niche, and it was for the same reason: both were governed by the same qualities of peasant good sense, unbending honesty and an extraordinary capacity for work.

For the public at large Marcel Pariaud is as obscure as Duboeuf is renowned, of course, but they are brothers in the sense that both are cut from the same vigneron cloth and represent the essence of what is the best in the Beaujolais. Fittingly, unsurprisingly, it was Duboeuf who had set me on the trail of Marcel in the first place—go see him, he's a good man. Quality knows quality. Duboeuf has introduced me to dozens of other winemakers over the years, but none of them can stand better than Marcel, I think, as a model for his caste. So for want of space to introduce them all, let his story represent the thousands of smallholder vignerons who make the Beaujolais what it is today.

"We weren't very well off," he explained when I asked him about his childhood in the forties and fifties. "Times weren't easy right after the war, and I can remember the days of bread rationing tickets. But we had a horse, which was more than a lot of other people who still had to do most of their work by hand. I began learning to plow at twelve. In 1958 I got my *certificat d'études*, my grade school diploma. I was fourteen when I came back from school and showed it to my father. With that, he took my book bag and put it away. 'No more school now,' he said. 'Go out and hay the horse.' From that time on, my life was in the vines.

"We had three cows, and in the worst years they were what kept us going. In 1951 and 1953 there were hailstorms, and in 1954 there was a drought. In 1955 the hail hit us again, and in 1957 worms ate most of the grapes. Things started to get better after 1960, but I can tell you we were happy to have the cows. I used to lead them out to graze by the roadside, because there were no real pastures—vines filled up all the available land. Sometimes my father hired himself out to plow with our horse in exchange for permission to graze the cows on other people's land.

"I suppose you could call those hard times, but I don't regret what we went through. Not at all. We had our pleasures, and the slightest little plus made us happy. When it rained, that meant we might find mushrooms, and that meant something like meat for the table. Same thing with the snails we gathered in the fields. Sundays, we took the horse to the Saône with a bottle of worms to fish for perch and catfish, or wheat grains to attract and net carp. Catching a carp was an event, a wonderful thing. It didn't take much to make us happy, you see? We don't have pleasures like that anymore. Today, we have everything too easy, and too much of it."

To an outsider, the Pariauds of Marcel's youth might have appeared as a curious family, but in many ways they were typical of rural France of the forties and fifties, scrambling to get by while mixing politics, economics and social relations with a degree of creative inconsistency that probably would have astounded Anglo-Saxons unfamiliar with the historical and ideological wake trailing behind them. Heirs to the anticlerical passion of the French Revolution and the turbulent rhetoric of the Popular Front in the thirties, Marcel's father and grandfather called themselves Communists, but nevertheless jealously guarded their prerogatives as landowners and private farmers. (Of course under real, Soviet-style communism they would have been expropriated without delay, sent to labor camps and shot if they protested, but in republican France they could safely indulge their political artistry.) Assuming their contradictions even further, the family went to mass every Sunday. The women insisted on that, and there was no gainsaying the women. Marcel's father agreed with them, anyway—religion helped maintain some values, he said. The real tough nut of the family was Grandfather, whose political faith was adamantine. Whatever one's political allegiance, though, the courtly, courteous manner that had always governed social intercourse in the Beaujolais clung on unchanged. Marcel recalled with enormous pleasure the anecdote about his grandfather and the village priest.

"Once the curé happened to pass my grandfather in the street when there were people around to hear the exchange. The curé said bonjour. 'I am obliged to greet you properly because I am a polite man,' my grandfather said. 'So bonjour. But since I am against the Church, please do not greet me anymore when we meet. That way, I won't have to do it again.'"

From age sixteen to twenty, Marcel was on his own as a day laborer, living at home in Lancié with his four brothers and sisters, working half the day for his father on the little 2.75-hectare family plot and the other half for a neighboring vigneron. Whenever he had a day or just a few hours free, he picked up extra pocket money by taking on jobs as a mason and helping with harvests. Strong guy—at age seventeen he was already measuring himself against the big men of the village, hefting 250-pound wheat sacks. Even as he labored, though, the lure of travel was upon him, and he dreamed of passing the test for the license to become a truck driver. He carried the dream with him when he was drafted for his two years of military service, but it ended when his father died, just after his return to civilian life. Sometimes fate makes the right choices: just as the world lost one more sports trainer and gained a uniquely talented selector and propagator of wine when young Georges Duboeuf got fed up with the Paris rush hour mob scene, it got a top-notch winemaker in place of just another truck driver when Marcel's father died.

As the oldest of the children, it was his duty to assume command of the farm and the vines and provide for the family. He was twenty-two and charged with energy and ambition when he took over the family plot. He contracted to tend a neighbor's vines and took on some added acreage in *vigneronnage* rental terms, some in Lancié's Beaujolais-Villages territory, some over in Morgon. All told, he was working twelve hectares, using the family horse and one other that he rented at 50 cents a day. It was an exceedingly heavy load, but Marcel was already something of a specialist in heavy loads. By any scale of cosmic justice he ought to have been handsomely rewarded for his courage and sweat, but when the west wind sweeps in from the Loire Valley laden with humidity picked up over the big river, hits the chill of the air high above the Beaujolais hills, then comes whistling down through the gaps, wildly unpredictable things can happen to the weather.

"May 4, 1966. Ascension Thursday," Marcel remembered. "Hail shredded the vines. Then in September, hail again. Harvest was set for September 15, and the hail hit us on the thirteenth. We got the total treatment. On the fourteenth, I picked up from the ground what grapes had survived the May storm. After I pressed them, I got a yield of six hectoliters per hectare, and the wine tasted of earth. Next year it froze. Those two years didn't make life easy for me. But I'm *combatif.* I'm a fighter."

Six hectoliters of wine, and earthy wine at that, when the normal yield at the time was seventy or eighty hectoliters—this was pathetic, derisory. Standing in his destroyed vineyard, it would have been easy, even understandable, for a man less resolute than he to give in to despair, but Marcel carried on. Those were the days when he tested to the limit the strength that his genes had provided him, because what he had undertaken was in fact a triple workload. At the same time as he tended his own and his neighbor's vines, he was building his *cuverie*, his vinifying and storage shed. He rose before first light, slipped his feet into his comfortable old birch wooden shoes, plowed, pruned, tied and treated his vines from 4 A.M. to 7, then did ten straight hours of masonry, putting the *cuverie* together block by block. After that, it was back to the vines, and finally to bed at about eleven, when there was no more light to work by.

"That's all right," he said with that ineradicably hearty earnestness of his. "I don't regret it. It's when you have difficulties that you make progress in life. I never was a big sleeper, anyway. Three or four hours were enough for me at that age. That allowed me to get a lot of work done. And it wasn't all that hard, anyway. I could take my time. I had my lunch with me out in the vines, and my flask of wine. I had a little snooze after eating. The only problem was that the work took up all my time. I love nature, but I've never been able to stroll around and just enjoy it. No sport, either — too much to do. I would have liked to try doing something with music, but the closest I got to that was in the army, when they made me a bugler."

Marcel is sleeping more these days. Now that he is in semi-retirement, he admits that he lies sluggishly abed until five in the morning. (There's another parallel with Duboeuf here. Georges told me the other day that after passing his seventieth birthday he began slowing down, because he slept all the way to 4:30 A.M. instead of the 4:15 that for decades had been his normal wakeup time.)

Marcel got his first tractor in 1967 — secondhand, of course, or perhaps thirdhand — but never felt entirely comfortable with its diesel clatter, the oil it leaked onto the ground or the suffocating smoke from the exhaust, as if somehow these signified that he was cheating on nature. "You've got to learn how to listen to nature, because she rewards those who love her," he says, virtually apologizing for the chemical treatments he parsimoniously applies to his vines and the minimal doses of SO_2 he injects into his wines to disinfect them and prevent them from clouding over, turning and becoming unsellable. An innate ethical sense—the rightful balance in all things—nags at him, and he cannot quite chase away the conviction that somehow it has to be better to do his plowing behind a horse, the way he used to do. And besides, he sincerely enjoys the partnership between man, beast and nature. So strong are that conviction and that enjoyment that he has not been able to entirely renounce the old ways. Which is why he keeps Hermine.

Hermine is Marcel's mistress, his joy and passion. She has soft brown eyes, a comely shock of black bangs, a pleasant disposition, a white flare on her forehead and weighs approximately fifteen hundred pounds. She is a *comtoise*, a workhorse whose ancestors originated in the Jura Mountains, from crossings between local animals and German stock from across the border. Marcel reserves her efforts for the small family plot of Beaujolais-Villages vines next to the house, the old vines that give the finest wine. Marcel admires Hermine and loves her dearly, but the partnership has its command structure, and he is not duped by her capricious ways, for she is a real Marie Antoinette.

"She's intelligent, but she's lazy," he said, laughing again and again as he told of their partnership. "She has a nice life out in the pasture I keep for her, you see, so she'd rather not work. The first time I hitched her up to the plow, she did very good work—very delicate, very careful— for a few rows. She understood exactly what she was supposed to do. Then, after a few more minutes, she decided that was enough, and she lay down. She lay down! Well, I made her get up and get going again. If you let them get away with something like that, it's finished.

"I know these animals. I had another experience like that a long time ago, when I was working for our neighbor, Monsieur Besson. He had a big Percheron, and one day he ran away when he wasn't hitched up. I had to go out after him on my motorbike. When I finally got to him, I swatted him good and hard. Marcel, that's no way to get him to cooperate with you, someone said, but I said: just you watch. I gave the horse a piece of bread from my lunch, and I spoke to him about the situation. 'I'm the boss,' I told him, 'and that's how it had to be.' I love horses, but you have to show them who's in charge. He understood. I was the only guy who could work with that Percheron."

The spectacle of Marcel plowing with Hermine is now part of the local color around Lancié and Romanèche, rare enough and colorful enough to draw an occasional article and photo in the local press, but the exercise isn't necessarily to everyone's liking. For one, it prodigiously irritates Paulo Cinquin. Very interesting man, this Cinquin. He makes wonderfully good wine from his vines in Régnié (Duboeuf is one of his customers), and is a self-taught specialist of grafting who grows and sells young plants to the trade. He is so concerned to get his vinifying right that at harvest time every year he sleeps on a cot in his *cuverie* during the first week or so, keeping an hour-by-hour watch over the baby wine developing in his vats. Cinquin is a perfectionist, then, but a thoroughly modern perfectionist, a man who embraces all the up-to-date techniques that can help Beaujolais wines to compete in the increasingly tight world marketplace. Which is why seeing Marcel plowing with Hermine really gets to him.

"He shouldn't do that, Marcel. He can work his vines that way because he's lucky—he's strong as a horse himself. But he's giving people the wrong idea. That's not how wine is made anymore. If you give people the idea that you have to use horses to make good wine, then everyone's going to leave the trade. I started with a horse, too, but I'm not going back to it. What Marcel is doing is just folklore for the press."

Jean-Pierre Labruyère, president of the Moulin-à-Vent winegrowers union, emphatically shared Cinquin's feelings about the old ways versus the new. Rich, well connected and quite influential in French political and economic circles, Labruyère inherited family vines in Moulin-à-Vent, but you won't find any dirt under his fingernails. About as far removed from the peasantry as wealth, bespoke suits and the signature Parisian manner can make a man, he has wide holdings in supermarkets and food distribution, owns vineyards in Bordeaux and California, is thoroughly accustomed to commanding and shows little patience with romantic notions or sentimentalism in the face of the hard-edged realities of commerce. At a quick business lunch shared with the mayor of Mâcon, he made a vibrant apologia for modern chemical treatment of vines and dismissed the return of grassy bands to the vineyards—and indeed, the entire movement toward organic agriculture in winemaking—as nothing better than a passing fashion. There was an edge of disdain in his voice when he delivered his verdict: "It's like short or long skirts for women. I'm not at all convinced that the quality of bio wines is any better than those made with chemical treatments. But grass is good for the image—*c'est une mode.*"

So much for Marcel, his bands of grass, his horse and his compunctions about using too much chemistry. In reality, though, he is the least fashion-conscious of men, and far from being a Luddite, he has used machinery all his professional life, so whatever the tough guys and the economic swaggerers may think, he is not attempting to turn back the clock or to suggest that vignerons should give up their tractors and treatments. It is simply that working with Hermine makes him feel good, and he can't avoid the suspicion that the wine they make together is a little bit better, too. But his hand on the plow behind his horse is irritating, because it is a reminder that there is another way, slower and harder though it may be. If his fellow winemakers see that as a kind of reproach, that's their problem. The nub of the issue is starkly simple: mechanization is faster and easier, and, like the chemical industry, it is here to stay. And even if they were interested in trying a different approach, the vast majority of the younger generation of vignerons, the Beaujolais baby boomers, have never even touched a handheld plow. They're tractor jockeys now, and plowing and treating the vines with a horse would be as mysterious to them as saddling a unicorn. Marcel and Hermine are true anachronisms, then, but there's nothing fake or insincere about their relationship. Nor, he insists, is working the vines with a horse all that difficult or impractical, even in the twenty-first century.

"It's free energy," he cried. "If I had a son, the two of us could handle fifteen hectares with two horses. I've even offered to teach some of the young local vignerons to work with horses, but they're not interested. I think it's a shame to lose these old techniques."

Marcel is far too good-natured to feel sorry for himself, but his single regret is his lack of offspring. His first marriage, in 1970, was childless and ended in divorce. When he remarried in 2004, it was too late for children. In between there were a few wild oats to be sown, but he was occupied mostly with work. The already generous helping that he had on his plate increased in 1971, when the town council voted him mayor of Lancié. This was an honor for a young man of only twenty-seven, of course, but the honor came at a price, because there was and is a central fact about French small-town politics: in exchange for the exalted title and the tricolor sash, the mayor is the one who is expected to do most of the work and to take all the criticisms. That Marcel was able to hang on in the office for twenty-four years was testimony not only to his capacity for work but his patience, too—and his firmness in enforcing the rules.

"They used to call me The Sheriff when I was mayor. I made some enemies. That didn't always make life simple, either."

It was during this long period of involvement in local politics that Marcel enjoyed a brief moment of fame, as the result of his one and only experience of competitive sport. In 1985 for a lark he accepted an invitation to join a Bordeaux-to-Paris bicycle race of French mayors. Never in his life had he participated in any such race before, and he was totally ignorant of specific training and racing technique, but he was strong, he was determined, and he knew how to pump the pedals. Faced with a pack of fancy city gents on fancy bikes, the Beaujolais peasant put his head down and worked—first and last race ever, and he won it—French national champion of mayors at age forty. The 615 kilometers were to be covered within a twenty-four-hour period, and he came in first: twenty-one hours.

By then, he had already developed his own very particular commercial style, building a customer base by direct individual contact. Quite apart from the high quality of his wines, his affable nature, his perpetual good humor and his willingness to go the extra mile—quite literally—built him an extraordinarily loyal clientele, because he offered an additional service: he delivered. Marcel finally got his long-awaited truck driver's license when he bought a secondhand tractor-trailer rig big enough to stash as many cartons of wine as he needed for his customers, anywhere in the country. Customers led to other customers, and at any time of the year his old white truck might have been seen rumbling over the back roads (by principle he avoided expensive toll roads—a penny saved is a penny earned) from Brittany to Alsace, Normandy, Picardy or wherever else anyone wanted the wines he was selling. Marcel the wanderer kept long, frugal hours, sleeping in the truck, eating his sandwiches in the cabin and dropping off his orders at any time of day or night because, on the road as at home, he never slept much. Over the years, clients accustomed themselves to his unpredictable hours and unorthodox delivery system: cases of Beaujolais delivered to their doorstep at three or four in the morning with the bill on top, to be paid at their leisure.

Marcel was Marcel. That was just how he did things. In Brittany he sponsored uniforms for a local soccer team by offering the players T-shirts emblazoned with a fetching slogan: MARCEL PARIAUD EN BEAU-JOLAIS. It was a clever little bit of marketing, because the simple word "Beaujolais" could have been construed as an incitement to drinking, and thereby fallen afoul of France's draconian laws against publicity for alcohol. His simple identity, on the other hand, could hardly be contested. The T-shirts weren't nearly as sumptuous as a first-class trip on the TGV or a three-star dinner with Paul Bocuse, but small-town athletes in the middle of nowhere in Brittany were glad to have them, and word got around that Marcel was a good man who sold good wine. And he was accommodating, too. If for some reason his wine didn't live up to expectations, he might push his service-oriented commercial approach to the point of offering something entirely novel in the wine business: a take-back guarantee. One evening, as we were sampling different years of his Morgon and Beaujolais in his *caveau*, he told me about a customer in Saint Brieuc.

"He hadn't paid me for the cartons of 1995 that he had ordered," he explained, "and I couldn't understand why. When I came by to see him the next year, he said the wine had a strange taste. Well, it turned out that he had stored the cartons next to a radiator in his kid's room. Never mind, I said, I'll take it back and give you some others. I'm happy I did it, too, because after I put those cartons in proper storage, they came right back. They're perfect now. I'm still drinking them."

Seeking to accommodate his clientele further, he extended his reach by registering as a *négociant* after some of his customers asked him to bring both Beaujolais and wines from outside the region. Sure, no problem. His was a decidedly small-time operation compared to Duboeuf, Jadot and the others, but it turned a tidy little profit, and he was beginning to feel like a real capitalist when disaster struck in 1994. It arrived in the form of two bailiffs rapping smartly on his front door. They had come on behalf of a couple of banks, they explained, to seize his furniture, his bed and anything else of commercial value they could find, including his wine business.

Marcel had been too accommodating, it turned out—not just once but twice. Two friends had asked him to stand as guarantor for loans they were negotiating. The first was his banker, who wanted to retire and open a bar in Marseille. Who would not back a loan to his own banker? Marcel signed. The other, a local man, planned to set up a bottle-washing business serving the wine industry. He already owed Marcel 125,000 francs, so that sum could be put toward a share in the new business. Marcel signed for him, too. Bad luck: both men went bust. Finding the beneficiaries of those loans insolvent, the banks behaved as banks do, and turned against the guarantor. Nothing personal, you understand, the bailiffs explained. You can demand the money from the friends you signed for. That was no comfort, and there was no way out—a signature was a signature. Over the next seven years, laying out increments month by month, Marcel paid back his friends' debts: somewhat more than $400,000 in capital and interest.

"I learned the hard way how business works," he said, smiling ruefully. "But I left this affair with my head held high and my honor intact."

My honor. It is difficult to overstate the absolutely central importance of the concept of honor for the Beaujolais peasantry. It is painful to lose money, to be sure, but dishonor in the community is intolerable. That, too, is a reminder of the old ways, and the cynical dealings and financial hanky-panky of big-money hustlers will always remain an inexplicable mystery to these people. Less than ten years after Marcel's catastrophe, two new incidents—far more sensational, these ones—would be underlining that importance, when first the collective Beaujolais winemaking community and then Georges Duboeuf in person would be suffering grievously for honor unjustly impugned.

For the moment, though, the order of the day was to celebrate the debts expunged. Marcel did it the best way possible: he got married. Nathalie Joanton was a northerner, a girl from Picardy, a radiant, fresh-faced blonde who had been working as a hairdresser when Marcel met her while on one of his delivery rounds. She moved down to Lancié in 1994, but there was no question of marriage just then, not with the debts and their various legal complications hanging over Marcel's head. They officialized their union in 2004, when Nathalie in white and Marcel in his Sunday suit trotted up to the Lancié *mairie* (town hall) in Marcel's best secondhand buggy, pulled by Hermine. Splendid in her tricolor sash, *Madame le Maire* read out the ceremonial republican marriage pronouncement with appropriate gravity while Marcel mentally mouthed the familiar words along with her. He had performed the same ceremony himself, dozens and dozens of times.

"You know," Marcel said, grinning enormously as he recalled that trip to the town hall with Nathalie, "I clearly remember my father telling me about the two things he had learned in life. Never get into politics, he said, and never marry without a contract. So of course what did I do? I got married twice without contracts, and I became mayor."

With Nathalie, a new project had arisen. Across the road from the Pariaud family house, on the other side of the village, there was the ruin of an old sheepfold and, on a rise above it, a deserted and slightly less dilapidated two-story stone house, both for sale and not too expensive.

Marcel snapped them up, brought out his mason's tools again and set to work, back into the rhythm of ten straight hours of masonry. Over the next few years he transformed the tumbledown sheepfold into a two-story, L-shaped building with four rooms on top and kitchen, dining room and storage space below. Tourism was bound to be growing in the Beaujolais, he reasoned, and modern, well-equipped rooms inside picturesque old stone would make an attractive bed-and-breakfast. As he withdrew progressively from working his vines, the B and B could provide a nice supplement to his state pension and send him and Nathalie into old age with something like security. Just to make sure that tourists would come and then pass the good word on to their friends, he added a heated swimming pool and one more room, larger this one, equipped as a studio. The Pariauds' Petit Nid de Pierre (Little Stone Nest), entirely run by Nathalie, is now Lancié's best B and B, and Marcel is working on making the old house comfortable for the day when he and Nathalie move in. When they do—no date determined yet—he will have a deeply satisfying view from the upper windows: his own mini-hotel compound overlooking vines stretching away toward Fleurie and Chiroubles, the medieval turrets of the Château de Corcelles looming in the distance and Belgian, Dutch and English tourists splashing in his pool. Not bad for a peasant who left school at fourteen. Characteristically, though, Marcel appraised his good fortune modestly—it was mostly, he insisted, the result of luck and timing.

"I had it easy because I got started just when Beaujolais was beginning to be popular. I feel sorry for the young guys who are just starting out now. It's tougher and tougher to be a vigneron these days. There are a lot of new problems that I never had—competition from foreign wines, overplanting and oversupply, the government's anti-drinking programs and the police controls on the roads, all that. Me, I'm all right. I've got enough to live on, and I'm basically retired. But I pity the guys who've got themselves in debt up to the ears for land and equipment because they wanted to make wine. Their future's not clear."

Marcel and I were once again in his *caveau*, dining on *boeuf bour-*

guignon that Nathalie had prepared for us and drinking his muscular 2003 Morgon with it. Although it might have been reasonable to suspect the judgment of a man whose idea of having it easy was his lifelong habit of nonstop work from sunrise to beyond sunset, Marcel's sympathy was not misplaced. By the time the twentieth century had creaked over into the twenty-first, the salad days of the French winemaking community had come and gone. The woe was largely apportioned out among the brotherhood, but it was felt with particular distress in the Beaujolais, because the peasant vignerons, poor cousins of the trade, had grown accustomed to being invited to the front parlor and having a bit of money in the bank. Now those whose vines grew in marginal *terroirs*, or who did not possess Marcel's strength, exuberant good health and nose for vinification, found to their stupefaction that bankruptcy was a very real menace.

Fashion was changing, as it always does, and in the great traditional markets for Beaujolais in France, England, Germany and Switzerland, the wine of the gamay grape—especially Beaujolais Nouveau—was edging toward the dreaded category of been there, done that. Sales were picking up abroad, especially in more exotic markets like Japan, China, India and Russia, but in spite of this, *primeur* production had dropped to one-third of the total of all Beaujolais wines by 2006. The edge was off the novelty.

The trouble was not limited to Beaujolais alone. Far from it: almost everywhere in France except for the haughty, insanely expensive growths of super prestige, vignerons found themselves with unsold stock on their hands as the world spiraled once more into a situation of oversupply. With the new century, an entirely different situation had arisen. Thanks to vigorous, enterprising new winemakers in the United States, Latin America, South Africa, Australia, New Zealand and elsewhere, the French monopoly on high-quality wines was under attack from all sides. The result was paradoxical: more and more people around the world were learning to appreciate good wine even as the French themselves were drinking less and less of it. And now, in large part thanks to the enormous influence of the American wine critic Robert Parker, the heavies—the dour, brooding Beethovens—were leading the pack of popularity. In the din, the melodies of the sprightly Vivaldis were being drowned out.

Within the cacophony of this overcrowded wine marketplace, *primeur* fell into an uncomfortable position. For as long as anyone could remember, it was Beaujolais Nouveau that had stood as the archetype of the Vivaldi category of wines, but it became a victim of its own success—exactly like the music of the Red Priest himself. When *The Four Seasons* reached the point of commercial exploitation where it was simultaneously wafting out of elevator loudspeakers in Omaha and Singapore and innumerable points between, it was soon condemned to that special purgatory reserved for Things We Don't Do Anymore. With that, a fundamental truth got eclipsed: elevators and cell phone rings notwithstanding, *The Four Seasons* was still a terrific piece of music, a superb and thoroughly estimable contribution to the European classical tradition. So it went for *primeur*. When too many people—especially too many "other" people—had latched onto the pleasure of a glassful of red fruit and field flowers as of the third Thursday of November, that pleasure became obsolete and somehow unworthy for those wine lovers who had been there earlier.

But that was not the end of the vexing story, because the *primeur* phenomenon proved to be a double-edged sword for the rest of the Beaujolais. With each new market it conquered, the juvenile wine created such a stir of publicity that, year by passing year, people unconsciously began to identify Beaujolais Nouveau with the totality of the area's wines, forgetting that they were not one but thirteen: Beaujolais, Beaujolais-Villages, the ten *crus*—and then *primeur*, too, like a jolly little bonus. But the baby wine, the little newcomer to the Beaujolais family, had a big voice, and that famous third Thursday of November crept surreptitiously into the public consciousness as the signal for a one-time celebration. Especially in foreign lands, too many of these seasonal drinkers assumed that after downing a glass of Beaujolais Noveau in November they could drop the wine of the gamay grape until the following year.

That was very bad karma for the *crus*. Wandering through those granite-speckled hills from Saint-Amour in the north to Brouilly in the south, I began hearing how distressingly these growths—rarer, more complex and more expensive—were suffering from the obtrusive presence of their cheerful little cousin. Sure we're Beaujolais, the vignerons of the *crus* were saying, but we're also Moulin-à-Vent and Fleurie and Morgon and Chénas. Our wines are exceptional, *vins de garde* that can keep for years and years. People should realize they can't compare them to *primeur*, and they shouldn't expect to be able to get them for the same price, either.

Most of these vignerons diplomatically refrained from using that fraught adjective "better" when they spoke of their wines, but of course that's what they meant. And they were right, too. Beaujolais Nouveau never pretended to be anything more than a little wine, a glass of fun, and not even the most chauvinistic producer would dare claim that his sunny, fruit-juicey *primeur* could match the depth and complexity of the ten *crus*—same region, same grape, same methods of vinification, but the wines were totally different. Even so, the baby wine with the big voice had tended to blur distinctions, creating the erroneous perception that Beaujolais—all Beaujolais—was about the same: an amusing wisp of a wine that was enjoyable, but not really to be taken seriously.

I had a nice occasion to see just how misguided this perception could be when, in June of 2006, I joined a tasting in Paris to which Georges Duboeuf had invited the elite of France's wine-tasting establishment. Two winners of the World's Best Sommelier contest, Olivier Poussier and Philippe Faure-Brac, were there, along with one Meilleur Ouvrier de France (Master Craftsman in Wine), a couple of newspaper wine specialists, and the famously outspoken critic Michel Bettane, author of France's most incisive wine guide. Georges had brought samples of all the *crus* with him, but the object of the tasting was not to put his guests through one of those blind which-one-is-which routines. He wanted to make a point about misperceptions of Beaujolais. All he asked his guests to do was to comment on their appreciation of different years of production—as far back as thirty years, as it turned out, because his first samples dated from 1976.

On the face of it this should have been an absurd exercise, because common wisdom had long ago decreed that Beaujolais wines do not keep longer than two or three years at the most. Common wisdom took a beating that morning as the wines succeeded one another. From the very first samples—Brouilly, Morgon and even one "ordinary" Beaujolais, all of them bottled in 1976—the adjectives flying around the spitting buckets were straight from the book of hyperbole usually reserved for *grands crus*: "elegant," "distinguished," "complex," "delicate," "structured," "balanced" and, perhaps most pertinently, "surprising."

Surprising, indeed, that Beaujolais wines could be so good and hold their strength so well after so many years, but Bettane only shrugged. He had known the secret all along. A man who takes great pleasure in knocking down popular misconceptions, he had already told me a thing or two, over lunch a few months earlier, about how and why the wines of the Beaujolais had become so *déconsidérés* in comparison with those of the officially pedigreed nobilities.

"The tragedy," he explained, "is that the Beaujolais was administratively connected to Burgundy, and the dealers—*les négociants*—were all Burgundians. These people liked hierarchies, and they decided once and for all that the gamay was an inferior *cépage*. They are the ones who established the notion that Beaujolais was a lesser wine that had to be sold much cheaper than even the cheapest of the Burgundies. So it was the *négoce* that established these hierarchies, and unfortunately sommeliers and others in a position to form people's opinions have been raised with these same ideas."

Bettane was not saying that all Beaujolais was wonderful; in fact he energetically railed against unscrupulous merchants who had sold poor, thin stuff that they picked up for a pittance, profiting from the renown that Duboeuf and other quality dealers like Louis Tête and Jadot had brought to the wines. But his central argument was that the pricing system had gone all cockeyed over the years.

"Duboeuf himself has been guilty in this—the simple fact is that he is selling the best wines too cheaply! Selling a Moulin-à-Vent for only 20 percent or 30 percent more than a *primeur* is a monstrous error, because it is worth much more. In the old days, a high-quality Moulin-à-Vent used to go for the same price as a Gevrey-Chambertin-Villages. I started buying wines when I was twenty, and at that time a Moulin-à-Vent commanded the same price as a Mercurey First Growth or a Crozes-Hermitage. Now the Crozes-Hermitage costs two and a half times more. Beaujolais is underrated today because people don't know it well enough."

As an element of proof, he reached back considerably further than Duboeuf had done with the samples he brought to Paris—nearly half a century further, in fact—to recount an experiment he had organized by asking Beaujolais vignerons of his acquaintance to open some of the oldest bottles from their cellars. "At the Château des Jacques, I drank a 1929 Moulin-à-Vent that was absolutely sublime—you could have easily mistaken it for a Chambertin. Another time I had a 1929 Morgon that was better than the Romanée Saint-Vivant or the Chambertin of that same year. I've got two bottles of 1911 Morgon in my cellar right now. I'm just waiting for the right occasion to uncork them. So yes—Beaujolais can be a truly great wine. In my opinion, if you look at the quality/price ratio, Moulin-à-Vent is the best deal you can get in French wines."

Frank Prial, the pope of American wine critics, went even further than Bettane. "I agree that Moulin-à-Vent is the best buy in French wines," he said without hesitation, "but I would include all the *crus*. Moulin-à-Vent is usually the best, but Morgons from the Côte de Py can be even better in some years. And Chénas is a real sleeper. It's right next to Moulin-à-Vent, and shares much of the same *terroir*."

Prial, whose astute and eminently readable wine articles in the *New York Times* were educating American readers on the subtle joys of the grape when today's generation of young critics were still in oenological swaddling clothes, has been around the business long enough and has popped enough corks to be able to offer some fairly trenchant illusion-killing of his own. "The great thing about Beaujolais for me," he said, "is its consistency when compared with Burgundy. Great Burgundy is much superior to Beaujolais, but you simply can't count on it and, truth to tell, it isn't 'great' very often. Even the finest producers let you down regularly. Worse, the prices are outrageous even when the wine is mediocre. There are years when a $12 bottle of *cru* Beaujolais will beat out $150 bottles from Vosne-Romanée, Bonnes Mares or Chambertin."

Prial's comment recalled an anecdote recounted by Pierre-Antoine Rovani, the former specialist of Burgundy wines for Robert Parker's *Wine Advocate*. Commenting on a 2004 tasting of a varied selection of unidentified wines, he singled out a 2003 Moulin-à-Vent from Duboeuf that had completely hornswoggled both him and his fellow Wine Nerds.

"Not a single member of the group guessed Beaujolais," he wrote, "believing it was a top-flight Hermitage or Burgundy. Bravo!"

So, paradox again: if many Burgundy wines were apparently more expensive than their inherent worth, at the same time a lot of Beaujolais wines were too cheap. Extraordinary: after more than six centuries, the protectionist anathema against the gamay grape launched by Burgundy's Philip the Bold in 1395 still holds fast. For the lean of wallet and pocketbook, this situation looks very much like an opportunity to be turned to advantage. If any of us had any brains, it would appear, we would all dash out and stock up forthwith on Moulin-à-Vent, Fleurie, Chénas, Morgon or their sister *crus*, leaving the great Burgundy growths and the noble Bordeaux châteaux to Bill Gates, Warren Buffet and our friendly neighborhood investment bankers.

After decades of tastings in company with Georges Duboeuf, his colleagues and vignerons too numerous to count, my education in the nuances of character and quality among the several wines of the Beaujolais has been fairly comprehensive, but none of this offered the sense of historical satisfaction that was delivered in another session, very recent this one, in the gloom of the huge, vaulted sixteenth-century cellar of the Château des Jacques in Romanèche-Thorins, the very place where

Michel Bettane had enjoyed his instructive encounter with a remark-able 1929 Moulin-à-Vent.

Duboeuf City Romanèche most certainly is, but this time it was not Georges who led me down the stone steps to where the wine lay, but rather his friend Pierre-Henry Gagey, boss of the rival wine house Louis Jadot. The historical satisfaction of the occasion lay in the fact that Jadot is a Burgundy company par excellence, based in Beaune and producer of some of the finest, most expensive growths of the Côte d'Or—but when (perhaps inspired by Duboeuf's tremendous success) they de-cided to establish their own official outpost in the Beaujolais, it looked very much like an act of commercial contrition. They were admitting that Beaujolais was OK, after all. In effect, the company was making amends for Burgundy's having been so beastly about the gamay grape for so long.

Jadot made a first tentative venture south when it began buying acreage in Beaujolais-Villages vines in 1987; then the house followed that with the purchase of Château des Jacques in Romanèche nine years later, then Morgon's Château Bellevue in 2001. With each of these pur-chases, Philip the Bold could distinctly be heard spinning in his fancy necropolis in Beaune, because that made it official: gamay was vile and noxious no more. The mountain had come to Mohammed.

How right Jadot was to have done it. The wines I tasted that afternoon—after a white Beaujolais of the chardonnay grape I was treat-ed to a magnificent procession of wines from the Jadot properties in Beaujolais-Villages, Morgon and Moulin-à-Vent—all of them rich and round, succulent with mature fruit and balanced with the acidity and the tannin to allow them to hold for years and years. They were little short of stupendous, and I was not surprised when Gagey assured me that Jadot took the same painstaking care with a $10 Beaujolais as they did with a $300 Chambertin. But his earnest sincerity only led me in the direction of subversive thoughts. With stuff like this, I couldn't help wondering, how could they manage to sell their top-of-the-line Burgun-dies at prices twenty or thirty times dearer? And when, at almost the very moment when I was tasting these fabulous gamays, the news emerged that the price of Bordeaux's great Château Pétrus, jewel of Pomerol, had just topped $3,000 for a single bottle, my thoughts grew considerably more subversive. If it was hard enough to swallow the notion of a Chambertin being thirty times "better" than these wonderful bottles Gagey had uncorked for me, was I now to accept that a Pétrus was somehow *three hundred times* better? This was ridiculous. Any wine lover with half a palate, I was certain, would gladly take three hundred of Jadot's wonderful gamays against a single Pétrus. Bettane and Prial had spoken lucidly: snobbery and the cash flowing from wine investors had created some very weird imbalances in the market.

Like Duboeuf, like Rougier, Bosse-Platière and, indeed, like everyone involved in the promotion and sale of Beaujolais, Jadot agreed that the region had been chastened by the explosive rise of foreign competition on the world wine market, but added that this very chastening had been salubrious in its effect: it had gone a long way toward eliminating the worst wines from the commercial circuit and persuading producers to lay off overreliance on the chemical industry for growing their grapes.

"Beaujolais wines have never been as good as they have become over the past five years or so," he insisted, and the samples he poured for me that afternoon easily bore him out. With quality of that standard, with the shared enthusiasm that greeted Duboeuf's selection at the Paris tasting session, with the kind of commentary delivered by connoisseurs like Bettane and Prial, it is always galling when Beaujolais wines are misapprehended as they frequently are, and all the more so when the disparagement arrives from within the camp, in France itself. In 2002, all the latent dread and insecurity that had been stalking the region's vignerons came together in a single flash point when a nasty little affair erupted like an echo of Philip the Bold's anathematizings. Starting from next to nothing, it blew out of all logical proportion and reached a point that threatened to do terrible damage to the reputation of the entire Beaujolais region. Around Beaujeu, Belleville and Villefranche it was known as *l'Affaire Lyon Mag*—or, in its most painful labeling, as *l'Affaire Vin de Merde*.

Lyon Mag is a glossy monthly similar to hundreds of other "city" magazines around the world, offering a predictable mix of local coverage—politics, sport, pocketbook economics, women's pages and the like—and a young, ambitious editorial staff with a marked penchant for seeking out the sensational kinds of stories that tend to boost newsstand sales. In the summer of 2002, after Beaujolais producers had requested a governmental subsidy for sending to the distillery one hundred thousand hectoliters of unsold wine from the weak 2001 vintage, the magazine opportunistically splashed an article denouncing the request, in the name of defending taxpayers' interests. The key to the article was a quote from François Mauss, a somewhat obscure Parisian wine personality: "They wanted to make money at all costs, and they are perfectly aware of selling a *vin de merde*. As a result, the Beaujolais producers don't deserve state assistance."

Vin de merde: shit wine. The quote was heaven-sent. AN EXPERT ACCUSES, the magazine breathlessly headlined, "Beaujolais, It's Not Wine." It was tendentious, mean-spirited stuff that picked up on all the old rumors, prejudices, jealousies and stereotypes that had been laid out against Beaujolais for centuries—in effect, kicking someone who was already down. But the ploy worked like magic, better than anything the editors could have hoped for: the vignerons snapped at the bait. Wounded in their pride, already punished by flagging sales, the growers' community saw red and reacted unthinkingly to defend its honor: sixty-three village and regional trade groups got together and sued *Lyon Mag* for denigration of their product.

With that, the ball got rolling, and soon it was out of control. The lawsuit turned a meretricious little article in an unimportant provincial magazine into a national cause célèbre. The Parisian press picked up the story, and from there it went international. As the most widely recognized name in red wines, Beaujolais had always made good copy, so this was much too good to miss. Within twenty-four hours, Beaujolais =

Vin de Merde had flashed around the world. Duboeuf was depressed and horrified by the producers' gaffe, because he guessed very accurately the path that the whole dreary business would be taking over the next few months.

"They should never have filed that lawsuit," he told me. "All they're accomplishing is to spread the calumny around the world. Things were already bad enough. Now they've made it much worse."

It happened exactly as he had feared, and through the next weeks and months he gazed in stunned disbelief at his fellow countrymen great and small as they assiduously engaged themselves in a national exercise of shooting themselves in the foot, while at the same time sinking the Beaujolais. In first judgment and appeal, *Lyon Mag* was twice condemned and heavily fined, which unsurprisingly caused the national press and civil liberties groups of all ilk to leap to defend the cause of freedom of the press. Meanwhile, a venomous political squabble was developing between the United States and France, whose national administration seemed hell-bent on destroying the last shreds of more than two centuries of American affection for the land of *liberté, égalité and fraternité*. President Jacques Chirac was at his pompous best in displaying undisguised contempt for President Bush and threatening to use his Security Council veto against any UN help with the Iraq adventure. (The idea was right, the diplomatic manner wasn't.) At the same time, his talented mouthpiece, Prime Minister Dominigue de Villepin, declaimed elegant polemics against America in general, and before anyone knew quite what was happening everything had spun into caricature: Uncle Sam was a warmonger, the entire French nation had been transmogrified into cheese-eating surrender monkeys, and Freedom Fries were just around the corner. Along with everything else French, sales of Beaujolais plummeted in the United States.

It was in this poisoned atmosphere that the Cour de Cassation, the French supreme court, finally threw out the earlier judgments against *Lyon Mag*, on the perfectly reasonable principle that the European Convention on Human Rights explicitly shielded freedom of speech.

That ended it. The episode had proven to be nothing more than a useless, costly exercise in emotional gesticulation, one that made Beaujolais look silly around the world and gave undeserved honor to *Lyon Mag* as a doughty little bastion of freedom of the press. "Undeserved" because Mauss, the man at the origin of the affair, was furious at the magazine for having pulled a sensational story from thin air by manipulating him and his words—the traditional sin of low-flying journalists masquerading as crusaders.

"You've got to know the truth," he told me urgently. "They called me at ten or ten-thirty at night, and we spoke about all sorts of things for almost an hour and a half. You know how it is when you talk on the phone, you let yourself go a little, so yes, I did say that those one hundred thousand hectoliters were *vin de merde*, but I was only referring to them, not all Beaujolais. When I finally saw the article in the magazine, I said damn—I've been had! I adore Beaujolais, and I absolutely didn't want to say that the producers were no good. If they had consulted me before filing that lawsuit, I would have presented them a formal apology. What came out in *Lyon Mag* didn't at all correspond to what I felt about Beaujolais wine."

Three years after the start of this doleful affair, Duboeuf had cause to be horrified yet again, when an internal audit showed that the chief of the impressive new winery he had built in 2002 had lamentably screwed up his job, mixing together different *crus* that were meant to be stored and sold separately, then compounding the bungles by mixing Beaujolais-Villages in with certain *crus*. (With everyone harvesting at once over a few mad, hectic days and grapes arriving all day long and well into the night, it was perhaps understandable that fatigue would take its toll and cause a mess, but this one was of truly awful proportions.) Ironically, the errors came to light because Georges had installed a computerized tracking system that followed each batch of grapes from vineyard to bottle. On learning of the screwup, he immediately suspended his employee and blocked the wines in vats before they could be bottled. Blocked or not, though, the mixes constituted a breach of AOC rules. The matter came to the attention of the local tax and customs authorities, and the zealous new Villefranche prosecutor decided to make an example of Duboeuf. Once again *Lyon Mag* splashed a big story—Beaujolais always made good copy, but Beaujolais *and* Duboeuf was even better. DUBOEUF ACCUSED OF FRAUD, the headline shouted, and at length the case came to a trial. Despite the fact that the 2,090 hectoliters involved—less than 1 percent of his output—had remained in-house and unbottled, Les Vins Georges Duboeuf was fined 30,000 euros, or about $36,000, for "trickery and attempted trickery." This looked like doubtful justice at best, but Duboeuf was not going to make the same mistake as the producers who sued *Lyon Mag* and see the humiliating story dragged out over years of appeals, judgments and further tendentious articles. He swallowed hard, shut up, downgraded all the litigious wines one notch, selling the *crus* as Beaujolais-Villages, and the Beaujolais-Villages as simple Beaujolais. In both cases, the wines had been ennobled by the mix with higher-value stuff, then sold beneath the price they would normally command, so the company took a beating and some customers got a good deal. But what counted most was this: although Les Vins Georges Duboeuf had been found guilty of unauthorized procedures, Georges himself was declared innocent. Honor was intact.

XI

WHITHER BEAUJOLAIS?

GLOBALIZATION AND THE RANSOM OF SUCCESS

*A*s satisfying as it was for honor to be proven and to walk exonerated from a courtroom, the economic consequences of bad publicity remained imponderable, and after the successive attacks of *l'Affaire Vin de Merde* and *l'Affaire Duboeuf,* the Beaujolais was in something like a state of shock: unpleasant, baffling new forces had come to cloud the optimism that had swept over the region in earlier decades. Dealers and vignerons alike could understand and accept that their wines were encountering fierce new competition from abroad, but what mystified and troubled them was to discover so much cold antipathy coming from the French themselves, the same ones who only a generation earlier had raised Beaujolais nearly to the status of a national treasure. What had gone wrong? The peasant smallholders of the Beaujolais were supposed to be the good guys, *les bons petits gars,* brave little villagers taking on their rich and powerful competitors with the magic potion they brewed from the gamay grape. Certainly some among them had resorted to easy outs, grown and overgrown grapes in ill-suited grain terrain and dumped poor quality wine onto the market—there wasn't a wine area anywhere in the world where hustlers hadn't been similarly cutting corners—but they were exceptions. Why should the finger be pointed only at the Beaujolais? Why this vendetta?

Over and over again as I rambled around villages and vineyards I met the same uncomprehending headshakes and heard the same comparison between France and the United States brought forth: in America you admire success and try to emulate it; here, they hate you for it and try to tear you down. And then there was the matter of Lyon. That really hurt. The wonderful, easygoing old town astride the confluence of the Saône and the Rhône was France's version of Chicago, the second city, with its own particular culture, history, folklore, slang and accent. It was the anti-Paris, laughing and insolent where the capital was pompous and self-important, comfortable with its frank accent on good living and sensuality where Paris was ambitious, proud and just a bit paranoiac; and, best of all, it was the national epicenter of good eating and good drinking, the gourmet's earthly paradise of food and wine, where great chefs like Paul Bocuse and Jean-Paul Lacombe were much better known and admired than whoever happened to be mayor of the moment—and this marvelous place had turned its back on Beaujolais. It was distressing, incomprehensible. In the wine country this abandonment was felt like the breakup of a love affair, and not one that ended by mutual consent but rather by unilateral rupture—the Beaujolais had been jilted. Dismayed, the vignerons discovered a character trait in the Lyonnais that they had never suspected: they weren't necessarily always so jolly, after all, *les gones*. They could be downright spiteful when they put their minds to it.

One drizzly April afternoon I drove down to Lyon to see for myself how bad the situation was. In a personal survey of no statistical value whatsoever, I visited ten cafés and bars in the vicinity of the sumptuous Part Dieu food market on the left bank of the Rhône, lifted a few glasses and asked a few bartenders and clients their opinion of Beaujolais wines. My first observation was that certain overriding national character traits always dominate: the French will be the French, whatever region or microculture they inhabit. As a kind of preamble to any opinion emitted on any subject, it was postulated by general agreement that (1) everyone always cheats, and (2) in any case the press is rotten and never tells anything but a pack of lies, so you can never really tell what's what. The vote on that was unanimous. That being said, Beaujolais was out, definitely out. And what was striking—astonishing even—was the degree of antagonism: *not a single one of these bars was even serving Beaujolais.* Lyon, the city that had been identified with the wine of the gamay like none other, had decided that it would now drink Côtes du Rhône. More than a mere change of fashion, this was a major, implacable pout.

"The Beaujolais people should have paid more attention to their French clients instead of the foreign market," sniffed the boss of a bar called the Aristo. Bingo—that was half the reason for the pout right there. The other half was articulated bluntly in another establishment a few blocks away. "Beaujolais is much more expensive than Côtes du Rhône," explained the owner of the Brasserie du Palais as he poured me a generous *ballon* of his 2003 Belleruche. "The quality-price ratio is better with this."

So it was about money, after all. But that wasn't the whole story. Emotions were involved, too, and a good deal more than most people realized or would admit. Beaujolais—our Beaujolais, the wine we Lyonnais just about invented—had gone off and danced with other partners, then had the nerve to raise its prices. The big man behind the bar in the Brasserie du Palais delivered a final cruel announcement like a knockout punch. "I inherited this place from my mother," he said with satisfaction. "When she had it, its name was Le Beaujolais."

Relaxing with a pre-lunch glass of Mâcon white in his comfortable Art Deco house near the university in downtown Lyon, Professor Garrier added a third angle to the explanation. "Toward the end of the last century there were two or three years when a lot of mediocre Beaujolais was produced. It was coming out acid and sometimes mildewed, while the Côtes du Rhône was OK. The old generation of vignerons from the days of *les trente glorieuses* hadn't always updated their equipment and had gotten a little bit sloppy about maintaining their installations. Not many of them were as scrupulous as Georges Duboeuf, so the result was poor wine. Add that to the snobbery of the Lyonnais—since the Japanese like our Beaujolais so much, we won't drink it anymore—and you've got a very powerful negative argument: *l'amour trompé*. Infidelity in love."

A few months after my lunch with Professor Garrier I dropped in on Michel Rougier, director-general of InterBeaujolais in Villefranche. As it happened, he was gazing at a selection of withering anti-wine articles and postings on his computer when I walked into his office. As the man whose job was to represent both the growers and the dealers, he was sorely vexed by what he was seeing.

"I don't know what to tell you," he said and sighed. "Yes, we're in a time of crisis now, and I'm afraid its going to last a number of years. Look at this." He made a gesture of disgust toward the screen. "The political class has been manipulated by health professionals. Now they're acting as if alcohol is a medicine, or a drug to be regulated. It's almost as if they want to prohibit wine. But we're Latins, not binge drinkers like the Anglo-Saxons or Scandinavians. We don't go out and get drunk on Saturday night. We drink regularly, but reasonably."

Undeniably, Rougier had a point. While the consumption of wine is an integral part of the French daily social routine, drinking alcohol fast and deep to get seriously drunk is not viewed as normal or acceptable behavior. Early in my years in France—the mid-sixties—when the average per capita consumption of wine was still over one hundred liters a year, a journalistic colleague of mine, himself no stranger to the charms of alcohol, was moved to a lapidary observation: "You know," he said with something like confraternal admiration, "I've rarely seen a Frenchman completely drunk. But then again I've rarely seen one completely sober, either."

That's changed. Today, average per capita consumption has dropped to less than fifty liters a year, and there are more and more French men and women who spend their entire lives dead sober. The decline in wine consumption has been slow but cumulative. Until recent times, the only signs of any anti-drink campaigning that anyone might have encountered were the work of vaguely prohibitionist do-good organizations that bought advertising space in busses and metro cars where they installed a clumsily drawn cartoon of a sad little girl addressing an admonition to her staggering father: "*Papa, ne bois pas, pense à moi.*" Daddy, don't drink, think of me. The campaign was remarkably ineffective.

Meanwhile, out in real life on the highways, French drivers reveled (or shrank in terror, depending on their psyche) in an environment that brought to mind images of a giant automotive pinball machine: enforcement of speed limits was virtually nonexistent, stop signs and red lights were viewed as optional and alcohol tests were unknown except ex post facto, at the sites of serious accidents. *Priorité à droite*—the horse-and-buggy rule obliging the car on the left to cede right of way to the car on the right—seemed to be the single, overriding rule that everyone knew by heart, and it was viewed as a driver's absolute entitlement, whatever the circumstance. Naturally, this caused mayhem at poorly marked crossroads, because drivers habitually entered them at breakneck speed. Lacking a national superhighway grid, the *routes nationales* of the old three-lane geometry, ideal for head-on collisions, were a murderous travel adventure. Successive French administrations, alarmed at the cost to the nation of road deaths and maimings, finally took a look at the figures, saw that their country was leading Western Europe as the most dangerous place to take to the highway, and decided to do something about it. The statistics were awful, it must be said. In the ghastly record year of 1972, 18,113 persons were killed on French roads. The first and most noticeable reaction of the authorities was to rush construction of what is now an admirable and thoroughly modern superhighway system. After that, the cops were given new powers and new equipment. By 2001, road deaths had fallen to 8,000, then down to 4,975 in 2005. *Le tout-répressif,* the new national policy was called: the crackdown. With automatic flash-camera radars installed throughout the country and speed traps and random gendarme checks becoming generalized, French drivers finally began resigning themselves to maybe obeying the traffic laws.

At the same time, the dreaded balloon became a fixture of everyday road life: the unannounced ambush by a squad of gendarmes, the smart military salute and the polite but totally imperative request to blow into the balloon. Anything more than the equivalent of a couple of glasses of wine led to a forced wait by the roadside to get the alcohol rate down, and a few points off the twelve-point driver's license. Higher rates meant immediate suspension of the license, immobilization of the car in situ and a trip to the gendarmerie or commissariat for a much longer sobering-up wait—in a cell or holding room this time—and loss of the license for up to six months. It was draconian and painful, but there was no arguing with the statistics of dramatically fewer road deaths. In the face of that, it was difficult to argue that people ought to be able to drink as much as they wanted at lunch or dinner and carry on with their lives as before. Professionals of wine were caught in an ethical and semantic bind.

"Everything's changing," said Rougier despondently. "The police, the market, the competition, the consumers, the techniques of production, the *cépages*, the public's tastes—everything. Tradition doesn't hold anymore."

There it was. Ad lib, Rougier had summed up the predicament facing winegrowers in every corner of France except a few niche producers of specialty wines and, of course, those with happy names like Pétrus, Richebourg, Krug or Yquem. The ones at the very high end were sitting as pretty as ever, but the vast middle ground was an overcrowded sea of trouble. *Everything's changing.* And it never stops changing, either—that's what was so unsettling about it. The primeval soup called globalization is a fantastic machine for creating wealth, variety and innovation, but it is also a kind of monster, a dog-eat-dog combat that permanently threatens the status quo. It is a very unsettling thing, and a great national debate rages in France, where the tug of tradition is strong, about how to come to terms with it. Nothing is sure anymore, nothing is safe, whether here or anywhere else—and that goes for every kind of enterprise, whether wine, warplanes or widgets. If everyone can do anything and sell it anywhere, the inescapable corollary is that today's darling is in permanent danger of being tomorrow's discard.

Seething at the bad news on his computer screen, Rougier railed against *"les vins body-buildés,"* the powerful, tannic Beethovens that had come to worldwide favor at the expense of less muscular stuff, while stubbornly predicting that drinkers around the world would soon tire of this strong medicine and return to the subtler, less overwhelming charms of the gamay grape. "Those heavy wines will finally become undrinkable," he insisted. "Beaujolais is a wine for *drinking*, not for winning complexity prizes at tasting sessions. With our *cépage*, we can't make heavy wines. Beaujolais is going to be the wine of the third millennium."

But he didn't really sound all that sure of himself. There was a lot of whistling in the dark going on in the Beaujolais. As 2006 moved into 2007 the region boasted fewer than thirty-five hundred individual exploitations, compared to five-thousand-plus in the glory days, and the number looked certain to drop even further. Even though the Beaujolais had not been nearly as overplanted as the vast Bordeaux region, it was looking at a probable loss of a further quarter of its acreage under vines. New measures were hastily installed to allow desperate Beaujolais vignerons to double their yields per acre — on condition of selling their output more cheaply as simple table wine or a new regional wine to be called Vin du Pays des Gaules. It was a depressing admission of defeat: Beaujolais, or certain parts of the Beaujolais, anyway, was seeking salvation by going down-market.

"We're at a turning point now," Marcel Laplanche said gravely. This veteran vigneron from Blacé, he of the prodigious memory and illusionless judgment, is one of the most respected sages of the Beaujolais, a man who has known every twist of the region's fortunes from well before World War II. "Twenty years ago we were able to sell as much as we could produce, but now we've hit the wall. A lot of the guys are facing bankruptcy. We've lost Lyon now. We're going to be seeing some deaths around here, for sure."

Suicides in the Beaujolais would have seemed unthinkable a decade or so earlier, but the economic realities of expenses too high for returns too small are the same for a stockbroker, a hairdresser or a vigneron. For

many, the numbers were adding up seriously wrong, and it was not difficult to understand expressions of gloom like the ones I met in the handsome reception room of the *cave coopérative* in Saint-Laurent-d'Oingt,
where twenty-five years earlier, in the golden days, I had accompanied
Georges Duboeuf and Patrick Léon on a part of their marathon wine-
tasting duties.

"Globalization is hitting all of us hard," admitted René Bothier,
president of the *cave*. "The competition's getting to be ferocious. Now
on top of that, everyone's afraid of the cops. Our *caveau* used to be full
on Sundays. People came from all over to have a drink, meet other people, talk and have a good time. Now it's empty here. Customers come
to buy their wine, but they don't even taste it, because the gendarmes
might be waiting for them down the road. Sales are down 20 percent
over the last five years."

The big rectangular room with the long bar, wooden tables and
sweeping panoramic view out over the vines had been purpose-built for
drinking, fun and partying—the old ways of the old days—but it was
now strangely incongruous and bereft, like a house without furniture.
Our voices echoed off the walls—just as they do, come to think of it,
in the empty churches all over the Beaujolais. A few decades earlier,
Joseph Berkmann had been fighting tooth and nail to get his *primeur* to
London faster than his competitors because the Brits were crazy about
French wines, and in particular the wines of the gamay grape. In those
days, French wines were miles ahead of all others in sales on the other
side of the Channel. But by the fall of 2006, they had fallen to third
place in UK sales, behind Australia (number one) and the United States
(number two).

The United States! To be outstripped in the great national specialty
by the hamburger-chomping philistines from across the pond, traditional butts of all French food and wine commentary, was a sobering comeuppance, but that, too, was globalization. Unquestionably, some serious
rethinking was called for, along with a good dose of commercial humil-
ity. The seller's market was finished; it was time to court the consumer.

To their credit, it has to be said that French producers and dealers recognized the danger and reacted as quickly and energetically as they could, within the bounds of what was permitted under INAO* regulations. A trip to Vinexpo, the enormous biennial trade show in Bordeaux, offered plenty of proof that everyone involved in the wine business had been thinking long and hard about ways to attract attention to their wares. From stand to stand, every imaginable, ingenious size, shape and color of bottle was on display—tall bottles, short bottles, thin bottles, fat bottles, squat bottles, twisted bottles, you name it—along with an anthology of polychrome labels screaming *buy me, buy me*. More than a few of them were shameless imitations of the most successful offbeat brand names and graphics from the United States and Australia, and there was a great profusion of *cépage* wines—varietals—that lay outside the grasp of INAO's AOC parameters: here a sauvignon, there a syrah, everywhere a chardonnay. They were trying hard.

At his big, double-sized stand, Georges Duboeuf was playing it cool, testing a few new approaches but not quite joining the feeding frenzy of graphics that had seized so many of his confrères. The man who had revolutionized wine labeling in the first place had expanded his now-classical (and endlessly plagiarized) floral labels through a wide range of his wines, but was also experimenting with some splashier stuff: labels and, in some cases, entire bottles decorated by the hand of the Lyon designer Alain Vavro, a man who goes for bright, eye-catching Matisse-like flashes of color. In addition to the traditional stock of wines with which he had begun his career, he had added a range from the Rhône Valley and, further south toward the Spanish frontier, the very interesting vinous regions of Languedoc-Roussillon. There were blended table wines like GD Red and GD White, varietals like gamay and viognier from the Ardèche, plenty of chardonnay, merlot and syrah, pinot noir from

---

*As of 2007, INAO officially changed its name to INAQ: *Institut National des Appellations et de la Qualité*, in an apparent effort to underline that the products (wines, cheeses, etc.) given its certification did not only originate in certain *terroirs*, but were also *good*. The nuance was significant, because over the years too many AOC labels had been handed out too easily, debasing the credibility of the certification.

the Pays d'Oc, an elegant muscat de Beaumes-de-Venise and even some Bordeaux. All of this proved that Georges was covering the bases, but a simple glance at his catalogue or his Web site was enough to show where both his heart and his pocketbook lay: the Beaujolais-Mâconnais, his beloved, was and always will be up front, and way above all the others.

The innovative spirit and workaholic ways that had led Georges to dominate all the other dealers in the business of selecting and selling the region's wines inevitably led to the idea—the hope, the wish, the desire—that somewhere within Duboeuf's well-made noggin might reside a magic formula that could somehow lead the Beaujolais out of crisis. He had become the region's icon and father figure, but now, with the arrival of hard times, a weightier role was thrust his way: he was the one, more than any other individual, to whom peasants, bourgeois and bureaucrats alike looked for a route toward salvation. Time after time in these last years I have heard variations on the theme of a wish I first heard expressed a few years ago by a winemaker in Saint-Amour: "If only we had ten Duboeufs, there would be no problems at all here in the Beaujolais."

A hint of a smile plays on Georges' face when he hears the compliment, but it is a pained and reluctant smile, because his native reserve and modesty make him mistrust hyperbole, and in any case there is only so much he can do. Businessmen are supposed to cause their companies to prosper, create jobs and spin money for themselves and others involved in their commerce. He already had done that. What else could be expected of him?

Everyone groped for an answer, but perhaps it was staring them right in the face after all, just across the way from the Duboeuf headquarters building in Romanèche. There was more than a bit of irony to this situation, too, because the solid, bricks-and-mortar outline of that possible answer was also the source of the worst pain and humbling that Georges had known in more than half a century in the wine business: *le vendangeoir*, the winery where his weary, muddleheaded employee had mixed his batches of grapes and gotten the company in trouble with the authorities. Sitting like a spaceship on a knoll amid the vines along the road to Fleurie, Duboeuf's enormous vinifying and storage plant is a strikingly elegant modern structure of sweeping Frank Lloyd Wright lines in black, white and raspberry sherbet colors, sharply contrasting with traditional Beaujolais village architecture.

It is a very new addition to his enterprise, unlike anything he had done before. Georges surprised many, friends as well as competitors, when he had it built in 2002. For as long as anyone could remember he had insisted that his business was strictly selecting, buying and selling wines, not making them. But he had understood that it was time to adapt, because change was in the air. It had been for several years, as Professor Garrier had explained to me over lunch in Lyon: many of the traditional Beaujolais vignerons had been unable or unwilling to keep up with the fast-moving technical expertise of their counterparts in the New World and Down Under, who were producing a steady flow of soft, pleasant, clearly recognizable, moderately priced wines whose taste and quality hardly varied from year to year—the Coca-Cola effect, some called it, and the image wasn't entirely fallacious. In contrast to this new, semi-industrial reality, most artisans of the Beaujolais had continued to follow their old habits, trusting their *terroirs* to deliver the gamay's familiar flower and fruit and keeping their fingers crossed that the weather would cooperate. When it did, in exceptional years like 2003 and 2005, it was not a great challenge to turn out fine wines, but when the rains were too persistent or the temperatures too flighty, only the best—vignerons as skilled as Nicole Savoye Descombes, Paulo Cinquin or Marcel Pariaud—could cope with the variables and save what otherwise would have been a poor year.

There was a new reality in the overcrowded wine market, one that was painful for French traditionalists to contemplate: poor years were no longer permissible. Until recent times French consumers, rooted as they were in custom and tradition reaching all the way back to the very first glimmers of their wine-drinking civilization a couple of thousand years ago, had been wedded to the concepts of *terroir* and vintages that changed from year to year. Accepting annual variations in the quality of wines as part of the natural course of things, they rather enjoyed the game of ferreting out good deals from among the offerings of the country's myriad producers. The impatient new generations, however, were not so easygoing. More and more of them were expecting to be able to find the wines they liked, as they liked them, right now and every year, too. With a plethoric supply of competing brands and labels crying out to seduce them, they could cherry-pick their choices and, if they weren't happy, abandon today what they had been drinking yesterday. Foreign consumers were even more demanding, more price-conscious and more fickle, and—here was the scary part—the Beaujolais sold half or more of its total production in export. What seemed to count most, then—especially in the overcrowded field of mid-range wines—was constancy of the product. The wise winemaker made sure that that he always had optimum conditions for treating and raising his grapes, for vinifying them, for bottling and storing them.

Modern vinification is very technical, very manipulative stuff, and if it cannot make good wine out of bad grapes, it can very much attenuate the negative effects of poor weather. Purists will often say that by lopping off the lows modern vinification also chops the highs, creating so-so wines that are always OK, but never truly great the way they had been in the old days. The debate is endless and insoluble, of course, but what is certain is that never in history has the bending of nature away from vinegar and into wine been studied as thoroughly and understood as well as today, and where serious producers are concerned, never has more care been lavished on the grapes from which wine is made.

All of which explains Duboeuf's *vendangeoir*. In the Beaujolais-Villages area and in certain of the *crus*, he knew many vignerons who were expert agronomists growing fine grapes on interesting *terroirs*, but whose talents and equipment for vinification were not always up to standard. After years of reflection and talking it over with them, he finally decided to go ahead and become a *négociant-producteur*—both a dealer and a producer. Rather than finished wine, it was the grapes alone he would be buying from these growers, in order to turn them into wine himself, using the most modern gear in the best possible conditions. It would not be all that much—the winery today represents no more than 5 percent of his total sales—but it would be the chance for him to put his hand to some potentially exceptional wines. And his new plant would place him in excellent company. His friend and colleague Marcel Guigal, the most famous dealer of Côtes du Rhône wines, much admired and covered with accolades by Robert Parker and England's wine goddess Jancis Robinson, had long been both *négociant* and producer, and Pierre-Henry Gagey of the Louis Jadot company had preceded him with a modern winery for his southern Beaujolais wines in 1998.

Georges finally took the step in 2002, and with that the wheel came full circle and then some. The peasant vigneron who had begun in revolt against the *négociant* cartel was not only a *négociant* himself but had become an important Beaujolais winemaker as well. The tool he built for attacking this new role was an impressive piece of work, and— typical of Duboeuf—it was original and unlike any others. Visitors making their way to the new winery on foot passed first through the pathways of *un jardin en Beaujolais*, the botanical garden that Georges had directed to be planted to the southeast of the entrance. Why a botanical garden should have been associated with a winery was never really explained, but around Romanèche the locals just shrugged—why not? That was just the Duboeuf way. He did things like that all the time, and by all appearances he was much more proud of the garden than of the multimillion-dollar behemoth that sat next to it. The garden—ever so carefully laid out, arrows pointing directions for a properly sequential stroll through a collection of trees, shrubs, plants, herbs and flowers, all of them didactically labeled—merited a special celebration and press conference for its opening, while the *vendangeoir*, the big tool, simply went to operation after a few workmanlike switches had been flipped.

The winery itself is open for guided tours. Visitors enter through a side door giving access to platforms from which some of the intricacies of vinification can be explained, but the real business end is at the front, where the grapes arrive to be inspected, weighed and tested for sugar content, after which they go onto conveyor belts for the journey toward the maceration vats, presses and storage tanks. People entering the building here pass through the fishbowl of a glassed-in laboratory where young technicians in white blouses man computers and manipulate the usual baffling array of beakers, test tubes, funnels and pipettes; then visitors continue into the main, cathedral-sized shell where a series of see-through stainless steel gratings stacked one above the other, like decks in some improbably vast cargo ship, give a direct view down to giant presses, pumps and soaring, silo-shaped towers for storing thousands of gallons of wine. More often than not the whole cavernous shebang, as spotless as a hospital, is shimmering from the latest hosing-down of Duboeuf's permanent cleanliness campaign. There is nothing more up-to-date than this winery in the Beaujolais, and probably few to rival its technical finesse anywhere else in the world, but just to be sure that it always receives the right stuff to work with, Georges backs up the machinery with human supervision in the field. A team of eight inspectors armed with laptops and refractometers roams the vineyards of Beaujolais-Villages and the *crus* for him, keeping an eye on the quality and ripeness of the grapes and coordinating harvest dates with the winery. With design and planning of this caliber as a foundation for the rest, his original hunch proved to be exactly right: the plant was almost immediately booked solid through the year, and Georges now has to turn away growers who would prefer to sell him their grapes rather than to make their wines themselves.

Given the tough new realities of the wine market created by the ferocious competition from abroad, it would have been surprising if Georges had not found himself faced with something else to turn away: land. He is endlessly solicited with offers of vineyards for sale, but he already has more than enough work, so his refusal to expand into ownership has been pretty systematic, but with one exception: he could not resist when the Château des Capitans in Juliénas came up for sale. It isn't really a showpiece, this domain, nothing to compare with eye stunners like Château de la Chaize or Château de Corcelles. Sited unobtrusively amid the vines, the main building is more like a *gentilhommière* (country gentleman's manor house) than a palace—but for Georges a whole world of nostalgia was contained within its stone, wood and tile and the accompanying 6.8 hectares of vines. Capitans had been the property of Victor Peyret, writer, restaurateur, raconteur, bon vivant and all-around local character of the Beaujolais, the man who had transformed a deconsecrated church into a drinking place, but also a man who had taken the callow young Duboeuf lad under his wing, advised him, introduced him around, encouraged him in his new approach to the trade. It was in Juliénas that Georges had done his first job of estate bottling, and in Peyret's church-*caveau* that he met Rolande, the baker's daughter who became his wife. For that marriage, Peyret lent Georges what was in 1957 the supreme symbol of pomp and luxury: *une belle américaine*, a big, fat, soft-springed American car, with a chauffeur to motor the young couple away in fitting grandeur to the reception they had organized at the restaurant Le Coq in Juliénas.

It was, then, something like a sentimental journey when Georges bought Capitans in 2004, but there was an extra little twist to the story, a practical, bread-and-butter angle for the benefit of the Beaujolais that Georges had seen from the start. The essential fact was that he bought the domain not by himself but in partnership with his longtime American distributor, Bill Deutsch. A big, relaxed, bespectacled, stentorian-voiced bear of a man, Deutsch loves the idea of being a *châtelain*, and loves telling the story of how it happened.

"One afternoon I get this call from Georges. 'Beel,' he says, 'there's this fantastic château for sale, good price, winery, vines, everything. It's just right for our grandchildren. Franck and Fabienne and Jean-Paul are already in. Why not bring the Deutsch family in, too?' So I said yes, and that made it a milestone—now we have two families across the ocean, united by the common bond of this domain."

A fine family holding it is, too—no doubt about that—but Georges also admits to a benign ulterior motive: to tie Deutsch (and his son, Peter, who will succeed him at the head of the business) sentimentally to the Beaujolais. Deutsch had built his business around the backbone of distributing Duboeuf wines, but later lucked into exclusive U.S. rights and co-ownership of Yellow Tail, the faintly sweet, phenomenally successful Australian wine that set sales records in America (dismaying wine purists in the process), far outstripped his sales of Beaujolais and made him a mountain of money. Georges knew that Capitans would always be sending Deutsch a message: no matter how rich you get, no matter how many bottles of that Aussie stuff you sell, don't forget us.

By "us," Georges meant Beaujolais wines in general, of course, but more specifically the family enterprise that is Les Vins Georges Duboeuf. Within that enterprise, there is never any doubt as to who is in final control and who selects and blends the wines that have acquainted so much of the bibulous world with *le goût Duboeuf*, the Duboeuf taste. The founder is so firmly fixed onto the rails of his toilsome daily routine that he literally suffers withdrawal symptoms if he has no work to occupy him, and his presence in and around the local *caveaux* and *caves coopératives* is as much a part of the Beaujolais scenery as the springtime flowering of the vines. This being said, he is not the only Stakhanovite in Romanèche. Entirely in charge of the office, the personnel and all the daily details of the company there is Rolande, as tireless as the Sisyphean vignerons of Papa Bréchard's youth, endlessly lugging 110-pound loads of eroded soil up to the top of their vineyards. Tireless, and tough, too. She can (and does) say no to people asking for favors; Georges is famous for having trouble uttering the N-word. But especially for the longer term of things, as Georges approaches the age and status of most ancient and venerable sage, there is Franck, the one and only Duboeuf son, born in 1960 when his parents were still running the business almost all by themselves.

After the usual errand boy, delivery truck driver and general factotum duties traditionally assigned to bosses' sons, Franck was installed in the Romanèche executive office in 1983 after a few years of business studies and a few more of learning the subtleties of wine tasting at Papa's side. There's no organization chart in the Duboeuf company, and no titles, but everyone knows who is in charge and who comes next. The closest that Franck will come to putting names on functions is to allow that his father might be called director-general and himself general manager. With more than enough work to occupy both of them, Franck specialized for several years in the technical side of things in Romanèche, designing and overseeing the construction of huge new warehouse facilities and then moving into the commercial, PR and marketing side, notably taking over Duboeuf's never-ending export drive. Between the United States, Canada, Japan, China, Russia and India alone he has racked up enough frequent flyer miles to be able to circle the globe for free several times over, but airplanes no longer hold any charm for him, and he much prefers to be back home whenever he can, with his wife, Anne, and their kids, Antonia, Aurélien and Angèle. Georges has been quoted as saying that Franck is the better *dégustateur* (wine taster) of the two, but no one believes him, and of course everyone wonders where Franck will take the company in that vague, distant future when Georges is no longer there.

Franck is noncommittal on the subject. But, gifted with a matinee idol's good looks, polite, circumspect, meticulously well dressed, gazing appraisingly out at the world from behind his wall of restraint, he is clearly a chip off the old Duboeuf block. He reflects before speaking an opinion, chooses his words with care, and his articulation is every bit as hushed and susurrant as his father's. ("We Duboeufs are very reserved," he says, and it isn't exactly a revelation.) He shrugs at the question of succession and cites Rostand, Dumas and Bach. There have been artistic dynasties, so why not something similar in the wine business? In any case Franck prefers to keep his thoughts to himself, but what people in the Beaujolais know about him is that he married rather late, he is devoted to his wife and kids, and he is determined to give himself more family time than his father was ever able to spare. As a consequence, he has deliberately shortened his workday compared to Georges', arriving in the office as late as 7 A.M. and remaining there only until 8:30 at night.

While Franck takes it easy with his mere thirteen- to fourteen-hour workdays, Georges continues at his immutable marathon man schedule, and when he has a few free moments he spends them cogitating—there's something going on behind that poker-faced visage all the time. In the early eighties, a couple of decades before his big vinification plant was even the shadow of an inkling of an idea, he put several moments of thought together and began sketching out a project of far-reaching amplitude and impact, one totally different from anything ever conceived in the Beaujolais—or anywhere else in the French wine country, for that matter. It cost him a small fortune that in all likelihood he will never recover, but it affords him an (understated) pride that by any measure he clearly deserves. Le Hameau du Vin, it is called, the Wine Hamlet. Georges wanted to show off the Beaujolais and his beloved gamay grape, and he did it by transforming the entire southeastern sector of Romanèche into a kind of exhibition park devoted to wine. The comparison to a miniature Disneyland immediately springs to mind, but this one is authentic, free of crass commercialism and as tasteful as the floral labels on his bottles. Beginning with the old Romanèche train station—he bought it outright from the state—and moving on to its adjacent storage sheds and workrooms, the visitor ambles through a series of tile-roofed, ochre- and beige-walled buildings housing here a collection of railroad memorabilia, there a terrific scale-model group of electric trains forever chugging through an idealized Beaujolais countryside; then the visitor moves farther on to an antique truck museum (his old Citröen Tube is there, as is his very first van and its primitive bottling equipment), then past an authentic, early twentieth-century iron horse with its coal-filled tender behind, pulled up on a siding by the parking lot.

Over on the other side of the road is the main attraction, the wine museum that Georges had been wanting to build for the Beaujolais ever since he was a teenager. He completely gutted the old buildings of Pierre Crozet's former establishment and made them over according to the ideas that he had been refining for years. Fronted by a flagstone terrace, the main reception room is a replica of a Belle Époque *salle des pas perdus*, the train station waiting room of a typical medium-sized French city, complete with Beaujolais country frescoes, ticket office, exhibition cases of period train equipment, the inevitable waiting room clock and the equally inevitable *buffet de gare* (station restaurant), offering a short menu of light meals, pâtés, salads and sandwiches. There are marble-topped bistro tables, a zinc bar and an unbeatable selection of Beaujolais and Mâconnais wines of every sort.

All that is only the start, though, for what lies beyond the waiting room on the other side of the ticket office turnstiles. Georges' wine museum is of a size and class that are probably unsurpassed anywhere in the world. For years he had been scrounging, buying, borrowing and wheedling old winemaking tools and equipment around the Beaujolais, and he brought them all together, cleaned them up, classified them and had display cases made to exhibit them in this personal space, unsubsidized and free of government interference. In his *musée du vin*, pruning knives and shears, sulfur-spraying tanks, hoes, picks and all the other tools of a vigneron's laborious existence are presented and lit with the same reverent care that museums elsewhere devote to Etruscan artifacts or Renaissance jewelry. The ingenious, often surprisingly delicate objects of quotidian winemaking are overwhelmed by the looming mass of two enormous eighteenth-century wooden wine presses, one activated by a vertical worm gear amazingly carved from a single tree trunk and the other by a pegged "squirrel cage" system whose motor power was delivered by the feet of men trudging grimly forward and upward on a handmade, all-wood treadmill that turned the axle that pulled the rope that moved the wheel that forced the great beam of the press down onto the grapes heaped below. From room to room the exhibits tell the story of wine in paintings, photographs, models, audiovisual presentations, dioramas, an art gallery, an animated puppet show, a 3-D movie, a waxworks of Beaujolais characters à la Madame Tussauds, and some nifty holographic tricks reproducing Noah, the Flood, the Ark and mankind's first plantings of vines. The tour passes by way of a second bistro, or wine bar, this one big enough for renting out to special events, with a stage for performers and a big, air-powered fairground organ equipped with a xylophone that tinkles out melodies via wooden hammers striking wine bottles filled with more or less water for higher or lower notes. The museum offers plenty of instruction, and art and humor, too, because from the start Georges insisted that the visit should be *ludique*—an entertaining experience—but whether it was intentional or not, there is a single, more somber bass note that underlies all the carefully prepared detail. The leitmotif that dominates from one end of the museum to the other is the same one that has marked Georges throughout his life: work. In view of the region's history, the poverty that had been its lot until recent times, and the life story of the man who brought it all together under the museum's several roofs, this emphasis is hardly surprising, but it is a salutary reminder of the centuries of plodding, unremitting labor that lie behind those friendly little glasses of gamay so lightheartedly tossed off in bistro and bar.

"He had been thinking about the museum since he was fifteen," Anne Duboeuf told me over a coffee in her bistro. (I say "her" bistro because as Franck's wife she has been assigned the duty of running the Hameau—Les Vins Duboeuf is not a family enterprise for nothing.) "He knew exactly what he wanted, and where. The architect just followed him from room to room as he explained how everything had to be laid out."

With that remark I was immediately reminded of a conversation several years earlier with Papa Bréchard. We had been talking about the Beaujolais in general, but whatever aspect of the country he touched on, the subject always swung back to Duboeuf, this extraordinary character unlike any others he had known. "You know," the old man confided, "a lot of vignerons had their doubts about him because of his great success, but that disappeared when he opened the museum. They all believe in him now. They come and visit *en famille*, right along with the tourists. It gives them tremendous pride to see their region and their history explained so handsomely. They can see that he did it for the Beaujolais—all the Beaujolais—and not just for himself."

When Anne revealed that there was one particular vigneron who had sent more clients to the museum than any other member of the brotherhood, I was naturally curious to know who it might be. When she told me his name, I could not have been more pleased, but upon reflection, I wasn't really surprised. Who else could it have been but my friend Marcel Pariaud, the prodigiously industrious, perpetually optimistic former mayor of Lancié? Better yet, Anne added, Marcel often personally brought guests of his B and B down to Romanèche in his big old carriage, talking and clucking to Hermine along the way. While the visitors he delivered were making the museum tour, Marcel habitually passed the time by giving kids impromptu horse-and-buggy rides around Romanèche. (At Christmastime, Marcel and Hermine deliver *le Père Noël*—Santa Claus—by wagon to the Lancié kindergarten.)

That was typical of him—*sacré Marcel*, he's always doing things like that. The day I watched him tromping on the grapes in his old press, without breaking stride he had waved me over to his workbench, where a thick sausage lay side by side with his pocketknife, a bottle of his Beaujolais-Villages, several of his tools and his wine-stained notebook filled with cabbalistic entries in reference to his vinification procedures. Munching my ration of sausage, I noticed several plastic buckets standing in a corner of the vinifying shed, all of them filled to the brim with *paradis*, the sweet, deep purple, partially fermented runoff. I could guess that some of them were for him and Nathalie, but I had no idea why there were so many others. It became clear moments later, when a dapper old man dressed in an immaculate Lacoste shirt—clearly this was a gent in retirement—arrived with a big plastic container of his own. His name was François Giroud; he had worked as the town's butcher, and like many others who habitually dropped by Marcel's place, he had come for some *paradis* and *gène* (pressed grape mash), in view of cooking one of the great seasonal specialties of the region: *saucisson au gène*.

"I soak the sausage all night in the *gène* and the *paradis*," Giroud explained, "then I cook them together for twenty minutes and serve it with steamed potatoes—that and a good Beaujolais, of course. The kind

Marcel makes." His eyes shone with pleasure at the prospect of his little feast.

"If you're looking for good wine—real wine, good wine, no mixes, no cheating—this is where to come for it." He gazed affectionately around him at Marcel's heroically disordered collection of equipment. "This place is like *la maison du bon dieu*, the house of charity. You can find anything you want here."

"*Mais non, mais non*," Marcel protested, smiling bashfully at the compliments as he scooped a pitcher into the *paradis* bucket to fill Giroud's container. Compared to Duboeuf's shiny installation in Romanèche, Marcel's anarchic jumble of mostly ancient winemaking gear was hopelessly behind the times, but in his hands it played like a Stradivarius, and the wine that came out of it was invariably as full and mellow as the best expression of the gamay grape should be. How he could manage such an exploit year after year was mysterious, but of course that was where the elusive quality known as talent found its definition. Marcel simply possessed it, as did a few thousand other winemakers around the world, and no amount of investment in space age technology or expert consultancy could replicate that.

"Education is the head," he said, tapping his temple, "but intelligence is the eyes."

The remark was as apt for his life story as it was for Georges Duboeuf's. Both men had started at approximately the same level, each had succeeded according to the particular little genies that drove him, and each was equally worthy of admiration for it. Whatever the future for the wines of the Beaujolais—favorite wine of the twenty-first century, as Michel Rougier would have it, or just another appellation, retrenched in its original *terroirs* and fighting to survive in the globalized market—it was certain that the Duboeuf and Pariaud kind of intelligence would be crucial for leading the way toward a healthy resolution of the present-day crisis.

"*Les plus courageux survivront*," Marcel said by way of summing up his view of the coming years. The toughest ones will survive.

"Travail, rigueur, qualité" was Duboeuf's prescription. Work, rigor, quality. He did not speak these words in answer to Marcel's prediction; the juxtaposition is mine. But those three words are a kind of mantra that he repeats frequently. In view of today's expanding wine production worldwide—and look out, here comes China—attention to that mantra is probably as good as any other recipe for ensuring safe passage to the wines of the Beaujolais through the twenty-first century.

But that's not the end of the story, or the whole story anyway. If, as appears more than likely, this century is to be characterized by a steadily increasing technicity and mechanization in winemaking, to the point of quasi-industrialization, I persist in believing that, however powerful the steamroller of globalization, the Beaujolais will remain just a bit different from the rest, still anchored to the old peasant smallholder traditions and mannerisms that Papa Bréchard used to talk about, and to which both Georges Duboeuf and Marcel Pariaud were born. I admit that this is arrant romanticism on my part, but the beauty of the countryside, the ineffable allure of its gorgeous villages and the rock-solid authenticity of the vigneron character forged by centuries of labor are so compelling that it is impossible to imagine this place becoming just one more reflection of the consumerist, assembly-line lifestyle that is so efficiently stalking the rest of the modern world.

I can't honestly say that Lancié and Romanèche-Thorins deserve to be cited among the architectural treasures of the Beaujolais. The first is a pleasant, workaday kind of town—one grocery store, one church, one bar—the second a larger yet undistinguished sprawl behind Duboeuf's installations; and neither one can withstand comparison to jewels like Chiroubles, Fleurie, Leynes, Bully, Oingt or Vaux-en-Beaujolais, the original Clochemerle itself. The list of rustic beauties could go on and on, but of course what makes these two otherwise ordinary towns exceptional is that in Romanèche there is Georges Duboeuf and in Lancié there is Marcel Pariaud.

"Le vin est la mémoire du temps," says Duboeuf gravely. Wine is the memory of time, and he has literally set that memory into stone

and brick. Marcel Pariaud's contribution to that memory is bound to be more ephemeral — the joviality, the force of character and the downright humanity that rubbed off on those who came into contact with him.

The last time I saw him after the 2006 harvest afforded me a nicely wrapped little vignette charged with all the symbolism I needed for viewing the future of this wonderful region. Supping joyously with his grape-picking crew, Marcel presided over the table like a benevolent despot of good cheer, forcing more helpings of Nathalie's *boeuf bourguignon* on youths a third his age, overwhelming them with his energy and his jubilant chatter, topping up their glasses of wine, regaling them with stories about years past and harvests good and bad. When someone pointed out the battered old bugle hanging on the wall, Marcel sprang up and unhooked it. Erect now, poised in regulation position, he told about his army days when he used to rouse the troops before dawn, then raised it to his lips and gave the assembled crew a few skillful riffs. Naturally that set off a generalized clamor for everyone else to give it a try, and the ear-shattering competition went on and on until I took my leave and returned to my room at the other end of town.

It was approaching 11 P.M. as I walked through the darkened village, and as the bugle blasts continued I could only assume that the Pariauds had understanding neighbors. At length the amateurish blarings petered out and Marcel himself took up the instrument again for one more performance before turning in. The easy, practiced notes made it clear that it could only be Marcel who was delivering this last nocturnal serenade over the sleeping landscape. You take your comfort and your symbols wherever you can find them, so at that moment the import of Marcel's spontaneous choice of repertory for a final musical offering could not have struck me as more fitting: any normal bugler would surely have selected taps to play out into the Beaujolais night, but Marcel was blowing reveille.

Acknowledgments

$\mathcal{M}$y first thanks go of course to Georges Duboeuf, "Monsieur Beaujolais" himself, who for more than thirty years educated me on the wines, the people, the geography, the history and folklore of the region that has come to be associated with his name. So dominant for the Beaujolais is the persona of Duboeuf that the equation for me was perfectly simple: no Duboeuf = no book. The other members of his family pitched in to the degree that their workaholic routines allowed them talking time: Rolande, his wife; Franck and Fabienne, his son and daughter; and Anne, his daughter-in-law, who brightens the day for the thousands of visitors who flock to the extraordinary Wine Hamlet that Georges designed and she runs. I add a word of respect and regret for Georges' older brother Roger, sage and historian, who died shortly after according me two long and fruitful interviews at the family homestead in Chaintré.

Apart from the Duboeuf clan, four persons were of exceptional importance in providing research material and/or helping ensure that I presented it accurately. Professor Gilbert Garrier of the University of Lyon, gourmet, oenologue, raconteur and unequaled historian of French wines, cheerfully opened his books, his mind, his cellar and his dining room door, and sent me on my way a more knowledgeable if not necessarily wiser person. Michel Brun, retired from the Duboeuf troop, where he soldiered for some thirty years, became the object of my daily persecution via e-mail, fax and telephone for any niggling wine detail that I couldn't get straight without his amiable patience. Edward Steeves, Massachusetts Yankee who spurned a teaching career for the love of wine, came to France and became boss of an important distribution house near Mâcon, freely offered his impressive erudition in matters of wine, history, culture and language, along with the unsuspected bonus of a redoubtable command of grammatical nuance in checking my text. And finally there is Marcel Pariaud, winemaker in Lancié, a true peasant seigneur of the Beaujolais, with whom I spent far more hours talking (or rather listening) than with any other single person. Marcel was my personal professor in agronomy and winemaking, and role model in human comportment.

In Beaujolais "officialdom," the various groupings that deal with organizing the trade and furthering its good health, I owe thanks to Michel Bosse-Platière and Michel Rougier, respectively president and director of InterBeaujolais when they received me, as well as Gérard Canard, the organization's retired director; to Maurice Large, former director of the Union Interprofessionnelle des Vins du Beaujolais; Michel Deflache, director of InterBeaujolais; Louis Pelletier, director de l'Union Viticole; and Jean-Luc Berger, technical director de l'Institut Technique de la Vigne et du Vin.

Among writers and journalists, Bernard Pivot afforded me an astute overview of the people and the Beaujolais culture into which he had been born, while Michel Bettane and Frank Prial added their forthright and sometimes dissident views as seasoned professionals of the world of wine criticism. Vincent Rocken, who covers the Beaujolais country for the daily *Progrès de Lyon*, gave me valuable background information, and Lionel Favrot, editorial director of *Lyon Mag*, offered a spirited defense of his magazine's approach to reporting on the region's events.

No profession follows wine matters more closely than the restaurant brotherhood. Within its ranks I owe special thanks to Paul Bocuse, Jean

Fleury and Jean-Paul Lacombe in Lyon; Georges Blanc and Marcel Perinet in Vonnas; Chantal Chagny in Fleurie; and Jean Ducloux in Tournus.

In the iconic village of Vaux, undisputed capital of the Beaujolais for readers of Gabriel Chevallier's classic *Clochemerle*, I respectfully salute the mayor, Raymond Philibert, the graphic artist Allain Renoux and the *artistes* of Beaujolais-Villages appreciation Roger de Vermont and René Tachon. My own enlightenment in matters vinous owes much to my honorable fellow members of the *Groupment des Organisations Sociales, Intellectuelles, Éducatives, Récréationelles, Sportives et Éducationnelles* (GOSIERSEC).

In various branches of the commerce of wine, I thank Pierre-Henry Gagey, president of the Maison Louis Jadot, and Guillaume de Castelnau, director of Château des Jacques; Jean-Marcel Jaegle, president of Tonnellerie Dargaud & Jaegle; Bill and Peter Deutsch of W. J. Deutsch & Sons; Jean-Pierre Labruyère, president of Moulin-à-Vent; Joseph Berkmann and Allen Cheesman of the Joseph Berkmann company in London; as well as the extremely knowledgeable Peter Vezan, wine broker in Paris.

For technical advice on the biophysics of vinification, I thank Dr. Björn Jäckisch of Honeywell.

Over the years I have bothered far too many winemakers to enumerate them all here, but I would like to single out the following for their welcome and dealing with my questions: Jacky Nove-Josserand of the *Cave Coopérative de Bully*; Jean-Pierre Thomas, president of the *Cave Coopérative de Liergues*; and René Bothier, president of the *Cave Coopérative de Saint-Laurent-d'Oingt*. Among individual vignerons, in no particular order, I offer particular thanks to Nicole Savoye Descombes, Daniel Buillat, Ghislain de Longevialle, Bruno Martray, Marcel Laplanche, Claude Beroujon, Pierre Siraudin, Gérard Large, Jean and Bruno Bererd, Monique and Georges Larochette, Marcel Lapierre, André Poitevin, Louis Durieux de la Carelle, Maxime Chervet, Paulo Cinquin and Jean-Guy and Evelyne Revillon.

And finally, a special note of personal thanks to my wife, Brien, for her patience, help, support and expert copy-reading eye, and to Bill Shinker, Lauren Marino, Hilary Terrell and Lisa Johnson of Gotham, for accompanying these pages from initial idea to its present finished form.

Glossary

AGRÉMENT: Approval (of wine samples)

ANCIEN RÉGIME: France's pre-Revolutionary political and social system (monarchy)

ANDOUILLETTE: Country sausage composed principally of tripe

ASCENSEUR: Elevator

AUBERGE: Inn

AUTOROUTE: Superhighway

BALLON: Typical bistro wineglass

BOUCHON: Lyonnais term for bistro

BOUILLIE BORDELAISE: Agricultural fungicide composed of slaked lime and copper sulfate

BOULODROME: An earthen pitch for playing *boules* or *pétanque*

BOURRU: Adjective designating wine not yet fully fermented

CANUT: Lyonnais silk weavers

CAVEAU: Wine-tasting cellar

CAVE COOPÉRATIVE: Co-op wine cellar

CÉPAGE: Variety of grape

CHAI: Wine storage building

CHAPTALISATION: Increasing wine's alcoholic content by adjunction of sugar in fermentation

CHÂTELAIN: Owner of a château

CHEF DE PARTIE: A senior cook in a large restaurant's kitchen brigade

COMMIS: A beginning cook just out of apprenticeship

COMTOIS(E): Adjective designating one from the Comté region of eastern France

CONCOURS DU MEILLEUR POT: Competition for bar offering the best Beaujolais Nouveau

COURTIER: Wine broker or scout

CONFRÈRE: A professional colleague

CRU: An officially recognized vineyard, usually of higher quality

CUVÉE: A selected batch of wine

CUVERIE: Storage building holding vats or tanks of wine

DÉGUSTATION: A tasting session

DE GUSTIBUS NON EST DISPUTANDUM: You can't argue about tastes

EAU-DE-VIE: A strong spirit distilled from wine

ÉCOLE LAÏQUE: A nonreligious school

FAIRE PISSER LA VIGNE: Overproduce by causing the vine to "piss"

FERMAGE: Renting land for planting vines

FÊTE: A party, celebration or feast; more broadly, a holiday

FOND DE VEAU, FOND DE VOLAILLE: Veal or chicken stock, usually as base for sauces

GONE: A typical Lyonnais (cf. *titi parisien*)

GRATIN DAUPHINOIS: Scalloped potatoes in cream

HECTARE: Metric system's land measurement: 2.471 acres

HECTOLITER: One hundred liters

LA MALO: Wine's secondary fermentation, known as malolactic

LOUP EN CROÛTE: Sea bass stuffed with lobster mousse, served in a pastry shell with a choron sauce. House specialty of Paul Bocuse's restaurant in Lyon.

LES TRENTE GLORIEUSES: Three decades of French economic growth, roughly 1960–1990

MARCOTTAGE: Air layering: burying a vine's branch to cause it to grow roots

MERDE: Shit

MILLISIME: Vintage, year of production

MISE EN BOUTEILLE: Bottling

MOÛT: Must, crushed and smashed fruit being readied for fermentation

NÉGOCIANT: Wine dealer or intermediary

NÉGOCIANT-PRODUCTEUR-ÉLEVEUR: Dealer who also grows, ages and refines wine

PARCELLE: A section or "parcel" of land

PARADIS: The first, slightly alcoholized, juice from the press, after maceration

PAYSAN: Peasant

PÉTANQUE: *Boules,* or the "bowling" game played with iron balls

PIERRES DORÉES: "Golden Stone" region of the Beaujolais

PIPETTE: Long glass tube for withdrawing wine samples from the barrel

PIQUETTE: Poor quality "wine" made by adding water to already pressed grapes and pressing again

POILUS: French soldiers of World War I

POULET EN VESSIE: Chicken cooked with cream and vegetables inside a pig's bladder

PRIMEUR: New wine; usually a synonym for Beaujolais Nouveau

PRIORITÉ À DROITE: In traffic, the vehicle on the left must cede to the one on the right

SUI GENERIS: Of its own kind, self-generated

SO₂: Sulfur dioxide, wine's most common preservative and disinfectant

TERROIR: Total natural environment of a vineyard or *parcelle's* site

TITI PARISIEN: Typical Parisian of folklore and myth, most usually of the working class

VENDANGE: The harvest

VENDANGEOIR: Plant to which grapes are brought to begin the process of vinification

VIGNERON: Winegrower

VIGNERONNAGE: Sharecropping on a 50–50 basis with the landowner

VINIFICATION: The process of turning grape juice into wine

VITICULTURE: The growing of grapes

VITIS VINIFERA: Vine species used for most of the world's wines

Index